Intricate Links:

Democratization and

Market Reforms

in Latin America

and Eastern Europe

Intricate Links:
Democratization
and Market Reforms
in Latin America
and Eastern Europe

■

Joan M. Nelson and contributors:

Jacek Kochanowicz
Kálmán Mizsei
Oscar Muñoz

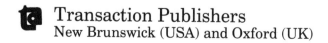 Transaction Publishers
New Brunswick (USA) and Oxford (UK)

Library of Congress Cataloging-in-Publication Data

Nelson, Joan M.
    Intricate links: democratization and market reforms in Latin America and Eastern Europe/Joan M. Nelson and contributors Jacek Kochanowicz, Kálmán Mizsei, Oscar Muñoz.

(U.S.-Third World Policy Perspectives, No. 20)
    1. Latin America—Economic policy.   2. Europe, Eastern—Economic policy.
3. Democracy—Latin America.   4. Democracy—Europe, Eastern.   5. Latin America—Politics and government—1980-.   6. Europe, Eastern—Politics and government—1989-.   I. Kochanowicz, Jacek.   II. Mizsei, Kálmán.   III. Muñoz, Oscar.   IV. Title.   V. Series.

HC125.N45   1994   338.98—dc20   94-39868 CIP

ISBN: 1-56000-177-1 (cloth)
ISBN: 1-56000-759-1 (paper)
Printed in the United States of America

Director of Publications: Christine E. Contee
Publications Editor: Jacqueline Edlund-Braun
Edited by Kallab Communications
Cover design: Snoreck Design Group
Book design: Tim Kenney Design Partners, Inc.

Contents

Foreword

In Eastern Europe and Latin America, two trends are under way: first, far-reaching reforms to convert economies from inward-oriented, state-dominated models to more open market-driven approaches, and second, efforts to consolidate democratic political openings replacing earlier authoritarian regimes. These reforms often conflict, yet paradoxically the success of each is crucial to the other.

Intricate Links: Democratization and Market Reforms in Latin America and Eastern Europe explores issues common to both regions and crucial to the prospects of economic and political reforms. This volume is the outgrowth of a multi-year collegial study on the interactions between the two processes of reform and transformation. The study focused on Latin America and Eastern Europe because in these two regions the reform trends have involved all or many nations (in contrast to Africa and Asia). Moreover, reforms in Latin America and Eastern Europe had moved furthest when the project began in 1991 (in contrast to the former Soviet Union).

The project was designed as a multilateral and cross-disciplinary effort from the outset. The first phase of the project focused on the experience of three countries in each region: Argentina, Bolivia, and Brazil in Latin America; Bulgaria, Hungary, and Poland in Eastern Europe. Because the project focused on interactions between economic reform and democratic consolidation when those two processes unfold roughly simultaneously, it did not examine the two Latin American cases where economic reforms have advanced the furthest: Chile and Mexico. In Eastern Europe, the project included at least one Balkan country rather than concentrating entirely on Central Europe and avoided the complexities of severe regional and ethnic divisions.

Twelve social scientists, all but one from Latin America or Eastern Europe, collaborated in the first phase. Authors for Eastern Europe were Jacek Kochanowicz, András Körösényi, Kálmán Mizsei, and Ekaterina Nikova. Latin American authors were Edmar Lisboa Bacha, Adolfo Canitrot, Marcelo Cavarozzi, Eduardo A. Gamarra, Bolivar Lamounir, Silvia Sigal, and Miguel Urrutia. Workshops in Budapest and Rio de Janeiro drew in a wider range of views from analysts in each region. A first step in the project was the compilation of country case studies and regional overviews based on the cases, which were published by the Institute for Contemporary Studies for the International Center for Economic Growth, in a pair of volumes entitled *A Precarious Balance: Democracy and Economic Reforms in Eastern Europe and Latin America*. Project Director Joan M. Nelson is a Senior Associate at ODC and one of the world's experts on the politics of economic adjustment and transformation. Her past published work in this area for ODC includes *Fragile Coalitions: The Politics of Economic Adjustment* (Transaction Publishers in cooperation with ODC, 1989); *Encouraging Democracy: What Role for Conditioned Aid?* (ODC, 1992); and *Global Goals, Contentious Means: Issues of Multiple Aid Conditionality* (ODC, 1993).

Within the larger group, four scholars in addition to Project Director Joan Nelson composed a core team, which helped in the design and recruitment stages of the project as well as contributing their own analyses. The core group included Argentine political scientist Marcelo Cavarozzi, Hungarian economist Kálmán Miszei, Polish economic historian Jacek Kochanowicz, and Colombian economist Miguel Urrutia. Chilean economist Oscar Muñoz joined the group for the last phase of the project, when Miguel Urrutia had to withdraw because of increasingly demanding responsibilities in Colombia.

In the second phase of the study, this core group focused on issues common to both regions and important for the consolidation of both market-oriented economic reforms and democratic consolidation: the restructuring of trade regimes, property rights reform, the roles of labor and business, and the roles of the state. Their analyses benefited greatly from the comments of participants in a series of workshops at the Overseas Development Council in March 1993. This volume presents the products of the second phase.

This project was made possible by a generous grant from The Pew Charitable Trusts, and by the support of The John D. and Catherine T. MacArthur Foundation for the ODC Fellows Program. The International Center for Economic Growth supported the two regional workshops in the first phase of the project.

ODC is also grateful for the ARCO Foundation's financial support for the project, and for the support of The Ford Foundation and The Rockefeller Foundation for ODC's overall program of policy research and education.

John W. Sewell
President
November 1994

Part I
Overview

How Market Reforms and Democratic Consolidation Affect Each Other

Joan M. Nelson

INTRODUCTION: SIMULTANEOUS TRANSITIONS

From the mid-1970s to the mid-1990s, two trends increasingly dominated events in most of the world outside the industrialized democracies. In Latin America and Africa, changes in the international economy exacerbated growing domestic economic difficulties; both prompted a basic reorientation toward more open, market-driven economic strategies. Different causes drove a similar shift in most of the communist and post-communist world. In some countries, such as Chile, that reorientation is now both largely completed and broadly accepted. In many other countries, it is incomplete or barely begun and widely viewed with deep skepticism. But everywhere the terms of debate regarding economic policy and strategy have changed profoundly since the early 1980s.

The second trend is political. First in Southern Europe, then in Latin America, and by the end of the 1980s in some of Sub-Saharan Africa and most of the communist world, discredited authoritarian political systems collapsed or were pushed aside and replaced by elected civilian governments committed to more open and competitive political systems. In much of East and Southeast Asia as well, formerly closed authoritarian systems were liberalized. The collapse of communism in the former Soviet Union not only ended 40 years of cold war in the international arena but also removed the most influential alternative to democracy as a long-run model for political systems around the world. As in the economic realm, the terms of debate were fundamentally altered.

In all of Eastern Europe and much of Latin America (as well as some countries in other regions), these two trends were intertwined and roughly simultaneous. This was not true throughout Latin America. Costa Rica, Jamaica, and several other small Caribbean nations, and later Venezuela and to a lesser degree Colombia, all faced the need for economic reforms within already established democratic contexts. Chile and Mexico carried out economic reforms under authoritarian or semi-authoritarian political systems; Chile's 1989 return to democracy came as economic reforms were largely completed. Much of the continent, however, moved toward more democratic politics at the same time that economic crisis demanded sweeping economic reform. In Eastern Europe, the dual transformation was still more radical and abrupt.

In many countries, a third transition coincided with political and economic liberalization. The collapse of Soviet communism was followed by the dissolution of the Soviet empire and its influence in Eastern Europe. Just how far that process will go, and what its consequences will be for border and ethnic disputes, remains to be seen. But for many countries in that former empire, the post-imperial consolidation of nationalism and independence is at least as important as political and economic liberalization. In some countries elsewhere, the third transition is not to a new independence, but from civil war to peace, as in El Salvador, Mozambique, and Cambodia. In terms of claims on the attention of national leadership and other scarce resources, this shift may well dominate or take priority over economic and democratic reforms.

This study, however, concentrates on cases where economic and political liberalization have dominated the agenda roughly simultaneously. It draws mainly on experience in a few countries in each region—particularly in Argentina, Bolivia, Brazil, Bulgaria, Hungary, and Poland.[1] In each of these countries, political opening coincided with pressure for far-reaching economic reform (though in some cases economic reforms had been launched prior to political transitions). In the Eastern European cases, the collapse of communism also ended Soviet domination. Especially in Hungary and Poland (as well as in the Czech Republic and the Baltics), resurgent national sovereignty was linked to a rush to "rejoin (Western) Europe." In these cases the third transition—enhanced independence and the turn to Western Europe—did not divert attention from, but rather merged with and facilitated, market-oriented economic reform and democratic consolidation. Indeed, fears that the Soviet Union (more recently, Russia) might try to reassert its dominance spurred Central European reformers to move as fast as possible.

The simultaneous introduction of democratic political institutions and radical, market-oriented economic reforms has few historical precedents. In Western Europe and North America, markets and democratic institutions evolved gradually over many decades or centuries. Since World War II and outside of Western Europe, strong market-oriented growth strategies or vigorous economic liberalization have been pursued more often by authoritarian than by democratic governments, while heightened democracy has frequently been associated with increased state economic intervention. Simultaneous economic and political liberalization, deliberately and rapidly introduced, is a largely new experiment on the world stage.

It is not at all clear that most simultaneous transitions will reach their objectives. The major risk is not reversion to old systems: communism in Eastern Europe, military government and strong state economic intervention in Latin America. Far more likely are partial and distorted semi-democratic political systems and poorly functioning versions of semi-market economies. Paralysis, disintegration, and chaos are also possible, leading to new forms of authoritarianism and state-controlled economies.

Outcomes are uncertain in a second sense. A wide variety of political arrangements are consistent with our basic definition of democracy: a system that permits substantial political competition, encourages widespread political participation, and protects civil and political liberties necessary for meaningful competition and participation. Similarly, a wide range of economic institutions and legal frameworks are consistent with the essence of a market economy, defined as a system that protects a broad range of property rights, relies primarily on market mechanisms to allocate resources, and is reasonably open to international trade and investment. Successful simultaneous transitions will create quite varied forms of democratic polities and market economies.

There is a massive literature on different aspects of market-oriented reform and a considerable body of writing on transitions from authoritarian to democratic political systems. But the two trends are usually analyzed separately. They are brought together in the growing literature on the politics of economic reform, but the focus is often short run and narrow on political obstacles to economic reform and on tactics to overcome these obstacles.

This volume and the project of which it is part view simultaneous transitions from a broader perspective. We start from a value judgment: Both democratic politics and market-oriented economic systems are important for liberty and prosperity. We want to understand how the processes of moving toward those goals—from authoritarian toward more open politics, and from heavily state-controlled toward freer markets—affect each other. Each of the two processes complements the other in some crucial respects and circumstances. But they also often conflict, not just in short-run hitches, but more fundamentally. This overview sketches major interactions. Later chapters explore some of these in greater detail.

There are fundamental contrasts between the economic and political transitions under way in Latin America and Eastern Europe (as well as immense differences in historic and cultural legacies). The depth and scope of change is obviously much greater in Eastern Europe. Indeed, post-communist societies are undergoing basic transformations rather than transitions from one form of economic or political organization to another: the fundamentals of market economies and democratic systems must be created, while in Latin America already largely market economies must be reoriented and strengthened, and older experience with democratic institutions must be revived and recast. This overview and later chapters note many contrasts between the regions (as well as important differentiation within each). But the interactions between economic and political reforms in the two regions are also similar in many respects. (For a historical view of state economic intervention in both regions, see the Appendix to this overview chapter.)

Launching, Sustaining, and Consolidating Reforms

Studies of the politics of economic reform have usually focused on overcoming obstacles to launching reforms. Somewhat similarly, studies of political opening have emphasized the processes leading up to the replacement of old rulers with more democratically selected political elites, and the varied nature of the transitions themselves—violent or peaceful, controlled from the top, or pushed from below.

Clearly, however, initial stabilization and liberalization packages and pathbreaking democratic elections are only the first steps in much longer and more complex processes. The initial democratic election marks the end of the old authoritarian political system and sets the stage for more open politics, but the process of building a viable democratic political system is a matter of years, or quite possibly decades. Though each country's experience has unique features, certain patterns and phases are common to most cases.

POLITICAL REFORM PHASES. The democratic political transitions of the 1980s were usually followed by a brief honeymoon. Not only the repression of authoritarian regimes but also the economic difficulties of past years were expected to be solved or eased in short order. Interests associated with the old regime were discredited and disorganized, or at a minimum thrown off balance. Where there had been strong anti-authoritarian movements, they normally disintegrated quickly, since their disparate members had little in common other than hostility to the old regime. New parties and interest associations usually mushroomed, as did the media.

To varying degrees (far more in Eastern Europe than in Latin America), the political transition also left major aspects of the new institutions and procedures undefined or vague, including relations between the executive and legislature, the relative authority of head of state and head of government (in parliamentary systems), powers of judicial review of government decrees and legislation, and sometimes even electoral arrangements. Unclear constitutional frameworks together with inexperience created considerable confusion. New political leaders also tended to be suspicious of hold-over bureaucrats, while civil servants were uncertain about the new system and fearful of retribution. The issue of retribution extended as well to the military and to others, since some groups pressed for widespread punishment for wrongs committed under the old regime.

The excitement, flux, and uncertainties of early post-transition politics were gradually replaced, in most of Eastern Europe and democratizing Latin America, with a trend toward "politics as usual." In Eastern Europe, many of those who had been active in the anti-authoritarian movement drew back from politics—disconcerted by the shift to intense rivalry and bickering. They were replaced by a new crop of more professional (and more self-interested) politicians. From the multitude of new political parties, a few began to emerge as more serious contenders, while others dissolved. Some of the parties and unions associated with the old system regained self-confidence and began to play active roles, often after considerable internal reorganization. High levels of political participation subsided, and many people lost interest or became alienated from politics.

In Latin America, the break with the past was much less sharp. Most major parties and interest groups carried over from the military period to the new democratic political arena, and much of the constitutional framework remained unchanged. Nevertheless, the broad features sketched above apply: initial euphoria and flux, followed by the emergence of some new actors and some reorientation of old parties and interest groups, constitutional debates, and later trends toward "normalization" and reduced political participation.

In both regions, normalization has been accompanied by some progress toward consolidation of democratic institutions. But consolidation is a very long process, measured less in terms of specific reforms or institutional characteristics than in the political attitudes and behavior of people and groups. Democratic consolidation requires that most major groups view representative institutions and procedures as their main channel for pressing claims on the state. To do so, they must accept the inherent uncertainty of democratic competition, which guarantees procedures but not outcomes. Consolidation also requires that most (preferably all) major social groups be reasonably represented,[2] through the party system and other channels of communication between the state and society, and that political parties and interest groups accept each other as legitimate contenders.

ECONOMIC REFORM PHASES. Like the process of consolidating democratic openings, converting a closed and state-controlled or heavily state-manipulated economy to one that is more open and largely market-driven takes years, or even decades. Reforms launched in Chile in 1975, for instance, were substantially reworked after the crash of 1982 and did not produce a well-functioning market economy until the late 1980s.

Economic restructuring includes several elements. In many countries, macroeconomic stabilization—the measures needed to correct an unsustainable balance-of-payments deficit or to control inflation—is a prerequisite for effective structural reforms. But some, like Czechoslovakia in 1989, start their reforms in reasonable macroeconomic balance. The second element in the economic reform agenda is the dismantling of the pervasive state controls that characterized the old regime, such as high tariff and nontariff trade barriers, extensive price controls, pervasive direct and indirect consumer and producer subsidies, and extremely detailed and rigid labor-market regulations. The third element is reorienting old agencies and institutions or creating new ones to perform the functions required for an efficient market economy. Those functions include effective financial institutions and regulations, comprehensive property rights and commercial laws, and appropriate regulations to restrain monopolies and protect public and consumer safety and the environment. Efficient markets are crucial for sustained economic growth but may not be sufficient to attain that goal. Therefore, in tandem with building market institutions and a market-friendly environment, many governments will also pursue short- or long-run measures to directly address growth bottlenecks or implement growth strategies.

The three elements of market-oriented reforms—macroeconomic stabilization, dismantling of old controls, and the strengthening or creation of new institutions and legal frameworks—are all in play throughout the reform process. Their relative importance, however, shifts in different phases. The launching phase usually includes stabilization measures (more or less radical depending on the severity of the imbalances) and those aspects of dismantling old controls that are comparatively easy to implement, such as reduction of trade barriers and decontrol of many prices. Stabilization requires tight budget constraints and therefore usually entails sharp cuts in the producer subsidies that were a key feature of the old state-centered systems. The easier segments of privatization are also often carried out as part of the initial phase.

Beyond the launching, careful macroeconomic management remains important—to encourage investment and promote efficiency (for instance, in the remaining state-owned enterprises). Emphasis shifts, however, to the more complex and delicate aspects of decontrol and the long and difficult process of institutional reforms including privatization of large state enterprises, financial sector reconstruction, and labor market liberalization.

Consolidation of market reforms, like consolidation of democratic openings, is less a matter of specific measures than of changes in the attitudes and behavior of economic actors. If market reforms are effective, they generate incentives for more and more firms and workers to direct their efforts to efficient production rather than to winning concessions from the government; and they attract growing domestic and foreign investment. Implicit in this behavior is the assumption that the new rules of the economic game are durable—not likely to be reversed or radically changed. As the market economy becomes more consolidated, economic actors also increasingly accept the uncertainty inherent in the system. Like democratic politics, market economies provide rules of the game but do not guarantee outcomes to specific actors.[3]

Given such uncertain outcomes, groups and individuals are likely to accept the rules of democratic politics and market economies only if three conditions are satisfied:

■ They believe that these rules offer the best assurances available for avoiding pitfalls they have come to fear: the repression of authoritarianism, and the stagnation and scarcities or inflation of state-guided economies (or, put differently, they come to believe that there are no longer any viable alternatives);

■ They believe that these rules will not produce disastrous political or economic outcomes for themselves or their own group (or put differently, the costs of losing will not put them out of the game entirely); and

■ They believe that the rules will be reasonably well enforced and that other players will observe them.

In any country, at any time, some individuals and some organized groups will not share these beliefs and will seek ways to evade or change the economic or political rules. The more widely shared these beliefs are, however, the more consolidated the democracy and the market system will be. It is particularly crucial for consolidation that elites share these beliefs.

Of course, neither economic nor political reforms move steadily and predictably through the phases described. Even if neither process is derailed, both may stall, or slip backwards in some respects, and then perhaps lurch forward, or take zig-zag courses. Even after democratic or market institutions are well-established, they can erode—as Venezuelan democracy has clearly done in recent years.

Nor are the phases of economic and political reforms tightly linked together. For instance, in Eastern Europe, economic reforms were launched before political transitions in Poland and especially in Hungary, and within a year or two after the political transitions in Czechoslovakia (then still unified) and Bulgaria. But in the Latin American cases we examined, economic reforms were delayed until well after the first phase of post-authoritarian politics. Each of the processes has its own dynamic and is affected by a great many forces. But each also affects the course and prospects of the other in many ways. These interactions change in different phases.

This chapter sketches some of these interactions. The next section examines how democratic openings are likely to affect initial and later stages of economic reform, and then reverses the causality and explores some of the ways in which market-oriented reforms affect the process and prospects for consolidating democracy. Next, the chapter turns to the relations between the state and economic and political reforms, and argues that rebuilding state capacities is crucial to both. Finally it suggests some perspectives for policymakers dedicated to both effective markets and consolidated democracy.

HOW DEMOCRACY AFFECTS ECONOMIC REFORM

The end of the 1980s saw a brief moment of euphoria among internationally oriented pro-democratic groups in North and South. The ultimate triumph of democratic governments and market-oriented economies seemed assured; in the United States and Western Europe, many assumed that the two were tightly interlinked. In four short years, that euphoria has given way to deep concerns regarding the compatibility of sustained deep economic reforms with efforts to consolidate democratic openings. Put simply: many of those primarily focusing on the promotion of economic reforms fear that democratic politics will abort or derail those reforms. And some of those mainly concerned with strengthening democracy fear that rapid and deep economic reforms may undermine tentative and fragile commitments to democratic processes or distort the nature of emerging democratic institutions.

Political Obstacles to Economic Reform

Any government attempting stabilization and market-oriented economic reforms, whether democratic or not, must cope with political problems inherent in the nature of these measures. Both stabilization and structural reforms impose costs that are immediate, certain, and often concentrated on specific groups. Where reforms are spurred by rapid inflation, or even hyperinflation, restoring fairly stable prices benefits almost everyone. But most other benefits of reforms—in contrast to the costs—are usually uncertain, delayed, and diffused. Losers know who they will be; gainers are much less certain. Moreover, the losers include powerful vested interests—many of them within the state apparatus. Even where much of the public is convinced that strong reforms are imperative, there are intense disagreements over the precise design and timing of reforms and who shall bear the costs.

Democratic governments, established or new, face additional risks when they undertake economic reforms but may also have certain advantages. By definition, democratic governments are more exposed to criticism and to opposition protests. Moreover, in democracies, decisions tend to be slow, especially if legislative action is required. And politicians' time horizons are usually bounded by the next election.

New democracies face additional problems. Especially in postcommunist cases, but also in some Latin American countries, the end of authoritarian rule triggered a mushrooming of new political parties and interest groups, competing with each other and with the (often disintegrating or reorienting) remnants of parties and interests linked to the old regime. The resulting babble may temporarily free government technocrats to act aggressively within the boundaries of their direct authority. But unless electoral and other laws reduce the multiplicity (by excluding the smallest parties and encouraging coalitions), legislative stalemate or paralysis is likely to slow more complex, later reforms.

Moreover, in new or recently renewed democracies, the usual problems of slow decision-making in democracies may also be exacerbated by still unclear relations and divisions of authority between the executive and the legislature as well as between cabinet and chief of state. Implementation of decisions is often hampered by confusion and insecurity within the bureaucracy: Many high and medium officials associated with the old regime are likely to be replaced by inexperienced newcomers, while the remaining hold-overs hesitate to exercise discretion or even attempt to sabotage changes in policy and procedure.

Countries with little or no experience with democratic politics may also face higher risks of grossly irresponsible protest and criticism. Both politicians and the public have exaggerated expectations and lack knowledge regarding the constraints facing the government. The tendency for irresponsible opposition and criticism is also fueled by the fierce competition among old and new parties and interest groups to hold on to former members and/or attract new followers. Closely related is the tendency for aspiring political leaders to use extreme or fantastic appeals like those of Stanislaw Tyminski in 1990 in Poland. The "political market" is untried and fluid, and it is not clear what approaches might attract sizable support. New democracies with deep ethnic or regional tensions of course face additional perils, often outweighing those examined here.[4]

Yet recent studies concur that there is no clear link between type of political regime and successful economic liberalization. Except in East Asia, authoritarianism has not been particularly successful in promoting economic reform, nor are democracies clearly less effective.[5] Indeed, democratic processes can complement economic reforms in several ways.

■ Although open debate and criticism of economic measures may slow and modify them, they can also broaden acceptance by spelling out the implications of superficially attractive alternatives or by providing procedural legitimacy.

■ Democratic processes can provide a safety valve for social frustrations, perhaps reducing the probability of severely disruptive protests. The Polish and Hungarian elections of autumn 1993 and spring 1994 illustrate the point.

■ In the longer run, democratic rules exert pressure on opposition parties and groups to consider realistic options rather than simply attacking the current government. In other words, the possibility of taking or sharing in power encourages learning regarding feasible policies.

More fundamentally, in Latin America and most of Eastern Europe in the 1990s, most major groups see no viable alternative to some version of democracy.[6] In both regions, the concept of efficient, growth-oriented authoritarian approaches has been thoroughly discredited. Some version of democracy is therefore a necessary, though far from sufficient, condition for sustainable and credible economic reforms.

Overcoming Political Obstacles: Initial Economic Reforms

Despite formidable obstacles, the fledgling democratic governments in Central Europe (and in the Baltic states) quite rapidly launched major economic reforms. So, too, did Argentina and Bolivia, but only after the second round of democratic elections.

Earlier research identifies several factors that help to explain why any government, democratic or not, decides to launch serious stabilization and structural reform measures, despite the considerable political risks.[7] These factors include the following:

- A serious economic crisis, often preceded by a long period of economic stagnation or deterioration, or by chronic instability;
- The perception (by technocrats, by political elites, and, in democracies, by much of the public) that less painful alternatives tried in the past have not worked;
- Sharply reduced political power of the groups with the strongest vested interests in old patterns of state intervention in the economy—usually as a result of a new government or even a change in the nature of the political system;
- Decisive political leadership, working in cooperation with a technically competent and cohesive economic team.

Pressure and technical and financial support from external agencies, including the International Monetary Fund and the World Bank, often reinforce these factors. But where governments launch reforms in response to external pressures alone, the measures are often abandoned or diluted in short order.

In strong authoritarian political systems, once leaders are committed to economic reforms, resistance from the public at large or from vested interests can be at least temporarily suppressed—as in Chile in the 1970s and 1980s, or in Turkey under military rule in 1980–83. But in democracies new or old, governments cannot resort to extensive repression (although they can repress specific groups, particularly if broader public opinion has come to view those groups as destructive of the broader national interest—as was the case in Bolivia in 1985, for instance, when the powerful tin miners' union was suppressed to contain hyperinflation). In democracies, therefore, the marginalization of old vested interests takes on added importance.

In democracies, it is also particularly important that not only technocrats and political leaders but also a large part of the public be convinced that there is no plausible alternative to market-oriented economic reform. This does not mean that there must be consensus on the design of reforms. As Jeffrey Sachs points out, "In deep crises, there simply is no consensus to build upon, only confusion, anxiety, and a cacophony of conflicting opinions."[8] Many elements of first-phase reforms—austerity measures (including sharp cuts in subsidies), trade liberalization, devaluation—are almost certain to provoke great disagreement. In the early phases of economic reform, however, agreement on specifics is not needed: Acquiescence based on the conviction that reform is imperative is sufficient.

From the 1970s forward, the Latin American and Eastern European countries that are the focus of this study were in deepening economic difficulties. In both regions, political transitions were facilitated, and often prompted, by the growing conviction among elites as well as much of the public that the old political systems could not solve the growing economic problems. In Eastern Europe, that belief was coupled with another: that communist economic arrangements had failed and must be replaced rather than repaired. And in the western tier of Eastern Europe (as well as in the Baltic states), there was widespread agreement that the Western European nations provided a feasible and desirable model to be pursued—a consensus reinforced by the prospect of eventual membership in the European Union. As a result, there was little political protest against draconian stabilization and sweeping liberalization programs in either Poland or Bulgaria, and still less against the structural reforms (without severe stabilization programs) in Hungary and Czechoslovakia.

Launching economic reforms in Central Europe was facilitated not only by broad agreement on the need for and direction of reforms, but also by the degree to which post-transition politics initially excluded and discredited the major political actors of the communist era. In 1989 and 1990, the former Communist parties, unions, and other organizations in Central Europe were thrown into disarray; most split, all lost much of their membership, and few were major political players. (Later, of course, both ex-Communist unions and many former Communist politicians did return to active roles.) In contrast, further to the east, the former Communist Party in Bulgaria won the first competitive election; and in much of the former Soviet Union, the Party (under new names), unions, and networks of state enterprise managers all retained a great deal of power.

Virtually all of the countries of the former Soviet bloc that have managed to bring inflation below 50 percent a year are also countries where the political break with the old regime was very sharp, and that break was reinforced by the reassertion of national sovereignty. Only in these countries have governments had enough autonomy from pressure by workers and managers in state enterprises to sever subsidies to those enterprises—an essential ingredient of stabilization.

In contrast to the Central European cases, in our Latin American cases, both widespread attitudes toward economic reform and the continued strength of old vested interests hampered initial economic reforms. In Argentina, Bolivia, and Brazil, at the time of democratic transitions, politicians, business leaders, technocrats and the public at large assumed that their economies were fundamentally sound but had been mismanaged by the military. Mismanagement then made the economies vulnerable, the argument continued, to adverse international events—the second oil price increase, the recession in the industrialized north, and the contagious impact of Mexico's default on its foreign debt in 1982. Bolivians in 1983, Argentines in 1984, and Brazilians in 1985 assumed that new democratic governments would correct the errors of their military predecessors and bring prosperity without pain. Political transition was de-coupled from economic reform. When growing economic difficulties nevertheless pushed each of the three initial democratic governments to attempt painful stabilization measures, opposition not only scuttled the economic reforms, but ultimately forced two of the first-round presidents to leave office early.

In Bolivia and Argentina, the picture then changed. Hyperinflation proved a watershed: The public, terrified, acquiesced in far more draconian reforms under second-round presidents. In Brazil, however, ten years after the return to civilian government, most political players were still not convinced that their economy, which had performed so strongly in the 1960s and 1970s, now required basic reforms. Some structural reforms were introduced piecemeal, and a fresh anti-inflationary program was launched in 1994, but as of mid-1994, Brazil had yet to undertake sustained stabilization and reform measures.

In short, where democratic transitions marginalize old political elites and actors, and where public opinion is prepared for fundamental economic changes (though not necessarily supportive of all, or even most, elements in the initial reform package), the launching of reforms is facilitated. In the absence of those conditions, other features of democratic transitions may well weaken or block economic reform.

Sustaining Economic Reforms in Democratic Settings: Growing Difficulties

It is often assumed that stabilization, with its painful austerity measures, is a higher political hurdle than the liberalization and institutional reform measures needed to reorient the economy. Yet many countries have launched promising efforts, and far fewer have sustained those efforts long and vigorously enough to produce results. The hardest political challenges often come after the initial package has been launched. The trajectory of political opposition over the course of a successful program to restructure an economy is likely to start moderately high, rise higher, and then gradually decline.

The political challenges tend to be greatest in the medium term for three reasons: the timing of costs and benefits, the character of later reforms as compared with initial steps, and the changing political context.

In many cases, economic reforms tend to impose severe costs early and produce benefits only more gradually (assuming the reforms are in fact sustained). Countries suffering high open or repressed inflation or hyperinflation—Argentina, Bolivia, Poland—display a different pattern. In Argentina and Bolivia stabilization rapidly brought down inflation to the great benefit of almost all the population; in Poland, the package of reforms launched at the beginning of 1990 promptly relieved many shortages. But further improvements were much slower to appear, while unemployment and other costs of adjustment built up rapidly in the next months. Even in Argentina, where the economy began to grow rapidly within months of the introduction of Minister of Economy Domingo Cavallo's program in April 1991, unemployment and poverty worsened. In spring 1994, a survey among Argentine firms found that three out of four planned to trim their labor force. Somewhat similarly, Poland's economy began to expand in 1992 and grew at a respectable 4.5 percent in 1994, yet surveys suggest that most state enterprises in Poland are still substantially overstaffed, and unemployment is expected to top 17 percent in 1994.[9] In Eastern Europe, only the Czech Republic has succeeded in combining vigorous structural reform with low unemployment—and correspondingly sustained political support.

After the initial phase, the reform agenda itself also changes in ways that do not reduce, and may heighten, political opposition. Despite the intense political controversies regarding first-phase stabilization and liberalization measures, many are administratively simple, in the sense that they can be decided and put into effect by a small circle of senior economic officials. Measures that usually come later—such as financial sector reforms, privatization or rationalization of large state enterprises, liberalization of labor markets, and restructuring of social services and social security—are much more complex. They require sweeping institutional and legal changes and involve the legislature, the courts, and multiple central and local government agencies. Therefore they are more vulnerable to dilution, delay, and derailing. Moreover, while many of the initial costs of stabilization are temporary and spread over much of the population, sectoral and institutional reforms usually impose permanent losses focused on specific interests. They therefore prompt tenacious resistance.

Later-phase reforms not only tend to be administratively more complex but also offer a wider range of technical options. The range of possibilities regarding stabilization measures is fairly narrow. In contrast, there is much more scope for variation in the design, pace, and sequencing of later reforms such as privatization or labor market liberalization. Such measures often generate as bitter debate as the earlier and more sweeping macroeconomic reforms.

Meanwhile the political context also shifts, particularly in new (or renewed) democracies. Honeymoons fade, and so does the ability to blame hard times on the old system. If acute economic crisis has been contained, willingness to sacrifice dwindles. But if initial results are disappointing, confidence in the government erodes. Either outcome heightens political difficulties.

Moreover, as noted earlier, in new democracies where the break with the old political regime was sharp, old vested interests are often discredited and disorganized initially. But with time, some will revive, as the successors to the former Communist labor unions have done in Eastern Europe. Anti-authoritarian groups also change their behavior. Unions originally affiliated with anti-Communist movements (Solidarity in Poland, Podkrepa in Bulgaria) hesitated to oppose their former allies in the early post-transition period. But in time they are likely to drop those inhibitions. By 1993, the Solidarity trade union federation—under new and younger leadership with few ties to the struggle of the early 1980s—had become strident and radical.

New parties, unions, business associations, and other groups also emerge on the political scene. They may try to block some aspects of economic reform; equally likely, they will try to steer other aspects to their own advantage. For example, after taking office in autumn 1991, the anti-Communist Bulgarian Union of Democratic Forces designed a program for breaking up the large agricultural cooperatives and returning rural land to pre-communist owners or their heirs. A major—perhaps dominant—motive clearly was to destroy the still considerable power of rural officials and managers from the old regime, whether or not this approach increased agricultural productivity. All this, of course, is part of the process of emerging democratic pluralism. But it does mean that reformist governments must cope with a wider and more pushy array of interests.

In intermediate phases of reform, even winners—those groups that benefit fairly early from reforms—may not provide much counterweight. Often they are not organized to protect their emerging stakes. As long as government policies are generally in their favor, they are less motivated than losers to try to influence the government. Indeed, winners may mobilize to protect their new interests only when losers threaten or succeed in rolling back reform. The result may be a zig-zag or stop-go course of reform.

For all these reasons, the pace of economic reform is likely to slow after the initial phase. Especially in post-communist countries, the slow-down itself creates new risks. Half-complete transitions have unattractive, even dangerous, features. Inconsistent and constantly changing laws and regulations discourage investment, while the absence of appropriate regulation encourages "raw capitalism": shoddy products, false advertising, financial scams, environmental abuse, labor exploitation. (Many of these problems also occurred under the old statist systems, of course.) The same half-dismantled, half-rebuilt, post-communist framework of laws and regulations—coupled with the breakdown of state capacity to enforce law and order (discussed more later)—spawns a frightening increase in organized illegal, mafia-style activities. In addition to their more specific costs, "raw capitalism" and crime discredit both market and democracy.

Sustaining Reforms in Democratic Settings: New Tactics and Approaches

Later-phase changes in the economic reform agenda and the political context require shifts in political tactics and strategies. In democracies, diffuse support (or tolerance) for first-phase macroeconomic measures must be replaced with more specific acceptance or support for narrower sectoral and institutional reforms.

Initial economic reforms are typically carried out with minimal consultation—even within the executive branch, and certainly with legislatures and interest groups. The crisis itself demands rapid action, and some aspects of first-phase reforms, such as devaluation, cannot be publicized ahead of time without destroying their effectiveness. Many measures are announced by executive decree; those requiring legislation are often rammed through with little debate. Later reforms, however, demand a much more consultative style. Implementing institutional reforms requires the understanding and cooperation of the public and of the private sector agencies and groups involved. The precise design of the measures needs to be fine-tuned to national (and sometimes local) circumstances; the groups most directly affected can provide information crucial to getting the design right.

Crafting piecemeal support through consultation is time-consuming and frustrating for reformers. But for the reasons just reviewed, the pace of reforms is virtually bound to slow in any event. Fuller consultation with the interests affected by specific reforms is part of the democratic process and can produce more legitimate and durable policies and institutions.

A more consultative approach carries two intertwined risks in addition to slowing the pace of reforms. First, truly representative partners for consultation often are lacking. Many interests are poorly organized; others are organized but lack internal democracy. Consultation tends to favor the most organized groups and often fails to distinguish representative from unrepresentative groups. Moreover, consultation is likely to produce agreements that sacrifice general to special interests, diluting or distorting reforms. Both risks are real, yet there are no good alternatives. Continued technocratic autocracy is a real threat to democratic processes. Intensified legislative involvement is another possibility. Legislatures are more broadly representative (though far from perfectly so), but they cannot process the entire agenda of varied and often highly technical reforms. Nor can legislative action commit or persuade interest group members to the degree that effective direct consultation can sometimes achieve. In practice, governments concerned about both sustaining reforms and protecting democracy are likely to continue to rely on technocratic decrees to some degree, but to make increasing use of legislative channels and of direct consultation with key interest groups.

To be constructive partners in policy consultations, interest groups themselves must evolve along lines that increase their sophistication and pragmatism and lengthen their time horizons, while preserving or enhancing their representativeness and capacity to influence the behavior of their own members. Especially in Latin America, where the break between old and new political regimes is much less sharp than in Eastern Europe, a key question regarding the crafting of consensus (or perhaps better, the bounding of conflict) is the degree to which traditional and non-negotiable party and interest group ideologies have faded, permitting new compromises consistent with both democratic politics and market reforms. A different way to phrase the same point is that, as faith in alternative political and economic approaches has dwindled, some groups—for instance, Argentine labor unions—have been forced to reappraise and lower their expectations of what is possible. Reduced expectations and narrowed alternatives can facilitate compromise—although there is no guarantee that they will do so. However, the same erosion of strength and confidence that lowers expectations may reduce the ability of unions and other associations to influence their members' behavior—and therefore to make credible commitments.

Consultation also requires rebuilding channels of communication among interest groups, legislatures and parties, and the state. The old regimes—authoritarian political systems characterized by extensive state intervention in the economy—often built elaborate channels for coopting and controlling interest groups. Communist labor unions were an obvious example. So too were the intricate links between business associations and state agencies in Brazil described in Oscar Muñoz' chapter in this volume. The collapse of the communist system destroyed these channels. In our Latin American cases, political transition brought less dramatic changes, but the later dismantling of state economic intervention is profoundly changing the nature of relations between state agencies and interest groups.

Interest groups' political roles and their communication with governments are closely related to the still emerging character of political parties and their links to interest groups. If parties themselves evolve into broad-based conglomerations of interests, then party platforms, campaigns, and party caucuses within legislatures become arenas where different interests can press their views, reconcile their goals, and work out concrete policy proposals. If the party system itself remains fragmented and parties are narrowly based, formal legislative proceedings become the main arena (other than direct contacts with the executive branch) for the clash of interests, and the result is often legislative paralysis.

Post-World War II corporatist arrangements among labor unions, business associations, and the state in several smaller Western and Northern European nations are often suggested as an attractive model for consultation in a democratic context. But the corporatist approach in Western Europe worked best where unions and business associations had large memberships, a small number of national confederations, and considerable discipline—so that they could enter into credible commitments with each other and the state. At present, those characteristics are lacking, or in a few cases only weakly approximated, in most Eastern European and Latin American nations. Not only structural features but also specific postwar historic contexts facilitated the Western European corporatist approach: memories of the economic and political debacle of the 1930s, and the more specific concerns of nations on the emerging Cold War frontier (Austria, Finland). The 1990s contexts in Eastern Europe and Latin America are obviously different—though some features may also favor social cooperation. Institutionalized arrangements with a corporatist flavor, including tripartite commissions to advise the government on labor issues, have been attempted in some dual transition countries, particularly in Eastern Europe, but thus far have usually worked poorly.

A more likely, though untidy, approach in most simultaneous-transition countries is what might be labeled "piecemeal crafting of enlarged consensus," tackling specific knotty issues such as privatization of large state enterprises, social security reform, labor market liberalization, or educational reform, and gradually reducing the scope and agenda of bitter conflict. In Eastern Europe, the same second-phase, post-transition trend toward somewhat more stable and coherent parties and interest groups that reduces the autonomy of technocrats may also facilitate the piecemeal crafting of enlarged consensus.

Building new or reoriented channels of communication between interest groups and the state, political parties, and the legislature is crucial for the piecemeal approach as well as for more ambitious corporatist arrangements. Some of the problems and possibilities are discussed in Nelson's chapter on business and labor in this volume, with emphasis on labor unions. The abortive Polish Pact on Enterprises proposed by the Hanna Suchocka government is a good example of an attempt to establish new channels; it sought to establish procedures for consultation and participation by unions in privatization or reform of large state enterprises. Constructing such channels is itself a long endeavor. Early failures do not mean the approach is wrong or unimportant.

Reformist parties and governments seeking to press forward with later-phase reforms must not only build channels for consultation with specific interest groups but also need to forge broader pro-reform coalitions. Parties and governments in any system have two main strategies for forging broader support: patronage (immediate material benefits for specific individuals and groups), or programmatic vision (deferred and broader benefits, usually for the nation as a whole or major segments of it). Most parties rely on a mixture of the two, although some (for instance, the major Bolivian parties) rely almost wholly on patronage.

Dual transitions offer some new opportunities for patronage. Allocation of privatized assets, for instance, has been a key feature of several different governing parties' strategies: the Czech government has used mass vouchers to build widespread support for both the governing party and market reforms; Mexico's government earmarked part of the proceeds from privatization for its National Solidarity Program of small public works and social projects; and in Argentina, in contrast, far narrower wealthy groups have been the major direct beneficiaries of privatization. More generally, however, the fiscal crunch and the goals of reduced state intervention sharply limit patronage, particularly in the form of public employment. This heightens the importance of a credible and appealing medium-term program or vision.

Not only practical constraints but also the psychological dynamics of the economic reform process put a premium on a broadened programmatic appeal. The launch phase of economic reforms is often accompanied by a "negative consensus": the urgent desire to get a crisis under control, and sometimes the further conviction that old economic strategies and institutions have failed. Later stages require the building of a more "positive consensus" regarding the principles that should guide further reforms. A positive consensus requires at least a rough sense of the kind of society that is sought—a "vision" of the goals of reform.

Several chapters in this book stress that the market-oriented agenda by itself does not provide an adequate vision. At least two crucial elements are missing. Prescriptions for more open, market-driven economies are silent on the issue of equity. Tolerance for considerable income inequality is a prerequisite for well-functioning market economies, and indeed the early effects of liberalization have almost always been sharp increases in inequality. Market mechanisms are acceptable in open democracies only with considerable mitigation of inequality. Some consensus on the extent and mechanisms for that goal are a key ingredient in a broader acceptance of market reforms.

The second missing ingredient is a plan for the rehabilitation of the disintegrated state. That goal is crucial both for a well-functioning market economy and for the consolidation of democratic opening. It is discussed later in this overview, and explored in greater depth by Jacek Kochanowicz in Chapter 4 in this volume.

A broadened vision of societal goals and strategy encompassing these missing elements is crucial for sustaining economic reforms. Without it, no durable social consensus is possible in new or recently renewed democracies. The credibility of economic reforms, and therefore a vigorous response by investors, depends on perceptions that the new policies will endure. In democracies, of course, governments are likely to change every few years. The credibility of economic reforms therefore depends not just on the commitment of the government launching and continuing them, but also on broad agreement among most contending parties and groups likely to take office regarding the basic direction of the reforms. Durable agreement on the neoliberal economic agenda is not likely unless the agenda is broadened to include progress toward equity and a revitalized state.

HOW MARKET-ORIENTED REFORMS AFFECT CONSOLIDATION OF DEMOCRACY

Thus far the discussion has focused mainly on the politics of economic reform in its initial and later phases in countries that have recently turned or returned to democratic politics. Of equal concern is the reverse causality: how market-oriented economic reforms affect fragile new democratic governments and the prospects for consolidated democracy. That is harder to assess, because many of the effects of economic reform on democratic prospects are indirect and delayed.

Views on the question vary dramatically. Two sets of propositions frame the parameters of debate. First, economic reforms are crucial to maintain the credibility of new democratic governments. In the medium and longer run, economic reforms are also vital to consolidation of democracy, in two ways: 1) by providing necessary (though often not sufficient) conditions for more dynamic and sustainable growth, and 2) by diffusing control of economic resources and therefore political power more broadly throughout society.

Second, from the other end of the spectrum of opinions, economic reforms threaten the stability and legitimacy of new democratic governments—by causing widespread suffering. Worse still, over the medium and long run, they may undermine the legitimacy and skew the representativeness of evolving democratic systems—by creating or enlarging an alienated underclass, impoverishing the middle classes, and enriching (and thereby increasing the political influence of) the already wealthy.

Despite their contrary positions, both assessments clearly capture aspects of reality. Economic reforms have benefits and costs for new democracies. The mix varies in different countries and for different groups; it also changes over time. And the political effects of economic outcomes are filtered through varied historical legacies and evolving political institutions. We should not be looking for neat and simple generalizations, but rather for a clearer grasp of the various channels linking economic reforms to political trends.

Four channels seem particularly important:

■ The effects of crisis control (or failure thereof) on the government's short- and medium-run political credibility and popularity, and therefore on its stability and capacity to cope with anti-democratic challenges;

■ Medium- and longer-run effects of economic reforms on poverty and inequality, with implications both for commitment to democracy and for political coalitions;

■ Effects of changing economic structure on the relative political power of different groups;

■ Medium- and longer-run effects of economic reforms on relations between the state and organized interest groups in civil society, and therefore on incentives and opportunities for different patterns of political behavior.

Economic reforms also affect prospects for democratic consolidation and the character of democracy through their impact on the functions and capacity of the state. Those linkages are considered later in this overview.

Crisis Containment, Credibility, and Popularity

Where newly elected governments have *failed* to adopt coherent reforms and economic crisis deepens, the credibility of the government and of democratic processes more generally does erode. This was clearly evident in the first civilian governments in Argentina, Bolivia, and Brazil. Economic tailspins played major roles in pushing Presidents Hernán Siles Zuazo and Raúl Alfonsín out of office early. Slovakia and Romania offer more current Eastern European examples.

Although failure to cope with economic crisis can destroy new governments, democracy itself may not be threatened immediately. The broader process of consolidating democratic transitions often has considerable autonomy from economic policies and performance. Arguably, aspects of Brazilian democracy are stronger now than when civilian government was resumed ten years ago, notwithstanding multiple failed stabilization programs and limited structural reforms. Similarly, Russia has made some progress on bitterly disputed constitutional issues—such as the role of the legislature or center-state relations—and its party system appears somewhat more workable, despite the indecisive and partial economic reforms of the past few years. In the longer run, however, continued economic chaos and disintegration clearly open the way for anti-democratic appeals.

Conversely, resumed economic growth reinforces democratic institutions by strengthening confidence in the government and the credibility of the new political system. Growth also generates resources that can be used in part to address problems of equity and rebuild state capacity. Perhaps the clearest example of this virtuous circle is the case of Chile after its return to democracy in 1989, when representatives of the business community agreed to accept a surtax on corporate income earmarked specifically to reduce poverty and inequity.

Confidence in democracy may be affected not only by economic performance but also—and perhaps in opposite directions—by the autocratic style of governing often associated with economic reforms. In several Latin American electoral campaigns in the late 1980s and early 1990s, candidates were silent regarding economic reforms or promised populist policies (as President Carlos Menem did before the Argentine elections of 1989), but once elected, introduced radical economic reforms. Both the reforms and the demonstrated capacity to act decisively and effectively proved popular in Argentina and Peru (though similar tactics by President Carlos Andrés Pérez in Venezuela were not welcomed by the public). Nevertheless, it has been persuasively argued that executive dominance, the subordination of the legislature and judiciary, and the use of deliberately misleading campaign tactics must eventually erode the credibility of democratic procedures and representative institutions.[10] Corrosive effects increase as the economic crisis is contained. This point adds to those noted earlier regarding the desirability of shifting to more consultative approaches in later stages of economic reform.

Distributive Effects: Poverty, Inequality, and Democratic Consolidation

Poverty and inequality in Latin America and Eastern Europe are not primarily the result of stabilization and market-oriented reforms.[11] In both regions, economic instability and/or stagnation eroded living standards and public services for years before economic reforms were introduced. Exogenous shocks shortly before or after political transitions—the debt crisis in Latin America; the collapse of the CMEA and the Gulf War for Eastern Europe—made things much worse. Economic reforms themselves have, however, damaged some groups—considerably (in some cases dramatically) increasing poverty and sharply worsening inequality.

In Eastern Europe, a new class of unemployed and unemployables may be emerging. Recent World Bank studies show that among the unemployed, the proportion who have been out of work for a year or more is rising sharply. The longer these people remain jobless, the less likely they are to find work. Particularly hard-hit are young and poorly educated people in smaller towns and rural areas, and older workers laid off from ailing industries. In Latin America, informal sectors swelled rapidly over the 1980s, undoubtedly forcing down incomes. Growing numbers of street children and exploding crime suggest not simply increased poverty, but an enlarged underclass. In addition to their obvious social costs, such trends raise risks of widespread alienation, easily exploitable by anti-democratic opportunists.

Perhaps still more problematic for democratic consolidation are trends toward the impoverishment of middle strata, including civil servants and the large public service sectors, unionized industrial workers, and pensioners. In Latin America, long-building fiscal crisis eroded real wages of civil servants and public service workers for many years; in both Eastern Europe and Latin America, stabilization programs then sharpened the pinch. Reports from Russia suggest that delays of many months in paying workers are now commonplace. Somewhat similar reports also come from Latin America. Even in Argentina, often labeled the most recent "success story" of market-oriented reform in Latin America, provincial governments (sometimes employing very high proportions of wage labor in their regions) are now under severe fiscal pressure and have delayed wages for months. The quality of public services—an important element in the living standards of most Eastern Europeans and for urban middle class and working class Latin Americans—has also dwindled under fiscal pressure. In both regions, pensioners—including substantial numbers of people who have always viewed themselves as middle class—feel that their incomes have eroded.[12]

Reduced standards of living and sharply increased insecurity for middle strata are likely to generate still stronger discontent because many of the wealthy are becoming richer still. And worse yet, much of the new wealth is widely viewed as illegitimate in any of several ways. Groups that were privileged under the old regime may use their positions to gain further wealth as a result of reforms. The *nomenklatura* in Eastern Europe are suspected of using old connections, and many managers of public enterprises have enriched themselves through "spontaneous privatization" while the authorities look the other way. In Argentina, some conglomerates that had close ties to the old military regimes have been conspicuous gainers from privatization. Others among the newly wealthy are suspected of Mafia-type connections (in Eastern Europe) or drug links (in parts of Latin America). Blatant increases in wealth and the dubious nature of some of the increases add intense feelings of injustice to the hardships of the middle classes and poor. Indeed, that sense of injustice may well be more corrosive of confidence in democratic institutions and market solutions than the hardship itself, which many (particularly in the middle classes) are prepared to view as temporary.

Changing Economic Structure and Relative Power

Shifts in income distribution and in economic structure affect not only attitudes and commitment to democracy but also relative political power. The wealthy are already very powerful politically in Latin America; they may be somewhat less so in Eastern Europe. Increased wealth is likely to increase their influence. Sometimes that influence is very obvious. In Bulgaria, for instance, by far the largest set of daily and periodic newspapers is published by the major business association. More "backdoor" lines of influence are still more worrisome.

In contrast, as discussed in Chapter 3 in this volume, market-oriented reforms quite clearly reduce the political power of labor unions, even though democratic openings have provided them a new autonomy in post-communist countries and have lifted their burden of repression in some Latin American countries. In most dual-transition nations, union membership has plummeted. Governments are retreating from their earlier roles in wage determination, and high unemployment and trade liberalization sharply reduce union bargaining power vis-à-vis private management. In Eastern Europe and in some Latin American countries, under the old systems, unions administered social security programs; reforms in these arrangements remove major resources from union control. Moreover, as economies modernize and privatize, employment in the heavy industries that were the core of industrial unions declines relative to employment in smaller and more flexible industries and services that are less prone to unionization. Some unions—especially in public services, such as teachers—will continue to be major players, but their importance in national politics and national economic policy is likely to shrink. This is true even in those countries—such as Poland—where unions currently play major roles. Effects on the quality of democracy will depend on whether alternative channels representing working-class concerns, mainly left-of-center parties, become effective power contenders. In Poland in September 1993 and in Hungary in May 1994 social democratic parties with strong ex-Communist involvement pulled broad support. The Workers' Party in Brazil proved a less strong contender in the elections of October 1994 than expected, but will probably remain a major player.

Especially in post-communist countries, market reforms have also created (or legitimized and greatly expanded) the class of small- and medium-scale entrepreneurs. These groups may become a counterweight to the declining state-dependent middle class. The potential support for democracy from a large and vigorous class of small and medium entrepreneurs is a strong theme in Kálmán Mizsei's chapter in this volume; this is one reason why Mizsei emphasizes the need to press ahead rapidly with basic property rights reforms. The design of aspects of later-phase reforms can also affect the stake of the broader population in private enterprise. A clear illustration is the Czech Republic's mass distribution of vouchers for shares in privatized enterprises. But such measures will not necessarily strengthen democracy (as distinct from making the economic reforms themselves more popular). Much will depend on whether new or broadened business classes and others with a stake in business interests believe that their best prospects for continued market-friendly policies are linked to stable democratic government. Chile's business classes came to that conclusion in 1990, but it will not be automatically replicated elsewhere.

Another possible effect of market-oriented reforms on emerging democracies bears mentioning here, although it is not strictly related to distributive outcomes. Earlier in this overview, the dangers of "raw capitalism" and the emergence of illegal Mafia-style organizations were mentioned as risks of half-complete transition. These excesses not only erode public confidence in market reforms and perhaps democracy as well, but also can more permanently distort the evolution of the emerging economic and political systems. The dramatic recent revelations of the extent to which illegal and Mafia-connected activities had penetrated the Italian political system offer a clear illustration of the risks for distorting the quality of democracy.

Market-Oriented Reforms, Relations Between State and Society, and Incentives for Political Behavior

Increased poverty and inequality appropriately worry those concerned about democratic consolidation. Much harder to track, but at least as important for democratic prospects, are the effects of market-oriented reforms on the relations between the state and various groups in society, and the resulting changes in incentives for different types of political organization and action.

Direct state controls over economic resources and rewards constrain the autonomy of those who depend on those resources. Centrally planned economies are of course the most extreme version of such controls, and the results—the stifling of independent criticism, autonomous associations, and political opposition—were obvious to all. Even where most economic activity is private, as in Latin America, extensive state controls and intervention in the economy powerfully shape the nature and extent of political organization and participation. Where businessmen or commercial farmers depend on the government for subsidies, protection, trade and foreign-exchange licenses, and even permission to expand or enter new lines of activity, they focus their energies on building contacts with the agencies and officials who control these decisions. Political parties and legislatures become relatively unimportant channels for promoting their interests. And supporting opposition parties or critical media can become risky for the pocketbook.

Similarly, not only under communism but also in many Latin American countries, wages and working conditions were (and in many cases still are) determined largely by state commissions or ministries. As a result, unions and workers direct their attention not to management nor to parties or legislatures, but to the state. The government is expected to mediate disputes between labor and management. Where lesser pressures fail, unions resort (unless repressed) to political strikes, including general strikes.

The essence of market-oriented economic reforms is to sharply reduce direct state intervention and discretion, such as the allocation of credit, direct and indirect subsidies, wage determination, and trade restrictions. Over time, as government agencies and officials exercise less and less direct control over crucial resources and decisions, entrepreneurs and workers shift their attention to the new channels for determining resource allocation and crucial policy decisions: market mechanisms, management-labor relations, and political pressures channeled through parties and legislatures. As Oscar Muñoz argues in Chapter 1, trade liberalization reduces the space for rent-seeking special relations between business and state agencies. In Chapter 2, Kálmán

Mizsei documents how credible property rights reforms similarly reduce rent-seeking, thereby changing the relationships between business and the state.

Altered state-society relations also affect the tactics and strategies available to political parties. As noted earlier, privatization may provide a one-time patronage windfall. But in the longer run, market reforms reduce the scope of state functions and the discretion of state officials to allocate economic resources, and patronage will dwindle. Old or new parties seeking to maintain or expand support in the evolving political system are indirectly pushed to emphasize patronage less and programmatic appeals more (though patronage will remain important especially where voter participation drops to low levels after the excitement of political transition fades). Like interest groups, parties must shift their attention from direct pressures for benefits distributed by the executive to the arenas of public and legislative debate regarding policies and programs. Distributive issues are no less important, but they are pursued in different, and more open, arenas. A major caveat is that the problem of financing party operations may push in a different and less constructive direction. Unless broad-based financing can be devised, political parties are likely to slide toward excessive dependence on contributions from business.

In general, then, market-oriented reforms are fundamental to the emergence of more autonomous interest groups, political parties, and media, and a much stronger legislative role in public policy. These are basic elements of democratic consolidation. But the substantial loosening of ties between state, economy, and civil society only creates a broad potential for democratic politics. It does not determine the detailed outcomes. Those all-important "details"—the changing relative power of different groups and interests, the character of evolving party systems, the orientation and tactics of emerging or reorienting interest groups—are shaped by other effects of economic reforms, by existing (though often rapidly changing) political institutions and rules of the game, and by historic legacies.

ECONOMIC REFORMS, DEMOCRATIC CONSOLIDATION, AND THE STATE

In both Latin America and Eastern Europe, new democratic governments must cope not only with urgent economic crises but also with demoralized and barely functioning state agencies. The overextended but virtually collapsed state is one of the most damaging legacies of the gradual disintegration of state-centered economic systems (see Appendix to this overview). Moreover, economic stabilization and restructuring exacerbate the decay in some ways, although they also can contribute to recovery.

The problem has drawn increasing recognition and concern since at least the late 1980s. For a time, debate was cast in terms of the desirable size of the state and scope of its functions. Neo-liberal economic reformers focused on encouraging markets and emphasized the need to slash the state's claims on resources and its direct state economic intervention. More recently, emphasis has shifted from questions of size and scope to issues of focus and effectiveness. There is broad agreement that a range of state functions is crucial for a healthy society and well-functioning markets and democratic institutions: States must shed certain functions, but they must strengthen and reorient others (such as social services) and add still other responsibilities (such as environmental protection).

As Jacek Kochanowicz points out in Chapter 4 in this volume, the more complex institutional and legal changes required after initial stabilization and liberalization measures must be initiated and designed by competent government agencies. Once reforms are launched, the vigor and intelligence with which they are implemented depends on the quality of government officials. And after reforms are largely complete, governments will still be responsible for a wide range of basic public services that underpin healthy markets and sustainable growth. Reasonably reliable and adequate state services are also important underpinnings for democratic political systems. Where basic functions such as capacity to maintain law and order, provide prompt and fair judicial services, and directly or indirectly ensure health and education break down, the legitimacy of government itself eventually dissolves. In Eastern Europe and Latin America in the 1990s, moreover, while much of the public is cynical about state capacities, one legacy of the extended state under the old regimes is a widespread tendency to look to the state to ease or solve a wide range of social and personal problems. Kochanowicz also calls attention to a more symbolic and less well recognized state function in Eastern Europe's current transformation: the creation, or reaffirmation and redefinition, of the sense of national cultural and political community.

In short, revitalized and reoriented state capacity is crucial to the success of both market-oriented reforms and consolidation of democracy. But do those processes themselves strengthen or weaken state capacity?

In the long run, successful market-oriented reforms should enhance the capacity of the state to perform its refocused functions. Eroding state revenues are probably the most basic cause of the state's decay; stabilization and tax reform are designed to create a sound fiscal basis. Adequate state revenues depend crucially on growth; stabilization and reforms are necessary—though often not sufficient—to prompt resumed growth. Moreover, deregulation shifts economic activities from the shadow economy or the illegal economy into the legal economy, where they can be taxed more readily. Reduced controls and subsidies shrink opportunities for rent-seeking and corruption. And transparency and greater distance between state agencies and special interests strengthens public confidence in the autonomy and integrity of the state. Moreover, in principle, a less ambitious state agenda should improve the quality of remaining functions.

In principle, established democratic institutions also contribute to strengthened state capacity. Ideally, elections enforce accountability; independent media enhance transparency; and decentralization permits more rapid, better-informed, and flexible responses to local problems and circumstances. (Decentralization is often associated with efforts to deepen democracy, but it is not always, especially in small nations, an inherent aspect of democratic systems.)

Reality of course often falls short of these ideals. New possibilities for rent-seeking open up even in the course of market-oriented reforms—though usually on a less pervasive scale than under the old system. Many democratic political systems entail extensive use of patronage; media (especially where not very responsible) may not only expose wrongdoing but also intimidate and squelch initiative; cozy ties tend to develop between legislators, bureaucrats, and interest groups. (These or worse failings also emerge in most authoritarian systems.)

In simultaneous transition countries, where market economies and democracy are far from established, the processes of economic and political reform may impair state capacity as much or more than they strengthen it. Continued fiscal austerity is the most obvious and important issue; long-drawn-out efforts to contain or cut spending inevitably undermine effectiveness and destroy morale. Implementing market reforms also temporarily adds to administrative burdens. For instance, privatization is a highly complex and lengthy administrative process, even though its goal is to reduce the scope of government activity. Pressures on high officials are particularly acute; they must design and administer extensive changes at the same time that they struggle to fulfill routine responsibilities. Democratic openings bring the responsibility of providing information and justifying actions to both legislatures and the media—in addition to the uncertainties of frequent changes of government. Where decentralization is an important aspect of political reforms, strengthened provinces or states can sometimes hamstring the central government, as Brazil and Russia illustrate.

In short, the processes of economic and political reform may for a time further weaken already crumbling states (although failure to reform would be still more damaging). The result may be a vicious circle: the state's inability to implement economic reforms hampers and may discredit those reforms, while incapacity to provide basic services discredits democratic governments and ultimately perhaps the idea of democracy itself. Growing dissatisfaction with both economic and political reforms, in turn, creates pressures which further weaken the state.

Growing concern about the need to rebuild state capacity has not usually been matched by high-priority efforts to do so (though economic reformers have emphasized improving central macroeconomic management capacity and insulating the key agencies from excessive political pressures).[13] The approaches most vigorously pursued concentrate on cutting back the functions of the state at the national level—by privatizing a great many activities and managing others through contracts with private groups; by decentralizing certain functions to state and local government; and by targeting remaining social programs to much narrower groups. Each of these approaches can be helpful for certain programs, in specific circumstances. But even if the state sheds many of its functions, a great many others will remain, including new tasks needed to support and regulate well-functioning markets. As Kochanowicz argues, rebuilding state capacity demands not only trimming and reorienting but also more positive (and costly) measures. The head-on conflict with the imperative of cautious fiscal policy will persist long into the future.

PERSPECTIVES FOR POLICYMAKERS

The difficulties of dual transitions are daunting. The complementarities between market-oriented economic reforms and efforts to consolidate democratic openings often seem outweighed by the tensions between the two. Worse still, those tensions frequently increase in later stages of reform. It is not surprising, then, that many economic reformers are attracted to the phased or sequenced approach to economic and political liberalization pursued by Korea, Taiwan, and Chile. China, Vietnam, and Indonesia claim they are following a similar course, postponing political opening until economic liberalization is largely accomplished.[14] That sequence, of course, has high costs in terms of human and political rights.

Even where authoritarian systems have been replaced by at least nominally competitive ones, the sequenced model tempts some economic reformers. President Alberto Fujimora's course in Peru is a radical example, but less blatant inroads on legislative prerogatives, judicial independence, media freedom, and the electoral process are widespread in both Eastern Europe and Latin America (sometimes in the name of speeding economic reform, and sometimes for other purposes). Yet broadly, in these two regions, and perhaps in some additional countries in other regions, neither economic nor political reform is likely to succeed fully and durably alone. The credibility of each depends on the progress of the other. In Eastern Europe and Latin America, abridgments of democracy will not long be accepted as legitimate, and the resulting political uncertainties will slow investment and economic recovery. Conversely, failure to address economic problems will ultimately undermine democracy. And broadly market-oriented reforms—as a direction rather than a rigid formula—are crucial (though in many cases not sufficient by themselves) for economic recovery and growth.

Therefore there is an urgent need for more creative thought and higher priority to reducing the tensions between the two processes, while maintaining the integrity of each. Policymakers must devise measures to mitigate those aspects of market-oriented economic reform that are most antithetical to consolidating democracy, and those aspects of democratic political systems that pose the greatest threats to effective market economies. The links are intricate and strongly shaped by each country's unique situation and history. No formula or specific list of measures can fit all countries. Two broad perspectives, however, may contribute to debate and thinking.

Selective Priorities Within a Broadened Agenda

This overview argues that after initial economic reforms are in place and the period of crisis politics fades, sustained macroeconomic prudence and difficult institutional reforms demand a new approach to sustaining political support. In democracies, and especially in fledgling democracies, the compatibility of later reforms with democratic consolidation may demand and is certainly enhanced by a credible and appealing vision of the emerging society. That vision includes an effective market economy (and concomitant economic growth) and the procedures of democracy, but must go beyond those goals. An appealing vision of the future must also include greater equity and the restoration of the basic functions of the state that affect the quality of life of almost all citizens. To be credible, the vision must be backed by some immediate steps toward those goals.

These points are increasing widely recognized both within dual-transition nations and in international development circles. But the broadened agenda promptly poses a dilemma: Fiscal pressures and the weakened state permit only a limited, highly selective program of action. Within the broadened agenda, therefore, it is crucial to select and press hard for a few priorities: measures that will relieve bottlenecks and reduce major risks to both economic reform and democratic consolidation. Political leaders must resist pressures to try to do more than financial and administrative resources permit and must also vigorously and continuously explain and defend their priorities. The key measures will vary, but the following considerations are likely to be relevant in many cases.

Simplified and better-enforced tax systems are an obvious and key priority for strengthening the state, since increased revenue is both a major element in sustainable fiscal balance and a prerequisite for many other improvements in state capacity. In addition, more effective tax collection can serve a crucial political objective of reducing anger over growing inequality. More effective collection does not mean increases and could even mean reductions in top-bracket rates. But the wealthy should not only pay, but be recognized as paying. In Argentina, for instance, effective tightening of tax collection not only helped improve fiscal balance, but was also politically popular.

Equally fundamental for a more effective state is the building of an elite corps of civil servants, characterized by good training, merit recruitment, and reasonable pay. A civil service commission is a closely related priority. The judiciary is also a key element of an effective state with special relevance both to effective market reforms and to citizens' confidence in democracy. These complex institutional reforms will produce major benefits only over a period of years, but they must be begun. Moreover, clear statements of objectives backed by action should draw considerable support (despite provoking intense resistance from vested interests).

With respect to *equity*, measures to buffer the temporary costs of economic transition for vulnerable groups are widely recognized as important for welfare and ethical reasons and for reducing political risks. More tightly targeted assistance programs are the conventional prescription for this purpose. That prescription is conveniently consistent with the need to contain fiscal pressures. Two other equity issues have received much less attention and action—in part because they are much more difficult to square with the continued need for sharply limited spending. Yet both pose at least as great and probably greater risks for democratic consolidation.

First, market reforms appear to be creating or enlarging a permanent underclass in some countries. Social safety nets usually try to provide basic consumption needs to groups particularly vulnerable to immediate harm from poverty, especially children and mothers, and the elderly. The goal of avoiding or minimizing a permanent underclass may demand attention to a quite different group: teenagers and young adults with little education or skills, in towns and rural areas particularly hard-hit by market reforms (in Eastern Europe) or in already severely overcrowded urban areas (in Latin America). Moreover, their need is not so much for immediate consumption as for skills and information that boost prospects for productive employment (and, of course, for actual expansion of job opportunities in the economy).

Second, in addition to the vulnerable and the excluded, the working and lower-middle classes, whose living standards have eroded drastically, pose an equity challenge and a potential or actual political risk. For these groups, the *quality* of public services—education, health, police, sanitation, utilities—is an important component of the quality of life, since most cannot afford private services. Reformist governments might therefore give high priority to at least one selected aspect of *improved* services—perhaps aspects of educational reform—as a "down-payment" on a broader array of future improvements for middle-class groups, even while focusing on benefiting poorer groups. Educational reforms are not easy; among other obstacles, resistance from powerful teachers' unions will be formidable and will not be overcome without a major and sustained effort by top political leadership. But improvements might yield considerable dividends in terms of broader political support. Moreover, there is now compelling evidence that well-designed social sector investments strongly reinforce economic growth.

Disaggregated Tactics and a Strategy of Enlarged Social Consensus

A second broad perspective for reformers focuses on tactics rather than the substance of policies and programs. This overview has emphasized that different phases of economic reform call for different strategies and tactics. Some leaders have been well aware of this; others have clung to their initial tactics even when these have begun to prove counterproductive. In new democracies, where consolidation of political openings is as important a goal as economic reform, a shift away from the typical first-phase autocratic tactics is particularly important. Tactics for later phases must emphasize increased public education regarding economic policies, consultation with interest groups and stake-holders, and active coalition-building.

The shift from crisis to normal politics and the increased importance of sectoral and sub-sectoral (rather than macroeconomic) reforms in the policy agenda demand *consideration of much more disaggregated tactical options regarding sequencing, timing, pace, and channels of con-*

sultation between the state and social groups. Early stages of reform often generate passionate debate on what might be labeled "macro" tactics, that is, tactics regarding each set of reforms in their entirety. For instance, the "macro" question regarding sequence is whether economic reforms should precede political liberalization. Questions regarding the speed of reform are often couched in terms of shock versus gradualism, with reference to the entire reform effort (or, with greater precision, to stabilization). And proposals to improve consultation between the state and social groups often call for grand social pacts or corporatist arrangements at the national level. In post-launch phases, however, most of the practical possibilities for sequencing and regulating the pace of reforms, and for strengthening the channels for consultation with societal groups, are likely to emerge in more disaggregated forms, tied to specific measures, groups, and localities.

While tactics must be disaggregated, reformers should not settle for a strategy of muddling through—that is, coping with issues as they arise and promoting specific reforms by whatever means seem feasible and promising. Instead, in later phases of both economic and political transformation, disaggregated tactics should be guided by *a strategy of enlarging the area of societal consensus regarding basic institutions.* That strategy may require accepting slower resolution of issues and sacrificing some economic efficiency in the design of solutions to problems.

Specific sequencing choices can be tremendously important for the interactions between market reforms and democratic consolidation. Should better channels for consultation with trade unions be devised before or after large state enterprises are privatized or restructured? The answer may well vary in different countries—but the question is probably important in many. Can credible measures for improved tax collection be introduced at the same time that unrealistically high taxes are reduced? If so, business compliance and broader popular acceptance are both likely to be enhanced.

In later stages of reform, decisions about the speed and timing of reforms are also likely to concern issues at the level of sectors, subsectors, firms, or localities: How fast should large state enterprises in one-industry localities be restructured or privatized? Which educational reforms should be introduced in a compressed period of time, and which should be phased in more gradually? Such choices need to be considered not only in terms of narrow political feasibility, but in terms of broadened societal consensus.

Approaches to building channels of communication between interest groups and the state also must be approached in a disaggregated way. While national social pacts or corporatist arrangements modeled after those of smaller Western European nations may not work in many dual-transition countries, narrower consultative arrangements can help to resolve more limited issues or reduce particular conflicts. For example, auto workers and affiliated groups in the São Paulo region of Brazil have recently abandoned their traditional militancy and entered into an intricate set of agreements with management and state government, including provisions for linking wage increases to productivity increases. Such arrangements not only ease specific problems, but also broaden the consensus in society regarding market and democratic institutions—and thereby contribute to consolidation of both sets of reforms.

This overview noted at the outset that simultaneous transitions are largely unprecedented historically. Politicians and reformers in dual transition countries cannot draw much on past experience, although they may be able to learn a good deal from each other. Once economic reforms are well launched and basic democratic procedures are in place, the risks of reversal are much less than the danger that half-built market and democratic institutions will evolve in directions that subvert their promise. The challenge, then, is not merely to continue reforms but to encourage markets that generate growth and democratic institutions that combine effective governance with participation and representation.

The perspectives offered here are far from prescriptions. To argue for selective priorities within a broadened agenda leaves open all the difficult questions regarding which priorities to choose. To urge disaggregated tactics within a strategy of broadened societal consensus is to gloss over all of the complexities of such an approach, including the fact that dual transitions create real losers. Yet the two perspectives do focus on the key issue of societal consensus. That consensus is crucial for investor confidence and growth, fulfilling the promise of market reforms. Enlarged consensus is also the essence of democratic consolidation. Neither goal can be reached and sustained without the other.

Notes

This overview draws extensively on the lively exchange of views and ideas over several years among the members of the core team of the Overseas Development Council's project on interactions between market-oriented reforms and democratic openings: Marcelo Cavarozzi, Jacek Kochanowicz, Kálmán Mizsei, Oscar Muñoz, and (for the first phase of the project) Miguel Urrutia. Extensive and thoughtful comments on an earlier draft by Albert Fishlow, Eric Hershberg, and Ben Slay also made important contributions.

[1] For detailed case studies of interactions between political and economic liberalization in these countries, see the two-volume series edited by Joan Nelson, *A Precarious Balance: Democratic and Economic Reforms in Eastern Europe and Latin America* (San Francisco: Institute for Contemporary Studies for the International Center for Economic Growth, 1994). Most references in this chapter to specific experience in these six countries are based on the evidence in these case studies.

[2] In principle, in a consolidated democracy, all major societal groups must regard themselves as reasonably represented. If this is not so, then the omitted group(s) are a potential threat to the system, since they will not be committed to playing by democratic rules. In practice, poorly organized groups (which are often also poor and socially marginalized) are weakly represented in many stable democracies. In other words, many reasonably consolidated democracies exclude or marginalize substantial groups. Ultimately, however, exclusion is likely to erode democracy.

[3] In practice, both consolidated democracies and established market economies often include special arrangements for specific groups or sectors, or even for individual firms, thereby guaranteeing some minimum level of representation or other political privileges, or establishing trigger mechanisms for preventing major economic losses. Where such arrangements are pervasive, however, the system can no longer be described as a democracy or a market economy.

[4] For more on new democracies and ethnic conflict, see Marina Ottaway, *Democratization and Ethnic Nationalism: African and Eastern European Experiences,* Policy Essay No. 14 (Washington, DC: Overseas Development Council, 1994), forthcoming.

[5] See, for instance, Barbara Geddes, "Economic Liberalization and Democracy," *Journal of Democracy* (Autumn 1994).

[6] In contrast, in East and Southeast Asia, the option of "developmental authoritarianism" continues to be viewed as both feasible and desirable among many groups. Communist China and Vietnam, and non-Communist Indonesia are pursuing economic development first, with political liberalization and democratization a more distant goal. The contrast in part reflects major differences in economic and social structure, as well as historical and cultural factors. See, for instance, Minxin Pei, "Reform and Neo-Autocracy," *Journal of Democracy* (Autumn 1994).

[7] See, for instance, Joan Nelson, ed., *Economic Crisis and Policy Choice* (Princeton, NJ: Princeton University Press, 1990), especially pp. 321–36; Stephan Haggard and Robert R. Kaufman, *The Political Economy of Democratic Transitions* (Princeton, NJ: Princeton University Press, forthcoming 1995); Karen Remmer, "Democracy and Economic Crisis: The Latin American Experience," *World Politics* (April 1990), pp. 315–35; and Barbara Geddes, "Democracy and Economic Crisis," *Journal of Democracy* (Autumn 1994).

[8] Jeffrey Sachs, "Life in the Emergency Room," in John Williamson, ed., *The Political Economy of Policy Reform* (Washington, DC: Institute of International Economics, 1994), p. 505.

[9] "Argentina: The Other Side of the Halo," *The Economist,* Vol. 330, (12 February 1994), p. 39; Brian Pinto, M. Belka, and S. Krajewski, "Transforming State Enterprise in Poland: Micro-Economic Evidence on Adjustment" (Washington, DC: World Bank, 1993).

[10] See Adam Przeworski, *Democracy and the Market: Political and Economic Reforms in Eastern Europe and Latin America* (New York: Cambridge University Press, 1991), pp. 183–87.

[11] For further discussion, see Samuel A. Morley, *Poverty and Inequality in Latin America: Past Evidence, Future Prospects,* Policy Essay No. 13 (Washington, DC: Overseas Development Council, 1994).

[12] Actual data on the extent to which pensions have eroded in East European and Latin American countries are ambiguous, but pensioners convinced that they are much worse off are building potent organizations in Bulgaria, Poland, Argentina, and Uruguay. Pension programs cover for more of the older population in Eastern Europe than in almost all Latin American countries.

[13] Some governments have given much more attention to state capacity than others. In Spain, for instance, the "modernization" of the state was the centerpiece of Felipe Gonzales's 1982 electoral campaign. Chile, under both Augusto Pinochet and his democratic successors, has also emphasized enhanced state capacity to support market-oriented development.

[14] Indeed, it is not all clear to what degree elites in Asian authoritarian systems are committed in principle to long-run political opening—though many concede that some liberalization is likely to prove both necessary and desirable eventually.

The Rise and Decline of State Economic Intervention

Kálmán Mizsei and Oscar Muñoz

The histories of Latin America and Eastern Europe in this century are in most respects quite different. However, the evolution of the state's role in the economy shows some strong parallels between the two regions that are particularly important from the perspective of this volume. In both regions, the state became much more deeply involved in the economy as an ad hoc response to the strains of the 1930s. State guidance and control of the economy was later justified and deepened by new ideologies, taking different forms in the two regions.

From the late 1960s or early 1970s forward, however, a combination of international changes and cumulative internal problems caused the gradual decay of effective state control. The unplanned weakening of the old systems set the stage for the third phase in this parallel trajectory: The deliberate dismantling of state economic intervention that started in the late 1970s or early 1980s in some of the nations of both regions gained speed and strength by the end of the 1980s and the early 1990s. The parallel trajectory not only is an interesting historical perspective but also explains the partly similar tasks of economic reorientation and revitalization in the two regions.

THE RISE OF STATE ECONOMIC INTERVENTION

In both regions (as in most of the rest of the world, including the United States), governments became much more directly and deeply involved in the economy in response to the shock of the Great Depression in the early 1930s. Initially, the expansion of the state role was somewhat spontaneous—as governments tried to respond to dramatically shrinking international demand for export products and to mounting social dislocations. Later, more systematic intellectual justifications emerged for an active state role; these began with anti-cyclical Keynesian prescriptions and were later bolstered with various versions of the newly emerging field of development economics as well as rising anti-capitalist ideologies.

In Latin America, the predominant reaction to the Great Depression was protectionist. Import restrictions were imposed in a desperate search for balance-of-payments equilibrium in the face of collapsed export values. Domestic effects were no less dramatic. Exports had been the prime mover of many Latin American economies, and their collapse created widespread unemployment and sharply reduced government revenues. Governments adopted expansionary anti-cyclical fiscal policies, deficits put pressure on a reduced aggregate supply of goods, and inflation accelerated. Governments then imposed price controls in the belief that inflation was more the result of speculative behavior than of basic disequilibria. Devaluations, exchange controls, and currency inconvertibility in the face of payments crisis only added fuel to the cost and demand pressures, accelerating inflation. In this way, states became increasingly involved in the management of very complex external and domestic disequilibria, while acute social inequalities became more visible.

Although Latin America was not directly involved in World War II, demand for exports from the region expanded at a time when import shortages were still in force, thus creating trade surpluses and reserve accumulations that added impetus to inflationary pressures. These reactions were much more visible in the Southern Cone countries than in those of northern Latin America or Central America, which were less industrialized and engaged in less complex trade.

It would be very difficult to understand the increasing role of the state without reference to the deep changes that were taking place within Latin American societies, especially in the more economically advanced countries. What cannot be ignored is that these societies were in the process of overcoming semi-colonial economic and social organization. Their economies relied heavily on a few primary export staples and were characterized by extremely backward agrarian structures, technological underdevelopment, and lack of infrastructure. Rising urban classes were composed mainly of industrial and service workers, professionals, and small entrepreneurs. By the 1930s, these urban groups were developing aspirations for rapid social mobility and reduced dependence on foreign capitalists. The shocks of the Great Depression and World War II stimulated all sorts of social mobilizations and political movements demanding that the state take a more active role. In particular, high expectations were invested in industrialization as the way to overcome underdevelopment—as had happened in most developed countries in Western Europe and the United States.

By the 1950s a new driving force heightened the tendency to look to state intervention to promote industrialization and development. The international community became aware of the wide income differentials among countries and the growing gap between the "developed" and "underdeveloped" countries. International agencies were set up to channel foreign aid, and the instrument for allocating international funds was the state. Furthermore, new economic theories (better known as development economics) denounced the many failures of the market, which impeded overcoming the "low level equilibrium trap" that affected developing countries. Among the factors that produced market failures were externalities, monopolies, and lack of mobility of factors of production. Extremely unequal income distribution and inadequate education also contributed to the trap—and were not effectively addressed by market forces. The new theories all emphasized the central role of the state in promoting economic development. Concepts like the "big push," "critical minimum effort," "balanced growth," and "industrial linkages" became common jargon, supporting the consensus on the need for an activist state. In hindsight, it is easy to see that too much was expected of the state, while the constraints of limited human, financial, and institutional resources were ignored. Populist and nationalist groups, strengthened by post-war domestic trends, were impressed by the growth of Soviet-type economies and favored state intervention and economic planning.

In Eastern Europe, the Great Depression also forced an unprecedented increase in the state role in guiding and controlling economic activity. Currency convertibility was perhaps most affected. With the exception of Poland, all Eastern European countries abandoned the gold standard and full convertibility during the crisis. The driving force of these changes was the deteriorating trade balance and its consequence, deepening debt. Some Eastern European countries were forced to default on their international debt. As in Latin America, in addition to foreign-exchange controls, far-reaching foreign trade controls were introduced.

By the late 1930s—again as in Latin America—spreading state interventionism, initially a pragmatic response to the Depression, began to be justified by ideologies. Theories of state-driven development and preparations for war visibly accelerated the growth of state economic intervention. Inflationary trends played a less important role in generating state controls in Eastern Europe than in Latin America; the state's role as owner of enterprises was more prominent. This was especially visible in shaping the Central Industrial District in Poland, which had already begun to emerge in the Depression period.

After 1933, institutional changes in the German economy began to replace the impact of the Depression as the external driving force shaping the management of Eastern European economies. The increasingly centralized conduct of the German economy caused a "super-Keynesian" boom in that economy. The boom, supplemented by deliberate policies on both sides, brought the Eastern European economies closer to the German giant. Their dependence on Germany grew yearly—as did Germany's institutional impact. For the smaller Eastern European economies, managed trade was almost a necessity, because Germany preferred barter solutions for its increasingly command, and therefore shortage, economy. Thus statist trends were already deeply entrenched before the beginning of World War II. As is well known, the need to extract more resources for war production then brought an unprecedented deepening of state control over the economies of Eastern Europe.

While the trajectory of growing state economic intervention in Latin America and Eastern Europe during the 1930s and 1940s was roughly parallel, trends in political ideologies diverged. Throughout this period, the rise of right-wing centralizing and authoritarian political ideologies went hand-in-hand with growing statist practices in Central and Eastern Europe. In Latin America, in contrast—at least in Brazil, Chile, Argentina, and Bolivia—political ideologies increasingly reflected left-wing, populist ideas. This trend was a mix of anti-capitalism, anti-imperialism, economic independence from foreign capital, and social mobilization. Obviously the explanations for these regional contrasts go further back in history. For Eastern Europe, World War I was an overwhelming trauma affecting political development in the 1930s. Latin America, on the other hand, had a long history (stretching from the nineteenth century) of foreign capital dominating local oligarchies and becoming a symbol of foreign exploitation.

After World War II, the histories of the two regions diverged sharply. Eastern Europe became communist and was incorporated into the Soviet bloc, while Latin America remained basically capitalist, closely linked economically to the United States. Despite this fundamental contrast—which placed each region within opposing parties in the emerging Cold War—there continued to be striking convergence in the increasing bureaucratization and the expanding role of the state within the economies of both regions. The Eastern European communist states energetically nationalized nearly all enterprises, including the small ones; many were amalgamated to create a more readily managed number of units. The command economy system was imposed. This was the historical extreme of state involvement in economics, joined to total mobilization politics of a kind seen elsewhere only under the German variant of fascism. In Latin America, acceptance of the logic of increased state intervention rolled ahead considerably, although statism in the region obviously did not proceed as far as in Eastern Europe.

During the 1940s, despite inflation and import shortages, growth performance in Latin America had been satisfactory. External demand and import substitution contributed to stimulating industrial growth. The perception was thus developed that the state-led road to development was the most appropriate one, which encouraged theories diverging from classical economic theory.

The formation of the Economic Commission for Latin America and the Caribbean (ECLAC) was a major milestone in this process. Under the leadership of Argentine economist Raúl Prebisch, ECLAC was able to articulate and gain international prestige for an interpretation of underdevelopment in the context of a world economy divided into a "center" and a "periphery." According to this view, this division biased the distribution of world progress against the "periphery" through deteriorating terms of trade. The seemingly successful experience of growth and industrialization of the Soviet bloc, as perceived by even some right-wing sectors in Western countries, added strong impetus to this emerging international consensus. These lines of thought, plus the pressures of major balance-of-payments problems, led most Latin American countries in the 1950s to extend and deepen state regulation—especially in foreign trade, but also in the areas of credit, prices, and wages. For the first time in the economic history of the region, state enterprises multiplied rapidly. Great enthusiasm for national economic planning became widespread, stimulated by both local thinking and the U.S. government's Alliance for Progress strategy of the early 1960s. Despite periodic liberalization episodes, these trends prevailed until the mid-1970s.

It is worth emphasizing that when ECLAC advocated protectionism and economic planning, it primarily sought more rapid growth of productivity through the greater absorption of technical progress and the acquisition of dynamic comparative advantage for the export of manufactures. Many feared that Latin America would stagnate if primary exports and raw materials remained the major source of revenues. But only parts of this set of ideas were actually implemented, and the partial measures contributed to rent-seeking activities and gave rise to what economist Fernando Fajnzylber baptized "frivolous protectionism."

For a time, both centrally planned development in Eastern Europe and import-substituting, state-led development in Latin America produced some positive results. Import substitution in Latin

America promoted rapid growth and stimulated a learning process. New entrepreneurial and labor skills were developed that contributed to supply an existing demand for consumer goods and created new markets for intermediate and even capital goods. In Eastern Europe as well, industrialization was rapid for a time—perhaps most markedly in those countries or regions that had been less advanced and less oriented to Western Europe. Urbanization and levels of education also increased dramatically.

THE TURN IN THE TRAJECTORY: DECREASED EFFECTIVENESS OF STATE-LED APPROACHES

Ultimately, however, Stalinist industrialization in Eastern Europe and import-substituting, state-led development in Latin America proved to have high costs. In Latin America, originally justifiable protectionism was maintained beyond the Depression crisis and the postwar phase—and even beyond reasonable "learning" periods. As a result, many distortions and inefficiencies evolved, including monopolistic practices, lack of concern for cost reduction, and low quality of production, all of which led not only to dwindling international competitiveness but also, more broadly, to the gradual loss of touch with the main currents of international technical and economic development. The distortions and inefficiencies of the centrally planned economies of Eastern Europe were, as is well known, still more extreme. Indeed, the paradoxical result of this economic process was that these countries, having a considerably lower share of foreign trade in their GDP than open economies of comparable size, became increasingly dependent (although in a different sense than traditional dependence) on the most developed countries—to a greater degree than countries that had energetically integrated into the world economy. In Latin America, diversification of exports into manufactures was impeded by extreme protectionism until well into the late 1960s. Balances of payments became more rigid, as these economies came to depend more heavily on a continued supply of foreign intermediate and capital goods as well as imported agricultural products (since the drive for industrialization led to the serious neglect of domestic agriculture).

The deeper (and for our investigation more interesting) problem was that the state more and more visibly *overcommitted itself* by undertaking developmental tasks that it was not prepared to fulfill effectively. The dysfunctions of state intervention also became more visible. In most of Latin America, the spirit and pattern of state regulation increasingly came to resemble that in Eastern Europe. Byzantine over-regulation gave actual power to bureaucrats, who often used it for corruption. In both regions, grey and black markets expanded greatly, although they took different forms.

In both regions, the overcommitment of the state had another important effect. The state's leading role in investment in direct production limited the resources available for infrastructure and for social policies, which are everywhere recognized as appropriate, high priority state functions. The postwar period also brought about marked state expansion in the developed regions—especially for the promotion of social development. Even in the industrial nations, ambitious health and education programs in many cases strained fiscal resources and produced budgetary crises. In Eastern Europe, governments overcommitted themselves in similar ways and with tremendous institutional inefficiencies. In Latin America, in contrast, the main problem was not overcommitment in absolute terms, but misallocation to middle- and high-income groups.

While the precise timing of the change varied among and within the two regions, from approximately the early 1970s, the historical trajectory we have been tracing began to turn in both Eastern Europe and Latin America. While government policies continued to rely primarily on interventionist strategies and instruments, intervention began to become less and less effective in promoting growth and welfare.

Moreover, the visibly eroding effectiveness of state intervention was mainly a result of the inherent dynamics of the approach. Erosion was accelerated and made more visible by the oil shock of the early 1970s, but that shock was not, as many analysts have tried to insist, the main cause of growing difficulties within interventionist economies. International shocks do occasionally occur, and it is utterly wrong to interpret external factors as dominant causes of domestic disequilibria without considering that reactions vary in different institutional and policy settings. For instance, oil-dependent Japan and Germany emerged from the incredible shock unscathed. But most of the Eastern European countries reacted to the crisis by increased reliance on autarky and state-led efforts to again spur growth. These efforts turned out to be economic and social disasters. In Latin America, Brazil pursued a somewhat similar course—in sharp contrast to the policies adopted by Colombia and Chile. Where governments did not seek to shield domestic businesses from most of the impact of external shocks, major shifts in the structure of production caused considerable short-run pain, but thereafter led to considerably more competitive and dynamic economies.

To some degree, these trends can be traced in quantitative data. The efficiency of the economies in both regions continuously deteriorated and lagged behind trends in the East Asian "tigers." In Latin America, the general indicator of the erosion of effective state control was obviously hyperinflation. In Eastern Europe, however, eroding effectiveness took the form of shortages rather than inflation. Shortages were not measured, but anecdotal evidence indicates that they were increasing. In those Eastern European countries that experimented early with some decentralization of controls (Hungary and to a lesser degree Poland), shortages were to some extent translated into inflation as well. To various degrees in the two regions, the widening gap between official and black-market exchange rates and declining ratios of savings to national product were also telling indicators of the disintegration. In Eastern Europe, the informal and initially illegal private economy played a growing role—largely outside state intervention and control. In Latin America as well, unregistered private activities in the burgeoning informal sector as well as growing corruption were important, though less easily quantifiable, indicators of the decline of effective state control.

DELIBERATE DISMANTLING: THE BEGINNINGS OF MARKET-ORIENTED REFORM

These troubling trends eventually shook the ideological consensus on state involvement in the economy—though naturally with a time lag. Reformist thinking was more repressed in Eastern Europe, but in the more enlightened parts of the region, reformers also offered a much more fundamental systemic critique. In Latin America, advocates of reform were more vocal (as the region had long been more politically open), yet a new consensus emerged more slowly as a direct consequence of a less severe system crisis. Indeed, the crisis of communism itself changed intellectual and ideological currents elsewhere in the world, providing a strong feedback to evolving ideologies in both regions. Increasingly, the International Monetary Fund and the World Bank also conditioned their assistance on liberalizing structural reforms. The message slowly penetrated that the key issue is not only opening versus closing the economy, but fundamental revision of the whole statist model.

In several Eastern European nations (most clearly in Hungary from 1968 and in Poland somewhat later and even more hesitantly) as well as in a number of Latin American countries, deliberate dismantling of distorted state intervention started with partial or tentative liberalization episodes. Many of these were later abandoned or reversed—since gross mistakes were also made in early, naive liberalizing strategies. These false starts fed back into and accelerated the unplanned process of economic deterioration and de facto disengagement. Where partial but deliberate reforms were more successful, as in Hungary, they eased unplanned distortions and slowed the ad hoc disintegration of control.

A firmer and more broadly based commitment to extensive liberalization and privatization has emerged only fairly recently in some Latin American countries. (Chile was well ahead of most.) In Eastern Europe, a clear commitment dates from 1989 or later—paralleling the sweeping political liberalization in the region.

In both regions, the dominant initial theme of economic liberalization has been basically negative: the deliberate dismantling of mechanisms of state control. A second, more positive theme is emerging, however, as planned liberalization proceeds. The state clearly should retain, in fact regain, crucial roles in regulating markets, providing infrastructure and basic social services, protecting the environment, and possibly promoting aspects of research and development. In addition to these enduring roles, it is increasingly (and ironically) clear that a successful transition to a largely market economy depends on certain key temporary tasks that must be performed—or at least coordinated—by the state. In short, as the Overview notes and Chapter 4 discusses, the drive to dismantle the state is now generating an intense debate on the new relationships taking shape between state, markets, and society.

For a visual summary of this historical trajectory, see Figure 1.

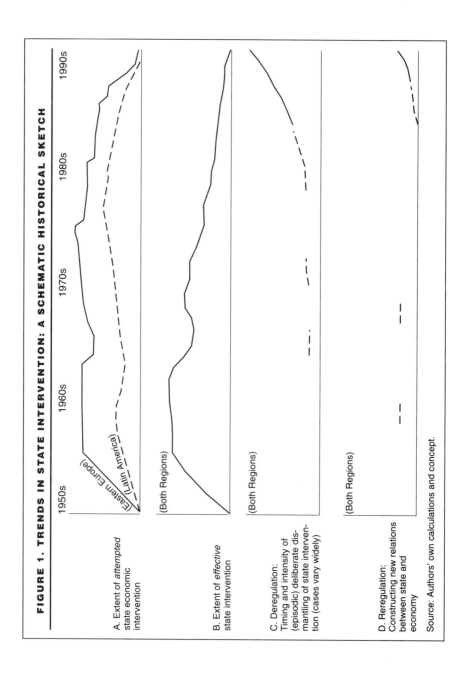

FIGURE 1. TRENDS IN STATE INTERVENTION: A SCHEMATIC HISTORICAL SKETCH

1950s   1960s   1970s   1980s   1990s

A. Extent of *attempted* state economic intervention

(Eastern Europe)

(Latin America)

B. Extent of *effective* state intervention

(Both Regions)

C. Deregulation: Timing and intensity of (episodic) deliberate dismantling of state intervention (cases vary widely)

(Both Regions)

D. Reregulation: Constructing new relations between state and economy

(Both Regions)

Source: Authors' own calculations and concept.

Part II
Chapter
Summaries

Chapter Summaries

Toward Trade Opening: Legacies and Current Strategies

Oscar Muñoz

This chapter analyzes the twin processes of economic reform and democratic transition with a special focus on the interactions between economic and political effects of trade liberalization in the context of transitions to democratic regimes. Similarities and contrasts between Eastern Europe and Latin America serve to illustrate the varying nature of these effects. Most of the observations and arguments refer to specific country cases (Argentina, Bolivia, and Brazil in Latin America, and Bulgaria, Hungary, and Poland in Eastern Europe) with no pretention to generalization.

Although these regions were characterized by quite different political and ideological regimes, in practice they shared inward-looking economic systems, high protectionism, widespread bureaucratism, and overwhelming state intervention. In both regions, growing economic inefficiencies negatively affected growth and stimulated increased indebtedness, which reached crisis proportions in the 1980s.

The chapter is organized with a historical perspective. Early trade reforms in Latin America were implemented to promote higher export growth, given that the import-substitution model was failing to alleviate chronic balance-of-payment problems. The main reforms were oriented to the exchange-rate policy and to tariff reductions. As a consequence, the growth of exports of manufactures increased substantially in the 1960s and 1970s. In some Eastern European countries, for example

Hungary and Poland, some decentralization and demonopolization of trade began back in the late 1960s. Increased demand for imported goods, especially capital goods, contributed to modernizing the economies, but inconsistencies with the rest of the economic system aggravated imbalances, leading to foreign borrowing and also to increased inflation.

With democratic transitions initiated in Eastern Europe in 1989, economic reforms accelerated rapidly. Trade liberalizations and price reforms, among other reforms, were rapidly implemented. The end of intra-CMEA and Soviet trade, however, was a severe shock to most countries in the region, contributing to output losses. Decentralization of state firms and loss of revenues further aggravated fiscal imbalances. Most countries suffered acute recessions and inflation during the first years of the transition. Shock therapy stabilization plans were implemented in most countries, although Hungary managed to follow a more gradual policy, consistent with earlier progress of economic reforms.

The circumstances of the initiation of deeper reforms in Latin America differed from those of Eastern Europe. In the three countries considered, the first democratic governments after the military regimes failed to start widespread reforms. As economic disequilibria deepened, the second round of democratic governments undertook more extended changes, although less radical in depth than in Eastern Europe. For instance, tariffs were lowered to a range between 10–35 percent. Also, since the privatization of state firms was a less radical departure from previous business organization than in Eastern Europe, and Latin American countries did not have to suffer a trade shock comparable to the loss of the Soviet market. Thus the output shock was much less severe.

Crucial for the success of stabilization is the enforcement of fiscal reforms to strengthen the budget. The contrast between the two regions in this respect is especially strong because of the experiences of Argentina and Bolivia. Brazil has had difficulty in attaining fiscal balance and thus has remained afflicted by high inflation. Eastern European countries are having great difficulty with enforcing effective tax collection on privatized enterprises, and fiscal expenditures show high downward rigidity because of welfare implications.

The other area of growing tension relates to management of the exchange rate. Under the open economy system that is being developed in both regions, the exchange rate becomes strongly influenced in the free market by the domestic interest rate. Economic reforms and stabilization policies have raised real interest rates and stimulated capital imports, which has led to appreciation of domestic currencies. This conflicts with the need to sustain depreciated currencies to stimulate exports. A sort of "premature appreciation trap" has developed in reforming countries that may hamper the export-led growth processes (even though appreciation usually contributes to lower inflation in the short run).

This complex set of interactions among economic policies and reforms has deep social and political consequences. Initial economic costs, such as output losses, unemployment, lower wages, and inflation hurt large social groupings. Opening the economies to international trade and capital imports strongly affects the traditional entrepreneurial coalitions that supported earlier phases of development. Resistance to many of those changes may create political instability and eventually impair democratic transitions. Reversals of economic reforms are also a potential danger. A lot depends on the capacity of governments to minimize unnecessary economic costs, as well as on their ability to mobilize institutional resources to increase the degree of social tolerance of those costs. This is crucial to improve credibility of the new policies and the expectation by people that future positive effects for their welfare will materialize.

From a longer-run point of view, widespread agreement has been reached in both regions that sustained growth and international competitiveness is crucial for the consolidation of democracy and improved distributive equity; stagnant economies would be the worst scenario for democratic progress. The East Asian experience provides useful lessons on the design of effective development strategies, yet mechanical application to individual cases is out of place. The "Washington consensus" also has been effective for the initiation phases of the transitions and for the basic reform of economic systems. But new strategies have to be devised that approach the challenge of international competitiveness with equity. This involves new roles for the state and the market, cooperative relationships between the state and the private sector, a regulatory framework that protects both the environment and society from market failures and abuses, and modernization of production structures by linking business with educational and technological institutions.

Property Rights Reform During Democratization

Kálmán Mizsei

Market-oriented economic reforms seek to create or strengthen a competitive, efficient, and enterprising private sector. Where the state has controlled most of the economy, or has deeply penetrated nominally private markets, creating a well-functioning private sector requires new or reoriented laws, regulations, and institutions affecting property rights in the broadest sense—that is, the incentives and constraints that mold the expansion of the private sector and prevent rent-seeking behavior.

Property rights reform, thus defined, includes a broad array of measures. This chapter selects four core categories from the larger array: privatization programs, banking reform, bankruptcy regulations, and rules affecting entry of new businesses. The discussion traces some of the main links between democratic politics and these reforms: how politics affects the reforms, and how the reforms in turn can influence the political scene and democratic prospects.

Democratic politics is often at odds with property rights reform. Electoral cycles press politicians to focus on short- or medium-run goals, whereas well-designed property rights reforms require a long-run perspective. Neutral market regulation benefits the public at large, but constituencies for such benefits are usually less organized and less vocal than the narrow interest groups that press for special privileges.

In some dual transition countries, a brief period of "extraordinary politics" eased these political pressures and permitted dedicated politicians to launch strong stabilization policies and initial property rights reforms. Successful macroeconomic stabilization itself greatly assists private sector growth both directly and indirectly. Moreover, a bold initial program generates momentum that almost automatically facilitates certain further reforms. Although fear of political backlash has blocked stabilization in many countries, strong stabilization programs in fact often generate political support, as in Argentina, Bolivia, and the Czech Republic.

Privatization can be viewed as two-pronged: the conversion of public enterprises into privately owned and managed enterprises, and the growth of new private firms. In Eastern Europe, governments have tried a wide variety of approaches to privatizing state enterprises. The mass voucher scheme pioneered in the Czech Republic has proved politically popular and permits rapid transfer of ownership, but company structure remains highly concentrated and effects on actual management are yet to be assessed. Hungary's contrasting, much more gradual approach had different political and economic costs and benefits. Farther east, political paralysis or chaos has blocked privatization in many countries; public tolerance (in Hungary and the Czech Republic) or antagonism (in Poland, and more strongly farther east) toward foreign participation has been an important factor shaping the design and progress of privatization programs.

Where private sector growth—through both privatization and new private investment—has been rapid, effects on politics have generally been positive: Extremist opposition parties get little popular support, and there is a growing social and political stratum of small owners who are likely to play a stabilizing role in politics. Yet, as some Latin

American cases suggest, privatization can also threaten democratic consolidation if it excessively favors already wealthy and powerful groups.

Regulation of banking is particularly sensitive because banking failures have immense repercussions for the state and society. It is very hard for governments to refrain from intervening to prevent such failures, and banks are therefore extremely prone to rent-seeking. Financial sector reform is also a particularly tempting area for political favoritism. In Central Europe, there has been some regulatory reform but a clear banking reform strategy has been slow to emerge; farther east, many countries still lack even basic regulatory changes. In Latin America, financial sector ownership is less distorted than in Eastern Europe, but regulatory frameworks need reform. In both regions, weak banking reforms perpetuate concentrations of political as well as economic power. Cutting the cord between the budget and the banking sector is a key area of democratic reform.

Bankruptcy laws—the regulation of business failure—is another crucial element for an efficient private sector. In this area as in the others examined, technical considerations must be combined with a sensitive calculation of administrative and political feasibility. In Hungary, for instance, particularly tough bankruptcy laws intended to sharply improve financial discipline backfired when a wave of failures swamped the courts' capacity to implement the laws. Worse, the failures set in motion a chain of bank bailouts that partly repoliticized state-business relations.

In Central Europe, *rules affecting the entry of new businesses* were dramatically deregulated immediately after the communist collapse, in part because there was a temporary vacuum in interest representation. This contrasts sharply with Latin America, where vested bureaucratic and private sector interests create high hurdles for new firms (except in Chile). From a political perspective, entry rules powerfully affect the rate of growth of a *Mittelstand* or bourgeoisie, which historically has supported the emergence of democracy. In the long run, entry rules also affect the size structure of firms in the economy; less centralized controls encourage a large number of small companies and reduce the risk of undue political influence by dominant large firms.

In short, while democratic politics often constrain property rights reforms, bold use of moments of "extraordinary politics" and politically acute policy design have permitted major progress in some dual transition countries. In turn, vigorous property rights reform (combined with macroeconomic stabilization) has won electoral rewards in several countries. In the longer run, privatization, banking reforms, and liberalization of entry rules should reduce (though not eliminate) pressure from special interests seeking direct or indirect subsidies and other favors from the state. The relative political strength of different business groups will also shift in favor of newer, more dynamic businesses. Finally, deregulation of entry rules and the emergence of new firms will strengthen the entrepreneurial middle strata, which tends to shun political extremism and value democratic openness.

Labor and Business Roles in Dual Transitions: Building Blocks or Stumbling Blocks?

Joan M. Nelson

Democratization and market-oriented economic reforms dramatically change the roles of major economic interests, including labor and business. In turn, how these groups adjust their goals, tactics, and organization powerfully affects the prospects for and nature of emerging market economies and democratic polities.

A common central theme underlies the changing roles of interest groups in Latin America and Eastern Europe. Where the state exercised pervasive controls, such groups focused their attention on influencing key officials in the agencies that administered the controls. Political parties and legislatures were not important channels for protecting or pursuing interests in either region, nor did public opinion play a role. Conflicts between groups were mediated by state agencies.

By sharply cutting state intervention, market-oriented reforms change these patterns. Unions, firms, and business associations must focus on new channels for resource allocation and key policy decisions: market mechanisms, labor-management relations, legislatures, political parties, and public opinion (which affects the behavior of legislatures and parties). These new channels require changes in organization and tactics. Moreover, simultaneous democratization changes the ground rules for exercising influence and transforms and multiplies the players. Interest groups have more freedom and autonomy, but also more rivals and complex choices.

Unions in dual transition countries often face particularly difficult dilemmas. Deregulation, privatization, and labor market liberalization usually impose severe costs on unionized labor (though not necessarily on the labor force as a whole) and reduce the strength and bargaining influence of unions as institutions. Yet union efforts to block reforms may isolate them politically, in situations where reforms have broad public support. In the early stages of reform in Eastern Europe, most unions were surprisingly passive, even cooperative. More recently, however, many have become more assertive. Where economic reforms have stalled and no workable party system has emerged, as in Romania, unions have been most confrontational and disruptive. In contrast, where reforms have moved ahead and workable parties provide reasonably effective government, as in the Czech Republic and Hungary, unions have been low-key and more flexible.

In Latin America, post-authoritarian union roles followed a different trajectory because the break with the past was much less marked and political opening was not linked initially to economic reform. Later, radical economic reforms in Argentina and Bolivia were accompanied by dramatic weakening of unions. In Brazil, in contrast, their political roles have strengthened. As in Eastern Europe, many Latin American unions are groping for new agendas and tactics appropriate for the radically altered economies.

In both regions, economic opening and labor market liberalization will put great pressure on unions to increase their flexibility, to shift from confrontational to consultative approaches to management, and to accept links between productivity and wages and benefits. Signs of these trends are already clear in some of the recent collective agreements. In some countries, rising center-left parties offer new channels for union political influence but also require new compromises.

In contrast to unions, the political influence of business groups has clearly increased in both regions. Business interests are heterogeneous, and business influence is exercised through many channels, including direct contacts with politicians and officials, forming or financing parties, and controlling the media. Business associations play a much more modest role in representing business interests than unions do in organizing and channeling workers' demands. Nevertheless, some Latin American associations have played significant roles in supporting democratic transitions and influencing aspects of economic reform, and their roles are growing in Eastern Europe.

In dual transition countries, the challenge is not only to contain and discourage interest group actions that may derail economic reforms or threaten fragile democracies, but to encourage more positive roles. Reorienting relations between the state and major economic interests in society is a key element in creating a well-functioning market economy. In industrial societies, the state must intervene extensively to protect and promote a range of public goals, including public health and safety, the environment, and the competitiveness of markets themselves. Interest associations can provide crucial information and facilitate implementation—ongoing, not solely transitional, requirements.

But it is a delicate task to retool state-interest group relations in ways that facilitate communication and consultation but minimize opportunities for rent-seeking or, worse still, the emergence of privatized areas of government activity, where state agencies and specific private interests collude to the exclusion of broader public surveillance and guidance. Retooled relations between the state and group interests must strike a fine balance between access and autonomy for both interest groups and state agencies.

There are no formulas for rebuilding channels of communication between the state and major interest groups and for creating incentives for those groups to play pragmatic and constructive roles. The social corporatist institutions that worked well in several small Western and Northern European countries for much of the post-World War II period were based on conditions lacking in most dual transition countries. Tripartite social pacts, even where feasible, are temporary. In most countries, the most promising approach might be described as the piecemeal engineering of consensus—a strategy guided by the goal of enlarging the area of societal consensus on basic institutions.

A few broad principles may help in pursuing such a strategy:

■ Encouraging internal democracy and accountability within interest associations (while preserving some autonomy for leaders);

■ Favoring consultative arrangements that bring together a broad array of interests;

■ Devising solutions to conflicts and problems that minimize and "download" state intervention and encourage direct communication and negotiations among groups whose interests are intertwined but may conflict; and

■ Establishing systems to monitor and review downloaded functions, to reduce risks of collusive behavior and rent-seeking.

Piecemeal engineering can gradually widen areas of consensus on controversial public policy issues. Broadened consensus in turn is crucial to the confidence of all groups that democratic rules and democratic changes in government will not reverse already accomplished reforms nor damage their most fundamental interests.

Reforming Weak States and Deficient Bureaucracies

Jacek Kochanowicz

The deep crisis in both Latin America and Eastern Europe—manifested in enormous foreign debt, huge budget deficits, inflation, and the disintegration of public services—is a result, of, among other things, the overextension of the state. For several decades, the state took upon itself enormous responsibilities in an attempt to fulfill a modernizing role. This role gradually became too heavy a burden and resulted in the exhaustion of state capabilities and the state's near collapse. This was more obvious in the case of the communist countries of Eastern Europe, where virtually all social life became subjected to state control. But it was also the case in Latin America, where the dominant role of the state was justified by developmentalist ideologies. The crisis in the countries of both regions is therefore a crisis of the state.

A standard recommendation for dealing with the crises in both of these regions (as well as elsewhere) is downsizing the state—through budget cuts, the reduction of social services, privatization of state enterprises, etc. While there is no question that this course is right, the central argument of this chapter is that it is not enough. In addition to reducing the state (which is inevitable whether one likes it or not), *reshaping* the state is necessary.

The standard recommendations, arguing simply for less of the state, tend to overlook its tremendous importance for the functioning of both the market economy and democracy. An effective state is important for the market as a guarantor of the "rules of the game," such as property rights. A well-functioning state is also crucial for democracy, since its basic services underpin community life and link ordinary citizens to the political system.

Nation-states, which emerged in Europe early in the modern period, facilitated the rise of capitalism. The state was even more of a contributor to economic development in such "latecomers" as Russia, Japan, and Germany at the end of the nineteenth century. In the second half of this century, the state was important in the postwar economic reconstruction of Europe and, even more so, in the achievement of the "Asian Miracle."

Somewhat paradoxically, the state also has a role to play in the process of transition from command to market economies in Eastern Europe, as well as in the shift to more market-oriented systems in Latin America. Critical transition tasks that cannot be fulfilled without the active, if temporary, participation of the state include:

- Construction or strengthening of the institutions needed to support the market;
- Investment in infrastructure;
- Temporary substitution for nonexistent, or underdeveloped voluntary associations;
- Reconstruction of social services;
- Roll back of environmental devastation;
- Investment in human capital;
- Reconstruction of industries, of which privatization is a part;
- "Debt management" (negotiations with creditors, and the mobilization of resources for repayment;

- Negotiations with such international institutions as the World Bank and the International Monetary Fund; and
- Administration of foreign aid.

Therefore, restructuring and reviving the state are as necessary as downsizing it. This chapter focuses on the restructuring of the state machinery and particularly on the creation of a highly qualified and motivated bureaucracy.

The bureaucracy is decisive in implementation and consolidation of democratic and market reforms. It is the most important "filter," or mediating mechanism, through which political ideas, programs, and projects are translated into everyday practice. Deficient bureaucracies—that is, those that are inefficient, embedded in informal patronage systems, or outright corrupt—can easily impede, if not derail, market and democratic reforms. It is also this particular part of the state that comes into contact with the public; its performance is therefore critical for how the state is perceived.

Bureaucracies, to fulfill their role, should therefore be reorganized as independent, apolitical civil services; they should be well-paid, carefully recruited, and promoted according to merit, as well as sufficiently insulated from undue interference by parties and politicians or business interests. Since countries in both regions are severely constrained by budgetary problems, their bureaucracies should not be large.

While the task of restructuring bureaucracies may seem technical, it in fact faces serious social and political obstacles rooted in the specific histories of countries in both regions. In Latin America, these legacies consist mostly of long traditions of patronage and clientelism. The state machineries in the region are too often treated as a source of jobs to be distributed among the winning parties. For their part, Eastern European nations—most of which were not independent throughout the nineteenth century's era of modernization—lack indigenous traditions of strong and effective states. Moreover, five decades of the communist system resulted in the excessive growth of the state, characterized by particularly deficient bureaucracies. Therefore, new democracies have very little experience upon which to build.

Despite these serious obstacles, however, there are chances for a change for the better, since the present ruling elites increasingly have to legitimize themselves by governing not only democratically, but also efficiently and honestly. For those chances to succeed, however, there must be greater recognition of the role of the state in the transformation to markets and democracy—both among the elites of the countries in question and within the international institutions.

Part III
Intricate
Links

Chapter One

Toward Trade Opening: Legacies and Current Strategies

Oscar Muñoz

This chapter compares aspects of Latin American and Eastern European experience with the dual transition process of market reform and democratization. The focus is on trade liberalization—one of the main challenges of market reform. Trade liberalization itself is much more than the manipulation of policy instruments. From an *economic* point of view, it links the domestic economy to international markets. But it also involves highly *political* choices: Changing a specific country's international economic relations strongly affects the power base of social actors, both domestic and foreign.

Following World War II, many Latin American countries experienced democratization after the collapse of oligarchic regimes or dictatorial populism. These processes were accompanied by rising nationalism as well as sustained efforts to industrialize. Mainstream thinking in these countries at the time interpreted traditional links with the international economy as detrimental to indigenous development. Protectionism was seen as a natural instrument to promote industrialization, which in turn provided the economic base for a rising middle class, an industrial labor force, and entrepreneurship. From this perspective, it is a paradox that, in the early 1990s, "trade opening" in several Latin American countries is being carried out by newly democratizing regimes disenchanted with protectionist practices.

In Eastern Europe, post–World War II official perspectives on trade were not very different, despite sharp contrasts in the political and ideological context. The regimes that gained power throughout the region sought to delink it from the West in order to build the material bases of a new communist order, expected to be more democratic and egalitarian. Both economic and political relations with the West were severed or subordinated to the dictates of the Soviet superpower. In contrast to Latin America, however—where each nation tried to individually pursue its economic strategy—the regional Council of Mutual Economic Assistance (CMEA) was organized, and to some extent the socialist division of labor provided the basic directions of trade and production. Today, the Eastern European countries, like those of Latin America, are striving to reconcile political democratization with economic and political opening to the West.

Long periods of frustration have thus led both regions to drop old expectations. In Latin America, those who valued development and reduced inequalities no longer think that economic nationalism and inward-oriented development represent an adequate policy course. In Eastern Europe, those who expected to sustain relative economic equality through economic and political isolationism have come to recognize the fragility of that approach. The fact that both regions, despite very different historical trajectories, now converge on reform processes aiming to build modern market economies and democratic institutions makes comparative analysis both attractive and useful.

Market reform processes generally pass through several stages. They are initiated under particular political and economic circumstances that discredit the status quo. What usually sets them off is a financial crisis due to unmanageable balance-of-payments problems or to uncontrolled hyperinflation. Widespread perceptions that the already tried policies are ineffective generally add strength to the feeling that deeper reforms are needed. Policymakers or politicians responsible for previous strategies are also discredited—making their replacement essential for building new expectations and confidence. Launching reforms is also facilitated by some political insulation of state elites from political parties or interest groups.

The actual implementation of reforms faces a number of problems. Tradeoffs between policy objectives raise difficult choices. The major tension in implementing trade reforms arises with stabilization policies. Since these reforms are usually initiated under strong instability, and themselves contribute to instability, sooner or later a choice must be made between macroeconomic equilibrium or further promoting trade opening. This conflict centers on the exchange market and fiscal equilibrium. Trade reforms usually require devaluation, which is inflationary. Tariff reductions also affect fiscal revenues. Implementing trade reforms also poses *political* tensions related to economic costs and power redistribution. These may create social resistance, and the management of this resistance within democratic institutions is in turn crucial for the survival of economic reform and for the ultimate consolidation of democracy.

The big question is how quickly economic reform *consolidation* can be achieved—that is, how quickly the new institutions of the economic system will be firmly accepted by political actors and society in general. Such consolidation is crucial for private economic agents to view the reforms as credible. There is an inherent contradiction between market reform consolidation and democratic consolidation, however, as the latter assumes the possibility of economic policy reversals and changes brought about through democratic procedures. Thus, it probably never can be said that market reforms, as understood in the 1990s, are consolidated once and for all. History teaches that institutions are dynamic and always subject to change. Furthermore, as contemporary experience clearly shows, there is no unique model of a market economy. But a crucial test of economic consolidation is whether growth resumes and stability is achieved. Economic crises that launch reforms are accompanied by stagnation or even recession. The ultimate success of an economic system depends on whether it can achieve growth and stability and then sustain both long enough for institutions to become credible and acceptable. This is the basis for predictability— a crucial ingredient of a decentralized economic system.

This chapter's discussion of the recent reform experience in Latin America and Eastern Europe is organized in terms of the initiation, implementation, and consolidation phases of reform.[1] Two other comments are in order. First, the *institutional* aspects of economic reform—for example, privatization, reorganization of the financial sector, and new economic laws—are not dealt with here because they are the subject of the chapter by Kálmán Mizsei in this volume. Second, although the chapter presents a general discussion of the issues involved, frequent references are made to specific country cases, especially to Argentina, Bolivia, Brazil, Bulgaria, Chile, Hungary, and Poland. All of these except Chile are simultaneous transition cases studied in an earlier phase of this project. Although Chile started economic reform under an authoritarian regime, two considerations justify references to this case. Even under authoritarianism, economic policy choices were not exempt from political debate and from pressure groups within social forces that supported the regime; there was thus a specific "political economy" of reform.[2] Moreover, the crucial test for the consolidation of economic reforms came just after the transition to democracy was started, as a large proportion of politicians expected strong reversals. Therefore it can be argued that, in Chile, market consolidation has taken place during the democratic transition in the 1990s.

LEGACIES OF INWARD-LOOKING INDUSTRIALIZATION

Building a market economy is a demanding objective. For most economies in the world of the 1990s, a growth strategy implies an international orientation. The inward orientation that both Latin American and Eastern European countries developed for many decades imposes a heavy burden on the present transition in both regions. The legacy is embodied in production structures, entrepreneurial experience, skill profiles, and social organizations that cannot easily be readjusted to the new conditions.

Historical Legacies

Despite obvious differences originating in history, geopolitics, institutions, ideologies, and value systems, the economic structures prevalent in Latin American and Eastern European countries in the late 1980s shared some common characteristics. In both regions, these structures were the outcome of an inward-looking development model and of macroeconomic disequilibria that developed in the 1980s.

In Latin America, the closed-economy model was the result of a gradually evolving mix of political and economic factors. The region started its industrial revolution in the nineteenth century as an open-economy system progressively integrated into the world system through its primary export structures and marked by a growing proportion of foreign capital ownership. In some countries, especially those of the Southern Cone (Argentina, Chile, and Uruguay), spontaneous industrialization was stimulated by dynamic export sectors. After the Great Depression and the collapse of foreign trade and finance, industrialization was further stimulated by import substitution. By that time, traditional oligarchic regimes were also breaking down, and the new middle-class or populist regimes rising to power were trying to promote income redistribution in highly stratified societies.

After World War II, the emergent social forces identified industrialization with their expectations of better wages, higher urban employment opportunities, more education, and other improvements. Urban entrepreneurial classes also saw industrialization as the best way to develop and become more independent of unstable mining or agriculture. Urban coalitions supported state policies leading to protectionism and to an institutional framework designed to reallocate resources from the primary sectors to the urban, industrial sector. Stronger pressures for democratization coincided with widespread nationalistic sentiment, strengthened by the feeling that foreign capital had achieved excessive political power and that the international economy was not favorable to primary exporters. The 1949 regional economic survey of the U.N. Economic Commission for Latin America (ECLA) gave intellectual and technical support to those trends and provided a rationale for explicit industrialization policies. The main objectives of the new strategies were the development of indigenous technological capabilities through a learning process and the transformation of production structures to incorporate a larger content of manufactures and to reduce raw materials, thus allowing the benefits of economies of scale and the dissemination of externalities typical of industrial production.

Several Latin American countries were able to achieve relatively high rates of growth of GDP and to successfully accelerate their industrialization processes through the 1940s and 1950s. However, the import-substitution model reproduced in Latin America some aspects of bureaucratic Soviet-type industrialization strategy. In both regions, a strong diversion from comparative advantage toward supplying domestic markets irrespective of international price ratios was the leading organizing principle for the allocation of economic resources. At the microeconomic level, both regions showed the typical disadvantages of a closed economy. Grossly distorted incentives stimulated inefficiencies, low quality of production, poor managerial capacities, technological backwardness, and vertical integration within firms. All of these factors contributed to a strong lack of international competitiveness.

Clearly there were sharp contrasts between the two regions, starting with the different nature of property regimes and ideological systems. In most of Latin America, the dominant regime was capitalism—notwithstanding widespread populism or centralized state intervention, which, according to critics, more than superficially resembled the Soviet-type model (e.g., Chile in the early 1970s). The basic contrast between mainly capitalist production structures and the centrally planned structures of Eastern European economies had far-reaching consequences for social relations in each region. Trade unions and business associations were very active in Latin America; they eventually mobilized wide public support and even challenged governments. Private lobbies and state clienteles in the region were basically organized on rent-seeking principles, whereas in Eastern Europe they were linked to Communist Party structures and ideological loyalties. Thus the political economy of industrialization was quite different in the two regions: in Latin America, it was the result of organized pressure from society, with a strong populist flavor; in Eastern Europe, it corresponded to a technocratic design by the state. Seen from this perspective, Latin American industrialization was more democratic—even though new urban elites developed strong ties with both domestic and international financial power groups. These ties prompted criticism by the new "dependency school," which argued against foreign social and economic domination implied by the alliance between domestic and transnational capital.

These regional differences in social relations were also expressed economically. In Eastern Europe, building heavy industry, even where it meant sacrificing consumption needs, was an explicit objective of economic planning. In Latin America, where the market still prevailed, despite distortions, industrialization first produced basic consumer goods in response to demand, and only then moved on to intermediate and light capital goods. As Albert Hirschman has remarked, by the early 1980s, discontent with their own production structures was widespread within both regions. In Eastern Europe the masses demanded the expansion of welfare and consumer goods, whereas in Latin America there was strong criticism of the underdeveloped nature of the industrial base.[3] Only a few countries—most clearly Argentina, Brazil, and Mexico—were able to achieve the more advanced industrial phase.

Brazil became a leading industrializing country in Latin America. An ambitious industrialization strategy began to be implemented in the 1950s; its goal was the development of an advanced industrial structure, including heavy industry, the production of capital goods, and access to high technology. Because foreign capital was considered necessary to the effort, the state developed a policy to actively stimulate foreign investment. Special privileges were granted to transnational firms. Thus emerged the so-called "triple alliance model" of political economy: The development process in Brazil was politically based on the converging interests of foreign capital and local private capital under the leadership of the state.

This model got special impetus under Brazil's military regime (1964–1984), especially after the failed experiment with economic liberalization (1964–67). For about six years, economic growth boomed at rates above 10 percent. This period came to be known as the "Brazilian miracle." Thereafter, several difficulties emerged. Prominent among these were 1) the oil shock of 1973–74, which hit the Brazilian economy very hard, due to its high oil-imports bill; and 2) the accumulated disequilibria of the import-substitution model, which reinforced a strong bias toward high inflation. Instead of facing these structural disequilibria (e.g., the extreme inward orientation of the economy and an intractable fiscal deficit), the military authorities chose to intensify the same strategy; at the cost of rising foreign indebtedness, they tried to further deepen the industrial structure.

The policy framework developed from the 1960s to the 1980s included a number of incentives and regulations that were progressively diversified and refined—especially in the 1980s, when the crisis intensified. Fiscal incentives were granted through the credits of the State Development Bank (BNDES). The promotion of non-competitive markets was a generalized practice through investment licensing, "sectoral agreements," or "local content requirements." Public procurement contracts were also used. Rent-seeking behavior pervaded the entrepreneurial sector. The need to develop technological capabilities was neglected.[4]

The proliferation of incentives and restrictions prompted the development of sectoral coordination mechanisms that further strengthened the influence of organized interests. Sectoral chambers were given powers to manage the "integrated sectoral programs."

Early Latin American Experiments with Trade Reform

In the 1960s, trade reforms were initiated in several Latin American countries with the aim of balancing import substitution with export growth. Incentives had been biased against exports under import-substituting industrialization, and trade balances were deteriorating. The main reforms were oriented toward more rational use of exchange-rate policy, gradual conversion of quantitative import restrictions to tariff restrictions, and compensation to exporters for tariffs paid on their imported inputs. Chile and Colombia had initiated new exchange-rate policies by the mid-1960s. In Brazil, strong incentives to promote the growth of manufactured exports were introduced in the late 1960s, after the military had taken over. Foreign investment in manufactures—either directly or in association with domestic investment—was also stimulated. Positive results were obtained in a short time. The share of manufactures in total Latin American exports doubled between 1965 and 1970 (rising from 4.5 to 9.1 percent, respectively) and doubled yet again over the next decade (reaching 20 percent by 1980).[5] Several efforts at regional integration were also initiated.

Reducing tariff protection was more difficult to accomplish. Vested interests permanently opposed the adjustment to more rational tariff structures. The Argentine case clearly illustrates this problem. The country implemented several trade reforms beginning in the 1960s, but these were always reversed—reflecting the political and economic instability that had affected Argentina since the 1940s. Trade liberalization was first attempted in the late 1960s, during the military regime of the time, but was later reversed as strong opposition mounted and the second Juan Perón government (1973–74) was installed.

During the military regime that followed, a new attempt at trade reform was started in 1976, in an approach similar to the strategy then being applied in Chile. Nontariff barriers were eliminated, and nominal tariffs were cut from an average of 94 to 44 percent.[6] Another tariff reduction (to 32 percent) followed, together with currency appreciation and growing foreign indebtedness. Large differentials among tariff categories were maintained, however, allowing industrial pressure groups to lobby for shifts from lower to higher tariff brackets. In several sectors (ranging from the automobile industry to the industrial-military complex and the steel industry), special quantitative restrictions were also maintained. It has been estimated that actual effective protection was not substantially reduced after 1977, when redundant tariffs were eliminated.[7] Furthermore, frequent reversals favoring specific lobbies contributed to the reform's loss of credibility.

Rising overvaluation of the exchange rate also acted as a disincentive to exports. With the financial crisis of 1982, the attempt at trade reform was sharply reversed, and by the mid-1980s, Argentina was back to a more traditional protectionist system marked by high and dispersed tariffs, quantitative import restrictions, special regimes, exceptions, and other characteristics making for a very complex bureaucratic system. Business associations such as the Unión Industrial Argentina became influential in the implementation of these restrictions in exchange for their support of the stabilization plans. Effective protection was very discretionary and depended on the bargaining power of rent-seeking groups, both sectoral and regional. As a trade policy instrument, ad-valorem tariffs lost importance relative to nontariff barriers, which included quantitative restrictions such as public health authorizations, approval by military and nuclear-energy commissions, antidumping legislation, "buy national" rules, and even would-be importers' sworn statements that there was no domestic supply of the goods they requested to import. Tariffs remained important only as a source of fiscal revenue. The private sector developed specialized capacities to maximize benefits from the protective system.[8]

Market Reforms Within Socialism

Traditional trade systems in Eastern Europe were not directly comparable to the classic Latin American protectionist system. In Eastern Europe, trade was subject to state monopoly and central rationing. Moreover, most of the region's trade was carried out within the CMEA, under bilateral agreements among governments. Thus neither a market nor private dealings existed. Trade had to be bilaterally balanced among countries, and enterprise managers had to bargain hard with state officials to obtain imported goods instead of optimizing according to economic criteria of decision-making. Prices of traded goods were determined by central planners without reference to international prices. Differentials were absorbed by the state. Tariffs were of minor importance—as in many Latin American countries, where significant exemptions prevailed. An important consequence was the inefficient use of prices in production decisions. Under a system of material balances, use of traded goods depends mainly on central planning rather than on economic calculations made by the managers themselves.

Within the region, Hungary started to reform its trade system in 1968. Dissatisfaction with the traditional command economy was by then a "tradition," and reformist thinking advocated gradual decentralization. In 1968, the planned economic system was abolished, and decentralized markets were stimulated. Managers of small- and medium-size enterprises were given more autonomy to bargain. Authorizations were granted to individual firms to engage in specific trade and to trading firms to compete among themselves; this meant a gradual de-monopolization of trade. Cost-benefit considerations began to be applied. A decade later, in the late 1970s, prices began to be liberalized in compensation for massive reductions in state subsidies. Then, in the first half of the 1980s, new market-oriented policies were implemented. These included the legalization of private partnership, self-management of large public enterprises, the use of international prices as guidelines for domestic prices, and further price liberalization.[9]

By the second half of the 1980s, conflicts between the reform movement and the traditional political elite became more open, as the latter opposed further reforms. Economic growth was slowing down, despite the Kádár regime's efforts to implement expansionary policies. The consequences were higher external indebtedness (total foreign debt almost doubled between 1984 and 1987), balance-of-payments disequilibrium, a rising fiscal deficit (3.9 percent of GDP in 1987), and inflation. Discontent spread, the movement for political reform intensified, and János Kádár was forced from power in 1989. The next government applied a highly restrictive monetary policy, making macroeconomic equilibrium the main target, and it implemented new structural reforms. Commercial banks were authorized, some privatizations were started, quantitative import controls were abolished, a reduction in tariffs was announced—and foreign investment was stimulated. In 1990, the communist regime came to an end, and democratic parliamentary elections were held.[10]

In Poland, growing dissatisfaction with economic performance emerged in the mid-1960s, after a period of rapid industrialization and improved social welfare. Symptoms of inefficiency became evident: growing shortages of factors of production, halted growth, increased costs of welfare programs, and accelerated inflation. Social unrest stimulated the introduction of market elements in a search for market socialism. The managers of state firms were given more autonomy, and both the linkage of wages to performance and the establishment of family-size private business were accepted.[11] During the 1970s, imports of Western technology and of consumer goods—financed with foreign credit—were increased. This led to rapid indebtedness, which reached crisis proportions in the early 1980s and mobilized the social opposition led by Solidarity.

New reforms were introduced in the course of the 1980s.[12] These included a larger voice for workers in the management of firms, partial price liberalization, state licenses to firms for trading directly with foreign countries, and the transformation of state plans into guidelines. A currency-exchange market was also established. In 1986, Poland joined the International Monetary Fund (IMF) and the World Bank. However, inflation started to accelerate in 1987 and reached the three-digit level (more than 600 percent) in 1990—after total price liberalization had been decreed in a context of wage indexation. The investment rate fell steadily during the 1980s, reaching a low of 11.6 percent of national income in 1990.[13] In July 1989, the first non-communist government was established.

SHAPING OPEN ECONOMIES UNDER NEW DEMOCRATIC GOVERNMENTS

In parts of Eastern Europe, when communist regimes collapsed in 1989, trade opened almost immediately as part of the overall drive to build an open market economy and to start a democratic transition. In Latin America, in contrast, democratic transitions had already started in Argentina, Bolivia, and Brazil. But the region's first transition governments opted to maintain protectionism together with varied mixtures of populist policies and structural adjustment, which only deepened the financial crisis that had been building since 1981. Only during the second round of democratic governments—in Bolivia in 1985, in Argentina in 1989, and then in Brazil in 1990—was it decided to embark upon more profound economic reforms.

Trade Reforms and Stabilization in Democratizing Eastern Europe

Post-communist Hungary and especially Poland moved rapidly to open their economies. In Hungary, trade liberalization was accelerated in 1989 and almost completed by 1991. Tariffs were reduced from an average level of 16 percent in 1986–89 to 13 percent in 1991.[14] In Poland, central control of foreign trade was totally eliminated in January 1990. Tariffs (averaging around 12 percent) became the only major import-control instrument, although specific tariffs still varied widely, and some temporary nontariff restrictions remained.[15]

POLAND. Price reforms carried out in 1989 in Poland included general price liberalization, a large devaluation, and full convertibility for current-account transactions. The effect of these reforms—aggravated by the trade shock from the breakup of the CMEA agreement and the loss of the Soviet market, as well as by falling output and a rising fiscal deficit (7.5 percent of GNP)—was to fuel inflation. Then a drastic stabilization plan, better known as the "big bang" shock therapy, was launched under the leadership of Deputy Prime Minister Leszek Balcerowicz; the plan aimed to lower fiscal expenditures, reduce subsidies drastically, increase taxes, and secure tight monetary policy. Wage ceilings were imposed, and increases in excess of the ceiling were made subject to stiff taxes in order to control inflation.[16] Foreign financing was also obtained to complement stabilization policy. Hyperinflation was halted, but inflation continued at relatively high levels. The recession that developed and the appreciation of the exchange rate to help stabilization in turn stimulated some trade-reform reversals. In August 1991, import tariffs for agricultural products were raised, and bans, quotas, and licenses were established for a few specific products, such as tobacco and alcohol. Other temporary restrictions have since been imposed on agricultural products.

HUNGARY. A major source of Hungary's economic disequilibrium has been the balance-of-payments deficit. As mentioned earlier, the external debt almost doubled during the mid-1980s, and this quickly imposed a very heavy burden of interest payments. By 1990, debt service absorbed 45 percent of exports. The strategy adopted by the government was further liberalization, maintenance of international credibility by keeping up debt payments, and more incentives to foreign investment. By 1991, prices of 90 percent of all goods had been liberalized; most of the exemptions were food products. These policies were accompanied by moderate devaluation and by pegging the forint to a basket of currencies. Foreign-exchange regulations were relaxed, and full convertibility was established for current-account transactions. The black market in foreign exchange collapsed. Since then, there has been a steady trend of appreciation in response to incentives to attract foreign investment (no limits have been imposed on profit remittances), high interest rates, and the government's efforts to stabilize by raising taxes and putting ceilings on wage adjustments.[17]

The stabilization policy pursued in Hungary has been relatively successful. Inflation did not jump either to Latin American levels or to those in some other Eastern European countries, and it has been kept at moderate levels (32 percent in 1991, but lower in 1992–93). A modest fall in real wages and currency appreciation contributed to reducing cost pressures. High interest rates helped increase private savings, reduced expenditures, and contributed to offsetting the high and stubborn fiscal deficit (around 8 percent of GDP in 1992), which remains one of the most difficult problems for stabilization.[18]

BULGARIA. Economic reforms in Bulgaria were initiated in early 1991, after the near collapse of the economy. Despite numerous attempts to introduce superficial reforms during the 1960s, 1970s, and 1980s, Bulgaria remained one of the most centralized countries of Eastern Europe. High dependence on Soviet and CMEA trade made for acute external vulnerability. During the 1980s, instead of adjusting to the oil shock and the international disturbances, Bulgaria followed a strategy aiming to deepen industrialization within the trading sphere of the Soviet bloc. Between 1984 and 1989, foreign debt increased more than threefold.[19] In February 1991, Bulgaria agreed with the IMF on a "shock treatment" stabilization plan that included price de-control, aggregate demand restriction, and trade and exchange-rate liberalization. Inflation accelerated, exceeding 480 percent in 1991.[20] A combination of external factors—the loss of the Soviet market, the Gulf War, and the embargo against Yugoslavia—affected the Bulgarian economy dramatically—probably more so than any other in Eastern Europe. It has been estimated that the country lost about 90 percent of its CMEA markets between 1990 and 1992. GDP fell by 17 percent and industrial output by about 22 percent in 1991.[21]

By 1992, economic distress characterized most Eastern European countries.[22] Domestic production was still about 30 percent below 1989 levels, and even lower in countries where the command economy had been more rigid (including Bulgaria). Massive unemployment and falling real wages have led to deterioration in the standard of living. However, improvements have been made in the control of inflation after the initial accelerations in 1989–1990, and by 1993 several countries—most clearly the Czech Republic and Poland—had resumed economic growth. Fiscal budgets remain the most intractable problem. Deficits have risen in most countries, mainly because of lower revenues associated with the recession, the increased autonomy of state enterprises, and institutional weakness in collecting taxes from the growing private sector. Since unemployment and reduced real wages have increased the need for social security, and the state also faces rising needs for public investment in infrastructure, the prospects for fiscal balance are somber.

The Hyperinflation Stimulus to Trade Reform in Latin America

Although various trade reforms were attempted in Latin America as early as the 1960s, the major sweep of trade reform was carried out, as already mentioned, in the relatively short time span between 1985 and 1992. Tariffs and other selective import restrictions were reduced drastically—to a range of 10–35 percent, somewhat above the predominant range of 10–15 percent in Eastern Europe. At the same time, most export subsidies were cut.

What ultimately prompted trade reform in Latin America was political acceptance that the rigid import-substitution model of industrialization had reached a dead end. The contrasting experience of East Asian countries greatly reinforced the belief that substantial reforms had to be applied. In several countries, however, the immediate catalyst of change was the severe hyperinflation that set in after the debt crisis of the early 1980s and the successive failures to face it within the context of protected economies. The situation unfolded in two ways that also reinforced each other. First, hyperinflation created a crisis environment and thus favored the adoption of radical policy changes, especially after previous experiments at control had failed. Second, trade liberalization was expected to provide a necessary check on the pricing abuses that follow price liberalization, which usually accompanies stabilization. To some extent, however, trade reforms also contributed to prolonging inflation, even if transitorily, due to relative price corrections.

BOLIVIA. The transition to democracy in Bolivia started in 1982, after years of military rule, strong repression, and corruption. The first democratic government, headed by President Hernán Siles Zuazo, had wide popular support but inherited the deepest economic crisis faced by the country in 30 years. With the economy bankrupt, the country was unable to service its foreign debt. Inflation was rising and GDP falling. The twin objectives of the Siles government were stabilization and democratization. Several stabilization programs were initiated with the support of the IMF, but the government proved unable to control the money supply (the expansion of which accelerated inflation), to raise taxes, or to reduce fiscal expenditures. The government also proved incapable of successfully bargaining with the opposition in Congress; or with the powerful labor federation, which became disaffected with the government; or with the Confederation of Bolivian Private Enterprises, which was intensely critical of the government's economic policies. Confrontation politics and the lack of a consensus contributed to hyperinflation, which reached 8,170 percent in 1985. The government ended in collapse, and President Siles had to resign before his term ran out—in a scenario similar to that later encountered by President Raúl Alfonsín in Argentina.[23]

His successor as President, Víctor Paz Estenssoro, a long-time leader and founder of the MNR, the revolutionary movement of the 1950s, applied one of Latin America's most radical and successful stabilization and market liberalization programs. Inflation was down to 66 percent by 1986, and to 11 percent by 1987; and in 1987, after years of GDP decline, growth resumed.[24] Called the New Economic Policy, the program was elaborated and implemented with great speed, at the presidential level, by a small group of young technocrats. What made this politically possible was the Democratic Pact signed by the leaders of the two major parties—President Paz Estenssoro and retired General Hugo Banzer, head of one of the opposition parties. This pact gave the government the necessary support in Congress and the political legitimacy to carry out the reform program. The main objectives of the program were stabilization (through a conventional program of fiscal and monetary adjustment), foreign debt renegotiation, price liberalization, wide opening to trade and to international capital movements, the introduction of more flexible labor-market regulations, and state decentralization (with many public firms transferred to regional state corporations or to municipalities).

The stabilization program relied heavily on fiscal adjustment. During 1982–85, the non-financial public deficit averaged 15 percent of GDP.[25] Tax revenues had fallen from 9.4 percent of GDP in 1980–81 to 4.2 percent in 1982–85. As part of the New Economic Policy, a tax reform and control of evasion were implemented, public employment was reduced, and prices charged by public enterprises were substantially adjusted. Due to the trade reform, taxes related to foreign trade diminished relative to taxes on domestic activity. Tax revenues as a proportion of GDP improved substantially in the second half of the 1980s. By 1986, they had recovered their 1980–81 level of 9.4 percent, and in 1988–89, they rose to more than 11 percent.[26]

Trade liberalization was initiated in 1985 with the elimination of quantitative restrictions on imports and a reduction in tariffs. This process continued for several years—until tariffs reached a common level of 10 percent on all imports except capital goods, for which a 5 percent level was established in 1990. Only a few tariff exemptions remained. On the export side, a "certificate of tariff refund" was created to stimulate exports that had imported inputs. This refund was 10 percent of the value of exports and remained effective until 1991. The response of exports, especially nontraditional exports, was very positive; the yearly rate of growth shifted from negative in the first half of the 1980s to 6.8 percent in 1986–1990.[27]

Financial liberalization was implemented simultaneously with trade reform. This included domestic interest rates and the capital account. Financial institutions were allowed to operate in foreign currency. However, interest rates remained high (in real terms) during most of the post-stabilization period, discouraging investment, which increased by only 2.2 percent a year over the second half of the 1980s.[28] This impeded strong economic recovery.

BRAZIL. The democratic regime in Brazil also inherited a badly shaken economy. Inflation had risen from 56 percent in 1979 to 210 percent in 1984. Public sector savings had dropped from 5.7 percent of GDP to 1.1 percent during 1980–84. The rate of capital formation had also greatly decreased. The only positive sign was a rising trade surplus, which facilitated a net real GDP transfer abroad of 7 percent in 1985 as a consequence of the adjustment after the debt crisis. In 1983–84, efforts to improve the trade balance, mainly through export promotion—that is, through exchange-rate devaluation, new export subsidies, tight monetary policy, and the transfer of private external debt to the public sector—aggravated the fiscal deficit. Subsequent efforts to reduce the deficit through expenditure cuts further contributed to stagnation.

The democratic scenario of the second half of the 1980s was characterized by several attempts to correct economic disequilibria. Successive efforts of President José Sarney's government to control inflation (starting with the Cruzado Plan) ended in failure. This government even contributed strongly to hyperinflation due to fiscal deterioration in the late 1980s. Government savings as a proportion of GDP fell from –0.4 percent in 1985 to –5.8 percent in 1989.[29] Revenues fell, and expenditures increased.

By the second half of the 1980s, a strong argument could be made that the problem was no longer the debt crisis. The return to democracy coincided with a worsening of the macroeconomic situation. Labor demands and political competition for resources were reinforced. Wage resistance increased. Indexation was generalized. Most important was the institutional weakness of the state to resist corporatist pressures for budget resources. This weakness was exacerbated by the proliferation of public agencies at the sectoral and regional levels. The growing autonomy of these agencies created a "political market for the budget."[30] The absence of presidential leadership also contributed to the lack of fiscal discipline.

Both corporatist ties between business and the state and the decentralization of governmental responsibilities contributed to a "privatization of the state." Special arrangements between private firms and government agencies proliferated as a consequence of an industrial policy characterized by a multiplication of incentives and import regulations. The large number of exemptions reduced tariffs to secondary importance as an instrument of import regulation.[31] Nontariff barriers and sectoral regimes—the "law of similars,"[32] local content requirements, or special regimes for some sectors (such as informatics)—were of far greater importance. The administration of these instruments involved private interests. There was a symbiosis between the regulators and the regulated: Business associations participated in the application of the law of similars or of "participation agreements" regulating local content. To avoid anti-export biases, exporters were granted special fiscal incentives that further aggravated the fiscal crisis.

Public opinion in favor of pro-market economic reforms swelled in the late 1980s. A "parliamentary bloc for the market economy" was organized by Delfim Netto, former Minister of the Economy (architect of the Brazilian "economic miracle" of 1968–1974, and also of the crisis of 1979–1984, both under the military regime).[33] In March 1988, a privatization law was approved authorizing the government to sell shares in public enterprises other than constitutional public monopolies (oil and telecommunications). Foreign capital was authorized to buy shares through debt-for-equity swaps.

Increasing awareness of the exhaustion of the historic development model contributed to a convergence of opinion among formerly contending economists. Besides privatization, a new industrial and trade policy—much more liberal than anything that had been attempted in Brazil before—was enacted by the newly elected government of President Fernando Collor de Mello. In March 1990, President Collor announced a new law reforming the regulatory framework for industrial and trade policy.[34] Despite widespread dissatisfaction with existing industrial institutions and laws, there was no consensus on the new policy in at least four areas: 1) the appropriate latitude for discretion on the part of government agencies in relations with the private sector; 2) the nature of industrial incentives (whether to grant them on an automatic basis or to condition them to performance); 3) the issue of competition versus concentration, especially in connection with foreign capital; and 4) the strategy for technological development.

The main objective of the new industrial policy was the achievement of a new style of industrial development based on efficiency and productivity growth and oriented to international competitiveness. The diagnosis driving the policy was that Brazilian industrial development had taken place in a very distorted framework, which had now been exhausted. Three types of instruments were proposed to achieve the new industrial style:

■ A gradual reduction of protection—in order to promote competition and liberalize markets;

- Rationalization of the great variety of selective incentives to a few linked to investment performance; and introduction of fiscal subsidies for the promotion of research and development projects, also linked to performance—in order to promote competitiveness; and

- Industrial restructuring, using special credit facilities as well as selective external protection—in order to upgrade industrial sectors with competitive potential.

The broad thrust of trade reform was toward the abolition of quantitative restrictions and "special regimes," and the gradual liberalization of tariffs, to be completed by 1994. However, the limited scope of this policy became evident from the retention of many nontariff barriers—for example, "similarity" criteria,[35] financing conditions, and requirements that producers rely substantially on local suppliers. Clearly tariffs were not expected to be the only trade restriction. This outcome was the result of pressure from very activist regional and sectoral lobbies in Congress.

The new tariff structure contemplated that by 1994 there would be a modal tariff of 20 percent, an average tariff of roughly 14 percent, and a tariff range from zero to 40 percent distributed in seven tariff groups. Initially, after the abolition of quantitative restrictions, the maximum tariff was 105 percent, and gradual reduction was to take place beginning in February 1991, with major reductions concentrated on intermediate and capital goods in the first two years. In practice, however, nontariff barriers for capital goods remained especially important; local content requirements and foreign financing conditions left this sector strongly protected. Local content requirements affect at least 50 percent of industrial production, so that this nontariff barrier is very significant and considerably reduces the extent of tariff liberalization. Special restrictions were also retained for components for the informatics sector—supported by a strong lobby headed by The National Council for Information and Automation (CONIN). Thus trade liberalization in intermediate and capital good sectors depends much more on nontariff policies than on nominal tariffs.

The export-incentive implications of these measures have been ambiguous. Several fiscal incentives have been abolished. But the most important effect comes from the exchange-rate policy, which has mainly been defined in terms of stabilization strategy. The overvaluation that has resulted is a disincentive to exports.

ARGENTINA. The experience of Argentina is of great interest, as extensive reforms have been carried out by precisely the political force that was most opposed to them during the previous government. This demonstrates the point made earlier that reforms are usually launched on the basis of urgent realities rather than on ideological grounds. When democracy was restored under the leadership of President Alfonsín, there was no perception of the extreme character of the economic disequilibria—despite the three-digit inflation inherited from the military regime. It was even expected that a strategy of growth with redistribution and stability could be achieved on the basis of the prestige of the newly elected civilian government and the support expected from the international financial institutions.[36] Real wages increased during the first year by more than 20 percent, under a strategy to counteract the strong influence of the Peronist party on the labor movement. The defeat of the Peronists was optimistically seen as the start of a new political era in Argentina—one that would end old corporatist practices and enable the country to start on a path of modernization and democratization. To achieve this, it was crucial to obtain the support of labor.

Inflation increased and reached a dangerous level by 1985, when the government implemented its first stabilization measures, known as the Austral Plan. The strategy, temporarily successful, was based on a mix of shock treatment, a generalized price freeze, and increased taxes on foreign trade. Delays in the application of fiscal-monetary restrictions, residual price increases, deterioration of the terms of trade, and new resort to indexed contracts led to the plan's failure and to renewed inflation after 1986.

Organized interests then increased pressures to defend their real incomes. Agricultural exporters pressed for compensation of their losses due to the overvaluation of the peso and to higher taxes on exports. Labor demanded wage adjustments. Provincial governments (mainly led by the opposition party) bargained through their political representatives in Congress for more credit from the central bank. The government lost popularity and credibility, and, lacking the support of an effective political alliance, became increasingly isolated. The Peronist party reinforced its opposition and anti-market rhetoric against the government just as the latter finally attempted more structural reforms, including partial privatization, trade liberalization, and deregulation.

Beginning in 1988, a new process of trade reform was started, in response to the "carrot" of World Bank lending. The 1988 trade reform, designed by then-Minister of Finance Adolfo Canitrot, was successful in reducing the higher tariff brackets (from 60 to 40 percent) and the average tariff level; but quotas for some products were maintained, specific tariffs were imposed, and special regimes with additional rates were established. Yet lack of trust in the government's capacity to stabilize the economy reinforced foreign-exchange speculation, and a new inflationary spiral developed. Total loss of control of the economy induced the early transfer of power to the newly elected Peronist government, with Carlos Menem as President, in mid-1989.

Benefiting from the experience of the previous government, President Menem lost no time in contesting the leadership of the General Labor Confederation; he quickly formed a new political alliance between his party and the entrepreneurial sector—inviting the major financial group in Argentina to head the Ministry of the Economy. The anti-market rhetoric that he had exhibited during the electoral campaign was quickly replaced by a fervent pro-market strategy. The military were also coopted through the granting of pardons to high-ranking officers previously imprisoned for the violation of human rights.

A new stabilization plan was organized, based on a tax reform effort to establish fiscal discipline. Initially successful, the plan nevertheless soon failed because of growing exchange-rate overvaluation that could not be maintained as the trade deficit increased. Following devaluation at the end of 1989, a new hyperinflation episode took place in the first quarter of 1990 and was in turn followed by another unsuccessful stabilization plan. Early in 1991, under the threat of further hyperinflation, recently installed Minister Domingo Cavallo decided that the time had come for an all-out reform strategy that should put in place measures to correct major disequilibria in the economy. This included a strong commitment to fiscal balance, a sweeping privatization of public enterprises, a convertibility plan that established by law a fixed value of the peso to the dollar, a totally passive monetary policy, and a drastic trade reform. Only three tariff brackets (0, 11, and 22 percent) were permitted, with the average level of tariffs lower than 10 percent. Special regimes and exceptions—negotiated with business groups in exchange for price restraint—nonetheless still remained.[37]

MACROECONOMIC TENSIONS FROM TRADE REFORM

The ultimate objective of trade opening is quite clear: a stable, internationally competitive economy. But the transition process itself is plagued with ambiguities and conflicts among opposing interests. Some of these originate at the macroeconomic level. As already mentioned, uncontrolled inflation is usually a main stimulus to the start of trade reform. However, trade reform itself creates new inflationary pressures which, if not offset by complementary policies, may abort the whole trade opening strategy. Two basic links between trade reform and macroeconomic stability are effects on the fiscal deficit and on the exchange rate.

Fiscal Imbalance

Tariff reductions shrink fiscal revenues.[38] Furthermore, devaluations increase the financial burden of the state's foreign debt. An increase in the deficit adds fuel to inflation. Yet changes in the fiscal balance ultimately depend on the ability of the state to restructure its revenues, compensating losses in tariff revenues with tax reforms designed to maintain an adequate revenue level. This is important not only for strengthening the state, but also for stabilization purposes and success in opening the economy. For instance, in Chile after 1974, trade reform was started just as a tax reform introducing the value-added tax was implemented. Tariff revenues as a proportion of GDP were reduced from 3.5 percent in 1974 to 1.5 percent in 1979, when the trade reform was already completed, but total tax revenues were significantly raised.[39] The fiscal deficit shifted from 25 percent of GDP in 1973 to a surplus of 1.7 percent of GDP in 1979.[40] In Bolivia, taxes on imports as a proportion of total tax revenues fell—from 19 percent in 1982–85 to 12 percent in 1986, and 10 percent in 1989. But total tax revenues as a proportion of GDP more than doubled, due to tax reforms and improved enforcement.[41]

There are certain common elements in the fiscal problem facing Latin American and Eastern European countries. In both regions, the main weakness is state incapacity to collect taxes. Reforming Latin American countries—for example Argentina quite recently, and Bolivia and Chile earlier—were able to substantially improve their tax-collecting capacity. This has not been the case in Brazil, where failure to reform the fiscal sector has maintained inflation at a high level.

Eastern European countries face additional fiscal challenges linked to the shrinking role of public enterprises (the main traditional sources of revenue) and to the lack of capacity to enforce tax payments by the expanding, newly created private sector. At the same time, rising social costs are imposing heavier burdens on social security payments by the state. Hungary, for instance, has suffered a worsening fiscal imbalance. Despite the sharp decrease in subsidies to state enterprises (from 21 percent of GDP in 1985 to 4.4 percent in 1992), the fiscal deficit has grown from nil in 1990 to almost 8 percent of GDP in 1992, dropping to 6 percent in 1993—mainly due to expanding expenditures on social security, which reached 37 percent of GDP in 1991 (a proportion comparable only to Western European countries). Total government expenditures have increased from about 62 percent of GDP in 1989–1990 to nearly 70 percent in 1992, while privatization and recession have reduced the tax base, and the new private sector resists accepting a high tax burden. Total revenues have increased only slightly—from about 61–62 percent of GDP in 1989–1990, to 62–64 percent in 1992. Though the state still commands a very high proportion of GDP, net performance compares unfavorably with reforming Latin American economies such as Argentina or Bolivia, where tax reforms were successfully implemented and did contribute to stabilization. Of course the trade-off in Eastern Europe is the higher social equality that the state is able to provide through social expenditures, in sharp contrast to most of Latin America. Sooner or later, Hungary will have to face the problem of fiscal reform—if stabilization is to be achieved at all, and if growth is to be resumed. To date, the fiscal deficit has been sufficiently offset by rising private savings (and stagnant investment), so that overall macroeconomic disequilibrium is not beyond control. Yet the effects of increased public borrowing under tight monetary policy are higher interest rates and a rising ratio between public debt and GDP, with future destabilizing effects. Bulgaria also faces high budget deficits, by one informed estimate reaching 11.9 percent of GDP in 1993. Poland, however, reduced its deficit to 3 percent of GDP in the same year.[42]

Problems of Exchange-Rate Management

The strategic nature of the exchange rate comes from its dual role. It is a measure of domestic prices relative to international prices, and thus influences the allocation of resources between domestic and internationally oriented activities. But it also influences the relationship between the domestic and the international rate of interest and thus affects capital movements. There is no guarantee that these two effects will complement one another, and more often than not, they conflict. A successful trade reform requires a reallocation of resources to the tradable goods sector, which is facilitated by a higher real exchange rate (or devaluation). Stabilization, on the other hand, is aided by currency appreciation, high interest rates, and the resulting capital inflows. Hence, the priority that governments give to stabilization often conflicts with the reallocation objective of trade reforms, unless very strict fiscal discipline is implemented.

In Latin America's old closed-economy model, the nominal exchange rate was fixed, capital movements were restricted, and interest rates were regulated. Fiscal and monetary policy were active and pulled aggregate demand, often destabilizing the balance of payments. The currency tended to be overvalued, and the domestic value of the dollar remained below its "real" value. Exports were discouraged and imports stimulated. When foreign reserves or foreign credit were exhausted, devaluation and fiscal and monetary restraints were required, though seldom vigorously pursued.

In the new, open-economy approaches followed in the 1980s by reforming Latin American countries, exchange-rate adjustments have been accompanied by trade liberalization and interest-rate flexibility. Control of the fiscal deficit and privatization also contributed to macroeconomic stabilization and to the improved credibility of domestic policies. New capital has been attracted, raising foreign reserves and turning initial depreciations into currency appreciations. This conflicts with the long-run objectives of trade reform, as it creates disincentives to exporters.

In industrialized countries, currency appreciates when international competitiveness is strong enough to create high trade surpluses. In developing, structurally adjusting economies in the early 1990s, currencies have tended to appreciate prematurely—not as a result of sound international competitiveness, but because capital inflows have been attracted by the very special circumstance that international interest rates have been extremely low, and important capital gains are expected from privatization processes. This kind of "premature appreciation trap" exacerbates the difficulties of implementing the new open-economy model. In addition, there are some social and political implications, which will be discussed below.

The clearest example of this predicament is Argentina after the introduction of Cavallo's plan for full convertibility in April 1991. Successive failures of stabilization plans led the government to declare the Argentine peso fully convertible to the dollar. This was accompanied by a drastic reduction of tariffs and import restrictions, a balanced budget, and extensive privatization of public enterprises. Inflation fell dramatically, and capital inflows soared. The exchange rate has remained nominally stable, despite accumulated domestic inflation of 40 percent during 1991–93.[43] The resulting currency appreciation has stimulated imports, and the trade surplus has turned into a deficit. Domestic industry and agricultural producers complain about losing competitiveness, and there is growing concern about the best way out. Devaluation would speed inflation—the last outcome President Menem wants now that he has declared his intention to fight for reelection in 1995. An alternative is further cuts in government expenditures to reduce domestic demand and force lower imports and higher exports. By reducing the interest rate, this policy would discourage capital imports and lower the relative price of non-tradables. But this alternative implies lowering growth and raising unemployment, which, by Argentine standards, is already high (10.6 percent in 1993 in Buenos Aires—up from 6.3 percent in 1991).[44]

Hungary is suffering from the same premature appreciation trap. The gradualness of the country's reform process, its success with stabilizing the balance of payments and avoiding accelerated inflation, its restrictive monetary policy with high interest rates, and its compliance with foreign debt-service payments were all factors that stimulated capital inflows, leading to appreciation. Confidence in the domestic currency improved, and people shifted savings from foreign currency to local money. While beneficial in the short run, this effect may be detrimental both to sustaining the growth of exports and to stimulating the growth of import-competing industries in the medium run. The only constructive alternative is to increase productivity, a subject that will be dealt with later in this chapter.

SOCIAL COSTS AND RESISTANCE DURING THE TRANSITION

Economic reforms impose social and economic costs during the transition. In the long run, they are supposed to increase the efficiency of the economic system, promote growth, and improve social welfare. That is their fundamental rationale, whatever the additional arguments based on the vested interests or ideological biases of the reformers. Chile's experience with reforms during the 1970s is an eloquent example of high social costs, in this case continuing for a period of about five years. Trade reforms in particular imposed costs on industries that were not competitive and relied on subsidies and protection. Adjustment to the new conditions created unemployment and inflation, and output fell.

While the hurtful effects of market reform are fast, positive responses to market incentives usually take longer. Expectations of future demand, the credibility of new policies, and technological and entrepreneurial adjustments all require considerable time to emerge. Furthermore, countries that have long been accustomed to an entrenched bureaucratic mentality do not easily shift to a Western-style "entrepreneurial" mentality. Even among those managers and investors who succeed in changing their outlook, "wait and see" behavior prevails until the environment becomes quite clearly conducive to undertaking major initiatives.

Aggregate Effects on Output

How severe are the economic costs of trade reform? Since trade liberalization has often taken place in a context of deep macroeconomic disequilibrium and external shocks, it is hard to gauge the costs of each separately. Furthermore, the relative importance of the main factors varies according to regions, countries, and periods. Some factors have both an aggregate and a structural effect. Devaluation of the exchange rate, for instance, negatively affects the real wage rate, thus creating a depressing aggregate effect on demand. At the same time, it changes the relative price of tradable versus non-tradable goods, imposing a structural effect. Preliminary empirical evidence suggests that in Chile in the 1970s, macroeconomic instability was more important than structural change.[45] The same result has been found for Bulgaria,[46] where a major factor of output decline was the shock from the crisis of CMEA trade; and for Poland, after the "big bang."[47] However, in Hungary, which followed a more gradual path to structural adjustment and stabilization, aggregate factors seem to have been less important.[48]

The effects of economic reform on output differ greatly in the two regions. Latin America began to suffer output declines in the early 1980s—when the debt crisis erupted, acute foreign-exchange scarcity set in, and inflation accelerated. Total GDP fell by almost 9 percent in per capita terms in 1981–1990.[49] Thus economic reforms were applied—first in Bolivia, then in Argentina, and then, timidly, in Brazil—in a context of profound macroeconomic disequilibrium and output stagnation or decline.

Except for Hungary and Poland, Eastern Europe did not suffer the massive debt crisis. The reasons for stagnation, which was already taking place in the 1980s, were more structural and had to do with the inefficiencies and progressive failures of planning systems. Even Hungary, which got off to an early start with price liberalization and decentralized decision-making at the firm level, grew by a mere 0.5 percent a year in the 1980s.[50] It has been estimated that Eastern European countries as a whole suffered an aggregate GDP loss of 20 percent in 1990–91. Hungary and Poland each lost between 12 and 20 percent in both years.[51] Bulgaria was hardest hit, experiencing a 9 percent loss in 1990, followed by 17 percent in 1991, and 12 percent in 1992.[52]

These figures may overestimate the actual output declines, as private-sector output has increased without adequately being incorporated in economic statistical information. Estimates of the share of private-sector output in total GDP in 1992 give 20 percent for Bulgaria, 40–42 percent for Hungary, and 45 percent for Poland.[53]

In analyzing aggregate factors behind the Eastern European recession, the evidence points to a major role of supply factors during the initial phase of recession.[54] Specifically, cost rigidities arising out of wage resistance and, above all, rising energy prices (oil was mainly imported from the Soviet Union) and interest rates restricted the conditions of supply. Mark-up margins were maintained, denoting resistance to adjustment on the part of managers—or at least expectations that governments would continue to use "soft budget" criteria.[55] These expectations were confirmed, directly or indirectly, in the form of tax payment arrears or rising inter-firm debt.

On the demand side, a major factor was the collapse of trade with the Soviet Union and within the CMEA area. Most economies, and especially Bulgaria, were heavily dependent on this trade. The sudden disruption of this trade is estimated to have reduced demand by 10 percent of GDP in Hungary (although the net reduction was in fact only about 3 percent, due to the fast expansion of exports to Western countries).[56] The impact was much smaller in Poland, but much stronger in Bulgaria.

The growth of exports to Western countries has helped reduce the impact of the collapse of trade with the former Soviet bloc. By strengthening the balance of trade, export growth has also stimulated the growth of imports from the West. Although this will improve competitiveness and the quality of goods in the long run, it has encouraged the substitution of foreign for domestic goods in the short run, thus creating demand problems in some industries. These problems are compounded by losses in real wages due to inflation. Moreover, these demand-related problems become more acute in the more advanced phase of the adjustment process, as corroborated by a survey of managers in Bulgaria.[57]

Theory predicts that the sectoral composition of output should alter substantially as the economy opens. This is because, under the influence of international relative prices, resources are allocated differently than in a protected economy. In this respect, there is a remarkable similarity between Latin America and Eastern Europe; in both regions, industry, especially its more technology-intensive sectors, has been most affected, in contrast to services, which have expanded.[58]

Paradoxically, the textile industry has also been strongly affected, despite its typically labor-intensive nature. This may be partly due to the modernization and robotization that this industry enjoyed in the 1970s and 1980s, which returned comparative advantage to the industrial countries or to the East Asian newly industrializing economies (NIEs).

In Latin America, restructuring has favored services, financial activities, and natural resource-intensive sectors. In Chile, the latter has expanded strongly due to technological and entrepreneurial transformations; this puts in question the past assumption that natural resource-based development lacks technological potential.[59] In Argentina, there has been a relative expansion of "industrial commodities"—steel, petrochemicals, pulp and paper, aluminum—at the cost of more elaborate capital-goods industries that developed in the 1960s; this is a result of an explicit industrial policy applied in the 1970s, which heavily subsidized investments in those sectors ("industrial commodities").[60] Nontradable goods and services also expanded strongly in the late 1980s, partly because of the privatization of public enterprises and major utilities.

In sum, two conclusions can be derived from this evidence. *First,* the recessions following structural adjustment have affected the Eastern European countries far more strongly than the Latin American countries. Although Chile was also severely hit in the mid-1970s, and most of the region suffered throughout the 1980s, this was a consequence of the debt crisis and of stabilization efforts. In Bolivia and Argentina, structural reforms such as trade opening and privatization in the late 1980s were not followed by recession, but by some output recovery. *Second,* in both regions, output losses have been mainly due to macroeconomic instability and financial adjustment rather than to trade opening, which mainly had the effect of reallocating productive factors away from heavy or technology-intensive industries into more labor-intensive sectors or those with a higher content of natural resources. This pattern of reallocation has been similar in both regions, although in Eastern Europe resources also shifted from the state to private firms. This reallocation implies static efficiency gains, but, if long-run growth strategies are not implemented, it may also discourage the introduction of more advanced technologies.

Winners and Losers: Balancing Conflicting Interests

Social costs and benefits derived from trade reforms have different effects on social groups—including state structures themselves. Several types of effects can be discerned: 1) impact on social inequality, 2) changes in productive structures affecting the power base of interest groups, and 3) impact on power relationships within the state itself.

IMPACT ON SOCIAL INEQUALITY. The impact of reform on income and social inequality is recognized to be especially relevant in Latin America. Income inequalities in the region are among the greatest in the world. The ratio between the income of the wealthiest 20 percent of households and that of the poorest 20 percent reached 40 in Ecuador and more than 30 in Brazil and Peru—compared to ratios below 8 in Canada and in Japan.[61] Moreover, the proportion of the population living below measured poverty lines increased during the 1980s as a consequence of stagnation and structural adjustments. In the region as a whole, the population living in poverty increased from 35 percent in 1980 to 39 percent in 1990, with the growth concentrated in urban areas.[62]

Many perceive a lack of minimum distributive equity as a serious threat to democratic consolidation. Thus, a highly relevant question is whether economic reforms, i.e., trade reforms, contribute to reducing inequality. Traditional economic orthodoxy supported the view that trade opening in less developed countries should reduce inequality because labor is a more abundant factor of production than capital. As trade opens, labor-intensive exports would grow faster, while capital-intensive industrial production would be reduced. These effects would strengthen the demand for labor, pulling the real wage upward. The return to capital would then be lowered. This outcome is consistent with the experience of East Asian countries, where export-led growth has been accompanied by more equal income distribution.

This process is of course more complex, and other relevant factors influence the relationship. For instance, during the 1970s and 1980s, Chile applied an export–led growth model, yet inequalities strongly increased. In the case of East Asian countries, it is widely recognized that a major factor contributing to less income inequality was land reform carried out in several countries in the early 1950s. Because the East Asian countries initially had a high proportion of population living in rural areas, land reform reduced nationwide inequalities and also helped to strengthen rural demand for manufactures—one of the fundamental factors stimulating high industrial growth and demand for labor in the following decade.

Two other elements that strongly influence the relationship between trade opening and income inequality are the endowments of human capital and natural resources. The two factors-of-production approach (capital and labor) is too simplified to adequately describe modern processes of production. The importance of human capital as the most relevant growth factor in the East Asian countries is well established. It not only contributes to international competitiveness but also to higher wages. This is a crucial link between export-led growth and distributive equity.

In contrast, Latin American countries are less well endowed with human capital but have much greater availability of land and natural resources than East Asian countries. Thus, in this region, exports have a high content of natural resources, which traditionally has stimulated the creation of rents. The more recent export expansion since the 1980s is no exception. Both theoretical and empirical analysis have persuasively shown that this kind of growth can increase inequalities.[63] Stronger demand for natural resources raises rents and stock prices, benefiting owners rather than labor, which tends to remain unskilled. This finding is consistent with the Chilean case, already mentioned, as well as with other countries in Latin America. In the longer run, this outcome could be reversed—provided there is enough capital accumulation and sustained growth.

Another factor intervening in the relationship between trade reform and income inequality concerns the role of the state. As mentioned, trade reform means tariff reductions and the elimination of import rationing. To the extent that these are sources of state revenues, government budgets become unbalanced unless other revenues are created. Trade reform also means real devaluations, which negatively affect state enterprises (except when they are exporting firms, as in Bolivia or Chile). Budget deficits that must be overcome lead to expenditure cuts, which usually affect social programs like education, health, housing, or pensions.

The poor are the most affected group, but the middle classes have also become involved in sharing these social costs in both Latin America and Eastern Europe. The latter region was traditionally characterized by low income inequality, but that was mainly due to the high degree of state involvement. The fiscal crisis these countries are facing, complicated by many other elements concomitant to macroeconomic mismanagement as well as to the general economic reform process, is strongly contributing to increased inequality, at least in the short run. In Latin America, the structural adjustment policies of the 1980s sharply affected the income shares of the middle class as well as of those in the bottom brackets, in favor of high–income groups. Reductions in state expenditures created unemployment among public employees and diminished the supply of those services. Real devaluations reduced real wages and salaries. Employees in the service sector had to cope with lower real salaries. These groups, as well as organized industrial workers, have a much greater capacity to organize and bargain than do the rural and urban poor.

Yet this capacity has not been used against democratic transitions and economic reforms, despite the high costs those groups have had to bear. Several factors could explain this. First, the middle class suffered human rights violations as much as workers and the poor, firmly establishing a more widely shared basic commitment to democracy. More realistically, however, reduced opposition to eventual negative effects of trade reforms can also be partly explained by the weakening of social organizations and political parties following the democratic and economic crisis. The Bolivian labor federation and the left were very much affected first by years of dictatorship and then by the hyperinflationary legacy of the leftist government of President Siles Zuazo. Another partial explanation is that tolerance and resistance also depend on people's expectations of the perceived alternatives. In times of revolutionary fervor, many people, especially the poor, believe that radical redistribution of wealth and power is a quick route to progress. This expectation leads them to reject any alternative strategy. The ineffectiveness of this approach in practice has moved people to realize the complexity of problems and to consider less radical alternatives. In Bulgaria, according to surveys conducted in March 1992, the number of people who did not accept the idea of the country being stratified into the rich and the poor dropped from 70 percent in January 1990 to 47 percent in March 1992.[64]

Corresponding to those factors, ideologies have also been adjusted, especially on the left of the political spectrum. Until the 1970s, it was unthinkable for the key social and political actors in Latin America to tolerate extensive trade opening; it was an anathema within their programs. But after a decade of stagnation and deep financial crisis during the 1980s, many things have changed, and what was earlier considered intolerable became conventional wisdom, even among militant leftists. In Chile, the Socialist Party—the country's most radical party in the postwar period in its anti-American and anti-imperialist positions—has, on the basis of a more pragmatic evaluation of benefits, incorporated into its program both the open market economy and acceptance of the social costs of economic change. The Socialist Party's strong influence among labor unions and rank-and-file workers has modified popular views concerning trade policies. In Bolivia, President Jaime Paz Zamora (elected in 1989), who had been an active opponent of President Paz Estenssoro's New Economic Policy, decided to endorse that policy and even to launch a privatization program. A similar evolution has taken place in President Menem's Argentina.

Finally, the appeal of benefits expected from trade opening—especially the most direct ones—must not be overlooked. For the typical consumer, imported goods were traditionally restricted and priced to include monopoly rents. With trade opening, supply has increased, and relative prices have been reduced. These effects of market reform are welcomed by the middle class and workers who see imported consumer durable goods as status goods. This is also true in Eastern Europe, where the lack of access to Western consumer goods was an added frustration for the middle class, on top of deep frustration with the political regimes. Thus, trade opening, especially to the European Union, raises expectations of access to the fruits of modernization.

In sum, following trade reforms, as part of wider economic reforms, a worsening of income distribution can be expected. In Latin America, the main beneficiaries are the owners of land and natural resources, whose products are exportable. Workers and the middle class are negatively affected by reduced social public expenditures, as a consequence of fiscal adjustments. This is more relevant in Eastern Europe, where a high degree of income equality had been achieved on the basis of state redistribution. These negative effects have not, however, raised strong political opposition to those reforms. Furthermore, to the extent that growth is recovered and sustained, the negative effects should be overcome and reversed.

CHANGES AFFECTING THE POWER BASE OF PRESSURE GROUPS. A second type of conflict that may be catalyzed by reform relates to corporatist pressures and supporting coalitions. As liberal trade reforms are consolidated, it can be presumed that they reduce the role of traditional import-substituting lobbies and urban labor unions. Furthermore, under the "closed economy" model, monopolies (private or public) enjoyed entry barriers that stimulated rent-seeking practices on the part of either business or labor, or both. With trade liberalization, these possibilities are reduced.

Thus, from a political economy point of view, consolidation of an open economy requires new coalitional support (formed mainly by exporters, traders, and financial intermediaries) to counter the import-competing coalition's efforts to reverse reforms. The new coalitions grow in importance as the reform process evolves. It can be assumed that the political decision to implement the initial phase of reforms is taken at the highest level of the state. But the twin processes of democratic transition and economic reform tend to raise the probability of reversals—*first,* because politically there are more opportunities to contest; and *second,* because, as the short-run social costs of economic reform become more evident, some sectors perceive that they can gain from reversals.

Yet it is difficult for the beneficiaries of the open economy to get organized, and they are often slow to do so. First, potential beneficiaries must be convinced that organizing is in their interest. Since for them economic conditions are improving under economic reform, they see no urgent reason to organize. Second, potential members of a coalition must become known to one another before they can mount a collective effort. This is more relevant under scenarios where potential exporters are dispersed rather than concentrated, and where they are new entrants into the export market rather than well-established interests.

There is asymmetry in this respect: import-competing coalitions, which are well established and have communication channels with the government, nevertheless remain in a better position to lobby than potential-exporter coalitions. They can also benefit from an "identity bias," in that an established identity has a stronger claim on political emotions than the case of the eventual winners, who are an abstract entity.[65] With the passage of time, however, the winners themselves acquire a "face" and an interest in the continuation of the new policies, improving the probability of economic consolidation.

Yet another difficulty is associated with the initial phase. As discussed above, in high-inflation contexts, trade reforms are usually undertaken simultaneously with stabilization policies. Then, even the most pro-export government must choose between maintaining export incentives and achieving macroeconomic stabilization. As already indicated, exchange-rate policy is the main victim of this difficult policy choice; by stimulating capital inflows and appreciating the currency, governments can secure stability more rapidly, but this weakens export incentives, even if tariffs are kept low. Argentina in the early 1990s and Chile in the late 1970s are clear cases in point. In Argentina, as already noted, there has been strong appreciation since the introduction of convertibility in 1991. Although inflation has been reduced to unprecedented levels, activities producing both import-competing goods and exports have lost competitiveness. Import-competing industrialists do not openly object to the general strategy of convertibility and trade liberalization (the ghost of hyperinflation lingers). Instead, for fear of bankruptcy, they press for subsidies, reduced taxes (especially social security taxes, which are very high), or import quotas. Exporters have also become outspoken opponents of the exchange-rate policy.

Distributive and power conflicts arise not only between exporters and traditional import-substituting industries oriented to the home market, but also between producers of *tradable* goods (import-substituting as well as exporting) and producers of *non-tradable* goods. Chile in the 1980s was a case where producers of tradables were winners, with exporters foremost among them, mainly because of the high real exchange-rate policy that was implemented after the debt crisis.[66] Argentina in the 1990s is a case where producers of non-tradables (services and the financial sector) are becoming the winners—through a stabilization policy similar to the one pursued in Chile in the late 1970s. In Eastern Europe, the main conflict of interest is between groups linked to state firms and the emerging private sector; so far, the former have tried to offset losses through informal privatization, lower tax payments, debt arrears, and indebtedness.

IMPACT ON INTRA-STATE RELATIONS. A third set of conflicting interests aroused by reform relates to the state itself. The state is not a homogeneous entity, but a mix of agencies and power structures embodying different interests and even different ideologies. Brazil provides numerous examples, since many agencies concerned with industrial policies have developed over time, and the groups they serve are differently affected by economic reforms. The transition from a very closed economy and a highly discretionary industrial policy to a more open and neutral system provides cases of internal conflict, or at least of conflicting interests.

Consider first the case of domestic competition policy under the traditional system. The basic framework of this policy was anti-monopoly legislation. Its philosophy was based on the idea that monopolistic practices result from abuses by firms rather than from special privileges granted by the vast proliferation of industrial selective measures. In the Ministry of Justice, an agency was created to control monopolistic practices—but another ministry, the Ministry of Planning, was in charge of providing special incentives and privileges, which usually stimulated monopolistic behavior. In practice, anti–monopoly legislation was never effective; since 1962, the anti–monopoly authority CADE (Conselho Administrativo de Defesa Economica, or Administrative Council for Economic Defense, under the Ministry of Justice) initiated 117 legal proceedings—of which only 14 percent ended up in actual sanctions, and many of these were reversed by ordinary courts.[67]

Conflicts of interest must be assessed in the context of the corporatist tradition of Brazilian industry. Traditional industrial strategy, especially in the 1970s, was based on stimulating the creation of strong industrial conglomerates (including both foreign and domestic firms) through special fiscal incentives, price guarantees, and entry barriers. A special agency, the Inter-Ministry Council of Prices (CIP), was created in 1967 under the Ministry of Planning. This Council, in charge of "competition administration" and price control, came to be a real sponsor of industrial groups and an actual regulatory mechanism, embodying the practice of corporatism. The anti-monopoly legislation was in a way a countervailing action located in the Ministry of Justice, but its goals were never given high priority on the reform agenda. The creation of new Sectoral Policies Executive Groups (GEPS) early in 1990, and then the "Sectoral Chambers" in early 1991, developed the corporatist idea even further by linking both private–sector interest groups and labor unions to the bureaucracy. The chambers collaborate in developing targeted sectoral policies to stimulate specific industries.[68]

The acceleration of inflation in the 1990s has deepened the conflicts among the different objectives of industrial policy as well as among the government agencies involved. With higher inflation, the various agencies blame each other for not fulfilling price control responsibilities that have been dispersed throughout the state.

Yet another Brazilian example is provided by the persistence of sectoral targeting within the new industrial law. An important "political economy" aspect of the industrial policy reform concerns the confrontation between two government agencies linked to industrial policy: The Department of Industry and Commerce (DIC), which is the coordination agency for industrial policy, and BNDES, which can autonomously allocate credit. The DIC selects the priorities in industrial targeting, and the BNDES applies the instruments. Tensions between the two agencies affect how industrial policy is implemented—and therefore which interests win and lose.

THE CONSOLIDATION OF ECONOMIC REFORMS

The consolidation of economic reforms depends on the credibility and political acceptance of the new system. The resumption of growth is crucial. But growth can be the result of particular circumstances originating in exogenous factors (such as an export boom) or transitory factors such as expansionary fiscal and monetary policies. More durable growth results from endogenous stimuli—for instance, the perception of private investors that the new rules are stable and provide sufficient incentives to undertake investments with longer maturity. A crucial test for investors is their assessment of the staying power of basic economic rules even during a change of government—especially a change from an authoritarian government to a democratic government.

A good example of this crucial test is provided by Chile's experience during the transition from the government of Augusto Pinochet (1981–1990), which implemented the economic reforms, and the democratic election of Patricio Aylwin's government in 1990. The successful performance of the Chilean economy during the second half of the 1980s convinced the democratic opposition that the new rules would in fact stimulate growth and private investment. But the private sector did not trust the new political leaders, and the presidential electoral campaign of 1989 was plagued with economic fears. Chaos and a return to the Salvador Allende period (1970–73) were predicted. Political and economic leaders of the democratic coalition tried hard to establish communication channels with the private sector and to find common ground for the discussion of economic policies. They were finally successful in persuading entrepreneurs that the basics of economic policies would be maintained, and that changes would only refer to social and labor policies. Ultimately, distrust gave way to acceptance and confidence, and the first year of the Aylwin government was marked by a dramatic increase in private investment.[69] By that time, it had become clear that economic reforms in Chile had been consolidated.

Markets and Institutions

A question crucial to consolidation is whether market liberalization is in itself sufficient to promote growth with equity or whether explicit strategies are required. Adjustment inevitably brings economic costs, and strategies differ on how to reduce their negative social effects. Until the late 1980s, the orthodox strategy was not greatly concerned with adverse social effects, which were viewed as inevitable and temporary concomitants of freeing resources for alternative, more productive uses. This strategy was criticized because of the human and social costs that accompany widespread unemployment.

An alternative, socially concerned strategy tries to compensate for negative social consequences arising from widespread unemployment and lower wages. Such an approach presents some risks. It can easily start a reform-reversing process by prolonging subsidies to declining industries. This delays adjustment and further increases its costs, because the surviving industries still compete for scarce, flexible resources like credits and skilled labor. But a socially concerned strategy need not be inefficient, provided that it differentiates between economic and social effects. While declining industries must be let down, complementary social policies can be directed toward unemployed workers as well as programs to stimulate worker retraining and reentry into the market. Since this implies using public resources, the strategy must also place high priority on improving tax-collecting capacity and tightening public expenditure screening.[70] Besides providing for social-impact alleviation—and thereby also for the political acceptability of adjustment—this strategy also helps reduce the negative multiplier effects of unemployment, which would otherwise deepen the recession. The right strategic choices are thus crucial to reducing unnecessary trade-offs.

An overwhelming body of evidence on the spectacular growth successes of the East Asian countries now provides a profile of socially efficient growth strategies. This is not the place to go into that subject in detail, but the basic characteristics of those East Asian strategies are:

■ Macroeconomic and financial stability as a basic, general condition for efficiency;

■ Close state-market cooperative relations that avoid the ideological confrontations typical of many Western countries; and state interventions that operate through, rather than suppress, market price mechanisms;

■ An industrial policy oriented to pursuing international competitiveness, including commitment to a long-run approach; incentives directly linked to performance within certain periods of time; high priority for technological development and learning capacity; enough flexibility to recognize mistakes, eliminate gross distortions, and put an end to failed policies; and

■ Social cohesiveness flowing from basic cultural and religious traditions, as well as from a broad-based education system.

Consolidation of economic reforms assumes that some kind of broad agreement on new ideas has been reached. Haggard and Kaufman compare the new consensus with other historical counterparts, such as the diffusion of Keynesian ideas in the developed countries and of import-substituting industrialization in the Third World during the postwar period.[71] More recently, the East Asian paradigm and the "Washington consensus" are leading to a new strategic thrust. But there is still considerable debate over the meaning of these proposals.[72] A wide range of changes in policies and institutions, extending far beyond trade reforms, are needed to develop an internationally competitive production system. In most dual transition countries, ideas regarding these changes are in flux, and the consensus needed for consolidation has yet to emerge, although important elements of consensus are appearing. Four areas of debate are particularly important: macroeconomic balance, the regulatory framework, labor market conditions, and industrial policies.

MACROECONOMIC BALANCE. Macroeconomic balance is now much more highly valued in the light of experience with hyperinflation and subsequent stabilization costs; economic agents are aware that fiscal and monetary laxity may appear attractive but prove to be very costly. A major obstacle to macroeconomic balance, however, is the classical free-rider problem: Each actor expects others to exercise restraint but in the meantime exerts all of his political power to obtain special concessions in his own interest. This also applies to the public-private expenditure balance. The private sector resents public expenditure increases, generally for fear of being crowded out through increases in interest rates or in taxes. Thus the fiscal balance becomes a permanent subject of debate and negotiation between state authorities and private-sector leaders.

Also receiving increased attention is the institutional insulation of some public agencies—particularly central banks, which in many countries are becoming autonomous of even central governments. This autonomy has both advantages and disadvantages, but the consensus is spreading that some type of relative insulation is a sound approach. Technical and political strengthening of budget offices is also a high priority if fiscal balance is to be maintained. The budget is where most social and political demands for public resources converge. Since the main channels for these demands are the sectoral ministries themselves, internal bargaining within the government may become very intense.

Finally, tax enforcement is also getting increased emphasis, because evasion and poor enforcement cause major losses of public revenues.

In sum, fiscal and monetary balance not only require efficient, macroeconomic policy design, but also reform and strengthening of the state apparatus that has to implement those policies. This involves not only technocratic and administrative capacities, but also political abilities to negotiate—both within the government and with key social actors.

A REGULATORY FRAMEWORK. A second major set of issues that affects market performance concerns the general regulatory framework. Although market reforms involve dismantling many regulations, such as price controls or trade restrictions, certain market imperfections and failures do demand state regulation. In open, small economies, classical imperfections associated with monopolies become less relevant, as foreign competition provides some checks—although monopolistic abuses may still persist in wholesale and retail trading, as well as in some sectors that have natural protection due to transportation costs or inadequate information on quality. State regulation is also necessary where natural monopolies are inevitable—for example, in public utilities and telecommunications. Although competition in many of these activities is growing, firms tend to behave monopolistically whenever they have a captive market. A reasonable question is whether the state is capable of regulating sectors that have become very complex technologically. There is also the problem of the capture of the regulatory agency by private firms;[73] this is another instance where state agencies have to be strengthened both technically and politically. Environmental protection is a further goal requiring regulation, and one that is becoming increasingly relevant, but most states are still very far behind needs in this area.

In most of these instances, regulation can be performed either by classical methods such as prohibition, price control, or bureaucratic restriction, or by methods that increasingly incorporate market incentives. The latter approach involves creating markets and property rights, as is evident in some current approaches to environmental protection or natural resource exploitation. For instance, traffic congestion imposes the need to create the right of access through payments. The same applies to the exploitation of common goods—for example, resources of the sea or the atmosphere. In the fishing industry, many governments have established special fishing rights, which are granted by regulatory agencies and can be traded in an open market. Similar rights are being created to regulate air pollution.

LABOR MARKET CONDITIONS. For many decades, the trend was toward strengthening labor protection, which was both a response to basic social justice expectations and to growing political pressures by labor unions and labor lobbies. This trend, however, presented a trade-off in terms of rising labor costs and lack of flexibility for firms to adjust employment to real needs. The neo-liberal reaction was wide deregulation and suppression of union rights. The challenge in democratizing and reforming countries, explored in more detail in Chapter 3 in this volume, is how to reconcile social justice with labor market flexibility without impairing market adjustments. Both entrepreneurs and workers are very sensitive to this issue. One principle guiding the new consensus is the need to differentiate between flexibility at the market level and social justice at the societal level. While private firms must respect certain fundamental labor rights that relate to prevalent conceptions of a civilized society, they must not be charged with responsibility to provide either job security or specified wages (above a certain minimum).[74] Economic security for workers must be provided at the societal level, through institutions like unemployment insurance, retraining mechanisms, and national health care programs. The financing of these institutions must be designed within the context of the financial system at the national or regional level.

COMPETITIVENESS VERSUS INDUSTRIAL POLICY. Traditional industrial policies viewed as mechanisms for protecting and subsidizing specific sectors have been questioned, especially as to their efficacy in promoting growth.[75] These policies are associated with closed economies, in which the state was the engine of growth through industrial targeting and "picking the winners." In the new consensus, competitiveness has come to be viewed as a comprehensive process, and the nation as a whole has to compete with the rest of the world. Economies are open to international investment, and risk assessment includes a significant political component. What matters is not only the competitiveness of domestic firms or the attractiveness of natural endowments, but also national institutions—political, social, and economic.

In Latin America, a strategy of "transformation with equity" is being widely advocated.[76] The emphasis of this approach is systemic: The whole social fabric must be transformed to carry out an effective productive restructuring that does not destroy social cohesion. A strong (but not oversized) state with a market-friendly orientation must be developed. Ultimately, the state is responsible not for picking the winners, but for creating a growth-oriented environment. Industrial competitiveness must rest on social creativity and non-antagonistic labor relations within enterprises. Education is crucial, and research and development efforts merit high priority. Similar issues are under heated debate in Eastern Europe, though there may be somewhat less consensus on the outlines of the new strategy.

For promoting industries able to compete in international markets, the precise mix of targeted or neutral domestic policies may be less relevant than the environment within which they are carried out. It is important for that environment to stimulate performance and initiative rather than bureaucratic norms. Basic policies under this approach include macroeconomic equilibrium, a trade policy oriented toward stimulating the growth of tradables production, active saving and investment policies, and social policies that avoid extreme poverty and stimulate investment in human resources. This approach of course requires sufficient openness to international trade and investment to provide a competitive environment. The approach also assumes incentives to foreign capital that are based on the assumption that profit rates on capital, net of political risks, are higher than in industrial countries. In this strategy, foreign capital and exports tend to perform as engines of growth.

Any long-run, export-oriented development strategy must recognize that dealing with the domestic environment, though crucial, is not sufficient. Protectionist practices still pervade world markets. It is not only explicit tariff restrictions that matter, but also quantitative restrictions, quotas, and, increasingly, restrictions related to environmental protection. Thus, domestic modernization policies are being complemented by internationally oriented trade strategies that recognize the bargaining component in most bilateral or multilateral trade agreements. This is another field where cooperative state–private sector relations are needed. Although trade bargaining is primarily a private sector concern, the state has a major role in negotiating with foreign governments and international organizations.

MARKETS, DEMOCRACY, AND UNCERTAINTIES

Market and democratic consolidation are not the end of history—not only because of the trivial observation that the future is uncertain, but also because of a more fundamental tension that will always be present in democratic, market-oriented societies. Democracy is uncertain with respect to its *results*. It is a fragile system, despite being the most accepted one universally. Majorities may opt for unexpected courses of political development. Democracy's main beneficiaries may turn against it. Attempts to protect democracy by means of coercion inevitably end up as dictatorships. There is no alternative to expecting that democratic values and cultures will prevail in the end. These values may be enhanced through education, participation, and cooperation. But uncertainty will always be present.

Markets, on the other hand, abhor uncertainty, since it undermines predictability, which is fundamental for undertaking strategic economic decisions. The greater the uncertainty, the shorter the term for predicting and the more volatile the decisions taken. Modern financial institutions have been created to deal with economic uncertainty, but political uncertainty is strongly punished by markets. As democracy is consolidated, in the more fundamental sense of permeating values and cultures, the range of political uncertainty or instability becomes almost negligible, and the tension between democratic politics and the market system is strongly reduced, as evidenced by the experience of industrially advanced market economies.

Are open economies more vulnerable to instability than protected systems? During the decades after the 1930s it was common wisdom among developing countries that closing the economy—i.e., prohibiting or restricting import and capital flows—would reduce economic vulnerability and associated strains on political stability. It was thought that economic vulnerability was mainly associated with international instability, especially with sharply fluctuating prices of exportable commodities. Experience teaches that Latin American protected economies were not immune to high instability. Export dependence on single commodities, fiscal vulnerability to foreign trade taxes, domestic disequilibria arising from populist policies, and weak commitments to democratic principles were some of the major factors contributing to uncertainty and lack of market predictability.

In contrast, the experience of small Western European countries after World War II shows that democratic consolidation and vigorous development of markets were possible within the framework of progressively open economies.[77] These countries followed a strategy of international competitiveness based on a free access to advanced imported goods, international cooperation for the development of science and technology, active involvement in international agencies supporting multilateral interchange and domestic stabilization policies geared to face international fluctuations and social inequities. These strategies were in turn politically based on social democratic systems that forced social actors to negotiate their demands with an awareness of national dependence on the international system.

Both Latin American and Eastern European countries are still experiencing the effects of the economic and political shocks of the 1980s. Economic adjustments have imposed high social costs in terms of unemployment, real wage reductions, and cuts in public social expenditures. In most cases, these effects cannot be attributed only to external factors. They have been consequences of domestic policies even in the presence of international shocks, such as the steep increases in interest rates in the early 1980s. The excessively indebted countries suffered most of the financial shocks, but even in these cases, the impact varied according to different domestic situations (for instance, Chile versus Brazil, or Hungary versus Poland).

Economic adjustment and trade opening have contributed to economic recovery in Latin America. While the industrial countries experienced an international recession, the Latin American countries as a whole grew by 3 percent in 1992 and 3.8 percent in 1993. Chile, with the most open economy of the region, experienced a much higher than average rate of growth of GDP: 6 percent in 1993.[78] Trade opening contributes to export diversification. Access to imported goods disseminates new technologies and improves the competitiveness of industries that use imported inputs. A higher share of trade in GDP, accompanied by larger financial flows (especially foreign direct investment), improves international reserves, strengthens the currency, and allows better access to voluntary international lending. All of these factors should increase economic flexibility and reduce vulnerability, provided they are complemented by prudent domestic policies designed to face and counteract unexpected external shocks.

Social learning takes time. Governments, social actors, and political parties must all experience the effects of reformed economic systems before these become incorporated into political programs. The adverse consequences of transition are still alive, and they can produce political instability as well as policy reversals. Most countries in Latin America and Eastern Europe are not yet in the consolidation phase, and most still face major uncertainties. The trends to date, however, suggest a positive rather than a negative prospect for democratic and economic progress.

Notes

The author wishes to thank Joan Nelson for her encouragement and valuable comments, and to acknowledge other important comments by Marcelo Cavarozzi, Sebastián Edwards, Albert Fishlow, Catherine Gwin, Robert Kaufman, Jacek Kochanowicz, Kálmán Mizsei, Ben Slay, and Andrés Solimano. Special thanks are also due to Paul Psaila and to Jean Fougerolles for helpful assistance in the bibliographical work.

[1] See Stephan Haggard and Robert R. Kaufman, "The State in the Initiation and Consolidation of Market-Oriented Reform," in Louis Putterman and Dietrich Rueschemeyer, eds., *State and Market in Development: Synergy or Rivalry?* (Boulder and London: Lynne Rienner Publishers, 1992).

[2] Eduardo Silva, "Capitalist Coalitions, the State, and Neoliberal Economic Restructuring: Chile, 1973–88," *World Politics,* Vol. 45, No. 4 (July 1993), pp. 526–59.

[3] Albert O. Hirschman, "Industrialization and Its Manifold Discontents: West, East and South," *World Development,* Vol. 20, No. 9 (September 1992).

[4] Winston Fritsch and Gustavo H. B. Franco, "The Political Economy of Trade and Industrial Policy Reform in Brazil in the 1990s," *Serie Reformas de Política Pública,* No. 6 (Santiago, Chile: CEPAL, 1993), pp. 7–45.

[5] Ricardo Ffrench-Davis, Oscar Muñoz, and Gabriel Palma, "Latin American Economies in 1950–1990," in Leslie Bethell (ed.), *Cambridge History of Latin America,* Vol. 6 (Cambridge, New York: Cambridge University Press, forthcoming).

6 Ricardo Ffrench-Davis and Manuel Agosin, *La liberalización comercial en América Latina: una evaluación* (Santiago, Chile: CEPAL, 1993).

7 FIEL, *Trade Agreements in the Americas: Argentina* (Buenos Aires: FIEL, 1992).

8 Adolfo Canitrot, "Inestabilidad macroeconómica y flujos de comercio en Argentina, 1978–1991," in *Serie Reformas de Política Pública*, No. 2 (Santiago, Chile: CEPAL, 1993), pp. 5–53.

9 András Körösényi, "Demobilization and Gradualism: The Political Economy of the Hungarian Transition, 1987–1991," *A Precarious Balance: Democracy in Eastern Europe and Latin America*, Vol. I (San Francisco: ICS Press for International Center for Economic Growth, 1994), Chapter 2.

10 Ibid.

11 Jacek Kochanowicz, "Transition to the Market and Democratization in Poland in the 1980s and 1990s," *A Precarious Balance*, op. cit., Vol. 1, Chapter 3.

12 Ibid.

13 Ibid., Figure 2.7, p.48.

14 Michael Bruno, *Stabilization and Reform in Eastern Europe: A Preliminary Evaluation*, IMF Working Paper, No. 92/30 (May 1992).

15 Paul Marer, "Foreign Economic Liberalization in Hungary and Poland," *American Economic Review, Papers and Proceedings* (May 1991), pp. 329–333.

16 Fabrizio Coricelli and Ana Revenga, (eds.), "Wage Policy During the Transition to a Market Economy: Poland 1990–91," *World Bank Discussion Paper 158* (Washington, DC: World Bank, 1992).

17 Körösényi, "Demobilization and Gradualism," op. cit.

18 Subsidies have been cut, but social security expenditures remain high. Revenues have not increased at the same pace as expenditures, state enterprises have suffered declining profits, and the private shadow economy has been the most dynamic sector.

19 Ekaterina Nikova, "The Bulgarian Transition: A Difficult Beginning," *A Precarious Balance*, op. cit., Vol I, Chapter 4, Table 4.2, p. 130.

20 Ibid., Table 4.4, p. 141.

21 Ibid., Table 4.4, p.141.

22 United Nations Conference on Trade and Development (UNCTAD), *Trade and Development Report* (New York: United Nations, 1993).

23 See Eduardo A. Gamarra, "Market-Oriented Reforms and Democratization in Bolivia," *A Precarious Balance*, op. cit., Vol. II, Chapter 2; and Juan Antonio Morales, "Política económica en Bolivia después de la transición a la democracia," in Juan Antonio Morales and Gary McMahon, (eds.), *La política económica en la transición a la democracia: lecciones de Argentina, Bolivia, Chile, Uruguay* (Santiago, Chile: CIEPLAN, 1993), pp. 97–115.

24 Morales, "Política económica en Bolivia," op. cit.

25 Ibid., Table 1, p. 108.

26 Juan Antonio Morales, "Reformas estructurales y crecimiento económico en Bolivia," in Joaquín Vial (ed.), *¿Adonde va América Latina? Balance de las Reformas Económicas* (Santiago, Chile: CIEPLAN, 1992) pp. 103–133, Table 3, p. 110.

27 Ibid., pp. 107, 115, 116.

28 Ibid., p. 107.

29 Fritsch and Franco, "The Political Economy of Trade," op. cit.

30 Ibid.

31 In 1989, nearly 70 percent of all imports enjoyed tariff reductions or exemptions.

32 The "law of similars" permits denial of any request to import a given product, if a "similar" product can be obtained from a domestic producer. See Fritsch and Franco, 1993, op. cit., p. 14.

33 Bolivar Lamounier and Edmar L. Bacha, "Democracy and Economic Reform in Brazil," *A Precarious Balance*, op. cit., Vol. II, Chapter 4.

34 Fritsch and Franco, "The Political Economy of Trade," op. cit.

35 See note 32.

36 Mario Damill and Roberto Frenkel, "Restauración democrática y política económica: Argentina, 1984–1991," in Juan Antonio Morales and Gary McMahon, (eds.), op. cit.

37 Canitrot, op. cit.

[38] Patricio Meller, "La apertura comercial chilena:lecciones de política," *Colección Estudios CIEPLAN*, No. 35 (September 1992), pp. 9–54.

[39] Meller, op. cit., Table 6, p. 24.

[40] Luis Felipe Lagos, "Estabilización en Chile, 1975–1980," in Daniel Wisecarver, (ed.), El modelo económico chileno (Santiago, Chile: Instituto de Economía de la Universidad Católica-Centro Internacional para el Desarrollo Económico, 1992), Table 1, p. 526.

[41] Morales, 1992, op. cit. Table 3, p. 110.

[42] Data for 1993 for Hungary, Bulgaria, and Poland from *Planecon Report*, issues from August 31, July 18, and July 5, respectively. Earlier data for Hungary is from Körösényi, op. cit.

[43] ECLAC, *Economic Panorama of Latin America* (Santiago: United Nations, 1993), p. 22.

[44] Ibid., p. 21.

[45] Sergio de la Cuadra and Dominique Hachette, "Chile," in Demetris Papageorgiou, Michael Michaely, and Armeane M. Choksi (eds.), *Liberalizing Foreign Trade*, Vol. 1 (Cambridge, MA: Basil Blackwell, 1991).

[46] Eduardo Borenzstein, Dimitri G. Demekas, and Jonothan D. Ostry, "An Empirical Analysis of the Output Decline in Three Eastern European Countries," *IMF Staff Papers*, Vol. 40, No. 1 (March 1993), pp. 1–31.

[47] Simon Commander and Fabrizio Coricelli, *Output Decline in Hungary and Poland in 1990–91*, World Bank, Policy Research Working Papers (Washington, DC: World Bank: November 1992).

[48] Ibid., p. 20.

[49] ECLAC, *Economic Panorama*, op. cit., p. 12.

[50] Michael Bruno, op. cit., Table 1, p. 6.

[51] Commander and Coricelli, op. cit., Table 2, p. 26.

[52] Nikova, op. cit., Table 4.

[53] From *Radio Free Europe/RL Research Report*, Vol. 2, No. 3, (13 August 1993), pp. 48–55.

[54] Borenzstein, Demekas, and Ostry, op. cit.

[55] Commander and Coricelli, op. cit.

[56] Ibid.

[57] Borenzstein, Demekas, and Ostry, op. cit., pp. 8–9.

[58] Commander and Coricelli, op. cit.; and Borenzstein, Demekas, and Ostry, op. cit.

[59] José Migguel Cruz, "La fruticultura de exportación: una experiencia de desarrollo empresarial," *Colección Estudios CIEPLAN*, No. 25 (December 1988), pp.79–114.

[60] Canitrot, op. cit., pp. 32–33.

[61] Inter-American Dialogue, *Convergence and Community: The Americas in 1993*, A Report of the Inter-American Dialogue (Washington, D.C.: The Aspen Institute, 1993).

[62] Oscar Altimir, "Income Distribution and Poverty Through Crisis and Adjustment," *Working Paper* No. 15 (Santiago, Chile: United Nations-ECLAC, 1993), Table 2.

[63] Ronald D. Fischer, "Efectos de una apertura comercial sobre la distribución del ingreso," *Colección Estudios CIEPLAN*, No. 33 (December 1991), pp. 95–121.

[64] Nikova, op. cit., p. 150.

[65] Ann Krueger, "Asymmetries in Policy between Exportables and Import-competing Goods," in Ronald W. Jones and Anne O. Krueger, (eds.), *The Political Economy of International Trade* (Oxford: Basil Blackwell, 1990).

[66] This approach to exchange rate management was influenced by the hard lesson of the late 1970s, when the government tried to stabilize by opening the economy to capital inflows and freezing the exchange rate—with disastrous results.

[67] Winston Fritsch and Gustavo Franco, "Los avances de la reforma de la politica comercial e industrial en Brasil," in J. Vial, (ed.), op. cit., 1992, pp. 137–157.

[68] Fritsch and Franco, "Los avances de la reforma," op. cit.

[69] Oscar Muñoz and Carmen Celedón, "Chile en transición: estrategia económica y política," in Morales and McMahon, op. cit.

[70] Giovanni Andrea Cornia and Frances Stewart, "Sistema fiscal, ajuste y pobreza," in *Colección Estudios CIEPLAN*, No. 31 (March 1991), pp. 77–106.

[71] Haggard and Kaufman, op. cit.

[72] Recent contributions to this debate are John Williamson, "Democracy and the 'Washington Consensus,'" *World Development,* Vol. 21, No. 8 (August 1993), pp. 1329–36; World Bank, *The East Asian Miracle: Economic Growth and Public Policy* (New York: Oxford University Press for the World Bank, 1993); Albert Fishlow et al., *Miracle or Design? Lessons from the East Asian Experience,* Policy Essay No. 11, (Washington, DC: Overseas Development Council, 1994).

[73] Eduardo Bitrán and Eduardo Saavedra, "Algunas reflexiones en torno al rol regulador y empresarial del Estado," in Oscar Muñoz, (ed.), *Después de las privatizaciones: Hacia el estado regulador* (Santiago, Chile: CIEPLAN, 1993).

[74] René Cortázar, *Política laboral en el Chile democrático: Avances y desafíos en los noventa* (Santiago: Ediciones Dolmen, 1993).

[75] See World Bank, *The East Asian Miracle,* op. cit. Note, however, that this study has been strongly criticized, and the controversy is still open. See Fishlow et al., op. cit.

[76] ECLAC, *Transformación productiva con equidad* (Santiago, Chile: United Nations-ECLAC, 1991).

[77] See Peter J. Katzenstein, *Small States in World Market: Industrial Policy in Europe* (Ithaca, New York: Cornell University Press, 1985), especially Chapter 2.

[78] ECLAC, *Economic Panorama,* op. cit., pp. 12, 40.

Chapter Two

Property Rights Reform During Democratization

Kálmán Mizsei

In Latin America in the past few years, and in Eastern Europe in the last decade or so, many democratic governments have achieved remarkable successes with economic stabilization. Poland, Hungary, the Czech Republic, and Estonia on the one hand, and Bolivia, Mexico, and Argentina on the other come to mind. But stabilization policies concentrate on the short term; even in the more sweeping cases, they only address a part of the underlying systemic problems that have been the main source of long-term economic imbalances and backwardness in the two regions. Stabilization policies by their very nature cannot address what seems to be the core problem of the economic systems in both regions: the *lack of a competitive and not overregulated environment for business activities.* Because of this, even the most successful economic reforms in the two regions need to be deepened through further, highly sensitive structural reforms.

In the very specific context of the interaction in Eastern Europe[1] and Latin America between the process of political democratization and economic reform, this chapter addresses the extent to which the newly emerging democratic politics are conducive to a continuation of property rights reform,[2] assesses how this reform influences the political landscape, and considers whether or not this reform contributes to the consolidation of the democratic order.

The author's personal and professional experience with Eastern Europe is intimate, while his knowledge of Latin America is admittedly sketchy; in fact, the author is not even a newcomer, but only a curious "guest" in Latin American studies. A second qualifying point is exogenous: Although the study of property rights reform is enormously relevant for the long-term perspective on both regions, the empirical work on this topic, especially concerning Latin America, is to date scarce.

Latin America shares many similarities with the Eastern European historical experience, making comparative study very relevant for a broader understanding of the two regions' distinct experiences. While examining the linkages between democratic politics and market reforms in countries undergoing this dual transition simultaneously, the impact of two extremely crucial factors should be kept in mind: 1) the influence of the outside world and 2) the impact of ideas at this point in time in particular countries. Outside influence may be more intense in the case of Eastern Europe, where the new political elites turned westward and expressed their desire to belong to the "Western" economic and political community. To be accepted, they continuously have to take into account the expectations and regulatory environments of centers of power such as the European Union and NATO.

References to "economic reform" in the literature show great diversity in the meanings assigned that term. Indeed, almost every type of major economic policy change or innovation has on occasion been called a "reform." While anyone is entitled to apply the term to any changes that appear to be desirable, the result is considerable confusion—especially in attempting inter-regional comparison. Variations in the use of the notion of reform within the two regions add to the general confusion. Since the early reform efforts in Poland and Hungary in 1956, in Eastern Europe reform has meant *decentralization-oriented*, or (after the radicalization of reform thinking) *market-oriented* changes in the economic order. In the literature on Latin America, the meaning of economic reform has been more varied, and in many cases (especially in the 1960s and 1970s, but sometimes also in the 1980s) has meant the *expansion of state regulation* and the *redistribution of wealth*—and this is precisely the opposite of what any Eastern European economist (or any other social scientist from the region) would now call economic reform.[3]

COMPONENTS OF ECONOMIC REFORM

This section will lay out what kinds of policies are considered reforms in this chapter and delineate a certain hierarchy among reforms leading to more market competition and less state interference in the economy.

Stabilization

All of the Eastern European and Latin American countries included in our larger study began their simultaneous transitions in an environment of serious macroeconomic disequilibrium; hence the need to *stabilize* was an urgent priority in each case.[4] In both regions, reform ideologies could become radical because the past crises had been protracted and brutal. In Eastern Europe, the system was understood to be in a deep and fundamental crisis. Economic reform and political democratization seemed to be two sides of the same coin, and both notions were in harmony on the need to remove the alien, imported system of Soviet-type socialism.[5] In Latin America, the situation was somewhat different. There, the "alien, imported" system was perceived by many among the elites to be U.S. domination, supportive of undemocratic, repressive military rule, and capitalism. Therefore the "reform" agenda of Latin American policymakers at the beginning of democratic rule was very different from that of their Eastern European counterparts.

Liberalization

The second type of economic reform action characterizing both regions is liberalization, or deregulation. In Eastern Europe, stabilization and liberalization are regarded as tightly linked, especially as far as price and foreign trade liberalization are concerned. The tone-setting precedent was the Polish macroeconomic stabilization program of 1990, which was accompanied by sweeping price and trade liberalizations. The Polish economic reformers' professional conviction (shared by this author) was that stabilization would not endure if major restrictions on prices and trade persisted. It is important to note that part of the economic literature (including earlier analyses prepared within the international financial institutions) also regards *non-liberalizing* stabilization as "reform," contributing with this to the terminology confusion.

The other reason for differentiating between the two types of reform is that many kinds of state controls and intervention other than price and trade controls can be deregulated (or liberalized) *after* stabilization. The most obvious candidate for a delayed reform is wage deregulation: first, because wage restrictions can be a very powerful tool for a radical break with high inflation in the *early* phase of reform, and second, because it is much easier to move away from wage restrictions later than from, for instance, a price freeze or high external tariffs. Furthermore, the "soft" budget constraint on state companies encourages them to increase wages above economically rational levels; in the early phase of the transition, one should assume that the threat of liberal wage increases in the wake of price increases is large, so that more restrictive wage policies are vital for the success of stabilization. This also applies to Latin America, where, however, the threat to reform is not so much the wage policy of state companies as the strength of the trade unions, which base their wage demands on *past* inflation, thereby prolonging high rates of inflation.

Property Rights Reform and Its Structural Reform Context

Property rights reform as defined here is a component of the "structural reforms" (in the World Bank vocabulary) that leads to less state ownership as well as less discretionary or arbitrary regulation and intervention in the economy by the state, thereby making the state a more neutral, regulatory actor. In other words, property rights reform is *rules, regulations, and state actions allowing private-sector expansion and preventing rent-seeking behavior.*[6] Property rights reform thus leads to "hardening the budget constraint," to use Janos Kornai's term; it covers issues of institutional reform that relate to the ownership structure in the economy and to the state's getting out of the business of supporting some businesses at the expense of the rest.[7]

An obvious goal of property rights reform is to secure the long-term efficiency of the economy by imposing competition and tough, normative rules. This is not, however, the only goal of these reforms. They are also indispensable components in the formation of an equitable society based on strong individual liberty. One foundation of such a society is the pair of principles that 1) any entrepreneurial activity should have a fair opportunity to succeed, and 2) entrepreneurs should bear responsibility for their own success or failure. These principles contrast sharply with the ideological assumptions of the collectivist (statist) society dominant—at least at the level of ideology—in pre-transition Eastern Europe.

In Latin America, state guidance of the economy was more limited, and private property rights were not eliminated. Yet even in Latin America, the pre-transition regulatory environment was very far from providing businesses and individuals equal chances to succeed in the marketplace. Most of the Latin American countries (with the clear exception of Chile) still have not addressed some of the important building blocks of property rights reform. Latin American experience seems to suggest that a high proportion of nominally private property in the economy is not by itself enough to create an efficient and just economy. Where access to discretionary state resources rather than efficient production and marketing is the key to business success, the incentives to economic agents do not differ fundamentally or sufficiently from those in socialist economies.

The issues of structural reform—even just those relating to the state-business relationship—are far too extensive to cover in so brief a study. This chapter will concentrate on issues—inevitably somewhat arbitrarily selected—that this author views as most crucial for overhauling the regulatory environment of businesses:[8]

■ *Privatization:* the extent of the state-owned versus the private sector.

■ *Banking reform:* the extent of "special regulation" and discretionary interference to avoid business failure and government use of the banking sector to provide "soft" rules for businesses.

■ *Bankruptcy regulation and its practical implementation:* rules and practices of exit for failing businesses.

■ *Rules of entry for new businesses:* ease of establishing new businesses; de-monopolization of once monopolized areas; and entry of foreign businesses.

The focus here is on the broad dynamics of interplay between democratization and this cluster of "core property right" reforms over time, in both regions, and a discussion of comparative themes at that level.[9] Obvious reform timing inconsistencies make the comparison quite complicated: The democratic transition started in Latin America much earlier than in Eastern Europe, making Latin America's accumulated experience with the interaction between the two types of changes much longer.

The following sections explore the linkages between politics in newly democratic systems and property rights reform. The discussion assesses the effects of democratic politics on the development of institutions generating competitive private markets more than the impact of property rights reform on political evolution, in part because the links are asymmetrical: The influence of democratic politics on property rights reform is more immediate and visible than the reverse. Interactions between property rights reform and democratic politics are also affected by the problem of timeframe inconsistency: The short-term cycle of democratic politics is in inherent tension with the long-term character of property rights reform.

A recurring theme throughout this chapter will be the enormously important influence of sustained macroeconomic stabilization on the development of property rights. Low inflation (in Eastern Europe accompanied by low or no shortages) is crucially important for property rights and state regulation of the business environment. For business, there is no more damaging uncertainty and arbitrariness than high and unpredictable inflation.[10] Stabilization should precede structural reform (although in some countries, notably Brazil and Russia, structural reforms are being attempted in a highly inflationary macroeconomic setting). Therefore, the politics associated with stabilization indirectly bears on property rights reform. In that connection, this chapter later explores Polish Deputy Prime Minister Leszek Balcerowicz's idea of a brief period of "extraordinary politics" and its relevance to economic reform. Even after the initial stabilization effort has been completed, fiscal constraints and budgetary considerations continue to operate as a powerful engine affecting the speed and design of property rights reform—often encouraging privatization even when the government's ideology would dictate otherwise.

The impact of property rights reform on politics and the evolution of political systems is very complex and less clearly visible. Three links will be explored in this chapter. The first link is via short-term electoral politics. Vigorous reforms in some cases have helped the parties or leaders responsible to get reelected, while slow reforms in fragile, post-crisis societies actually increase the chances of future electoral failure. The second link operates through longer-term shifts in political incentives. Credible property rights reform reduces the strength of rent-seeking lobbies by making it less profitable to organize pressure groups and invest in "government relations." The third link involves changes in social structure. Particularly in Eastern Europe, but to some extent also in Latin America, the reforms discussed here more or less directly help to *generate a broad-based entrepreneurial class;* this changes the political culture of a society.

DEMOCRATIC POLITICS AND PROPERTY RIGHTS REFORM: THE MAIN LINKAGES

Politics influences decisions concerning private-sector expansion, the treatment of business failure, banking reform, and the deregulation of market entry much more visibly and directly than these particular economic reforms affect the political landscape. Once implemented, specific economic reforms shape the nature and agenda of politics over a much longer period of time, primarily through the transmission of changing perceptions and the changing social composition of society. Privatization and liberalization of market entry may, however, have a more direct feedback into politics—especially in Eastern Europe, because the reforms were very rapid and started almost from point zero. Banking reform and revised bankruptcy laws affect politics and political evolution through more indirect links. A more direct link is that radical banking reforms reduce the chances of the political elites in power to use state-owned banks as supporters of particular political groups, especially in election periods. Yet, the entire set of policy reforms feeds back into politics (especially in the long run) far more than any particular one of the reforms does individually.

Influence of Democratic Politics on Property Rights Reform

The principal tension in the relationship between democratic reform and property rights reform lies in the difficulty of achieving short-term political gains while introducing long-term economic reform. There is a conflict between, on the one hand, the short- to medium-term scope of the electoral cycle and the desire of politicians to shape processes and institutions accordingly, and on the other hand, the long-term approach needed for property rights reform. Overcoming this inherent contradiction (which historically has led to certain unpleasant outcomes even in mature democracies) requires either that the electorate force the politicians to "act on the long run," or that some public-spirited politicians act that way on their own—perhaps even against their own short-term career interests.

A second major tension is that "neutral" market regulation benefits the public at large; in democratic politics, there is always inherent pressure to introduce preferences for certain interest groups.[11] Again, a popular consensus regarding the benefits of neutral regulation (as well as, in some cases, the ideological commitment of dedicated political leaders) can counter interest-group demands and help the state maintain fiscal discipline.

THE OPPORTUNITY OF EXTRAORDINARY POLITICS. Early in a democratic transition, it is relatively easy for the new government to introduce a broad range of reform measures if the leaders are so inclined (as was the case in numerous Eastern European countries). However, "extraordinary politics" does not last forever. As the overview of this volume notes, the consolidation of democracy is characterized by the emergence of more organized interest groups and more pressure on governments to favor one or another business or labor interest. "Normal" politics also means that dedicated reformists give way to professional politicians who are much more driven by considerations such as maintaining electoral influence, power, and the like. Pursuing highly sensitive structural reforms in this environment is a more complex political goal than early stabilization. In Latin America, where the discontinuity that democratization brought about was less dramatic than in Eastern Europe, the window of opportunity for reform has been smaller. Therefore (and because recognition of the urgency of sweeping reform was not present), the initial move toward economic reform was also less clear-cut than in the most radically reforming Eastern European countries, such as Poland and Czechoslovakia in 1990 and 1991, respectively, and Russia in 1992.

Balcerowicz has described these windows of opportunity as periods of extraordinary politics—times of radical democratization, when the change from authoritarian to democratic politics confers an *unusual degree of legitimacy* upon the new politicians because they were among the principal fighters for democracy. In such situations as in Eastern Europe in 1989 and 1990, there is a certain likelihood that public-spirited politicians will emerge. However, successful ones with enough power to influence the course of events have been very rare. Balcerowicz himself in Poland, and Václav Klaus in Czechoslovakia have been such politicians; both were able to grasp the benefits of the unusual political situation on behalf of their nations. In Russia at the end of 1991, Yegor Gaidar's team also took the historic opportunity to push ahead with market reforms.

To what extent can we regard the post-military Latin American political situations as "extraordinary"? The political situation *was* extraordinary immediately after the ouster of military dictatorships, and the newly elected leaders (in our sample, especially Argentina's President Raúl Alfonsín) did receive a great bonus of confidence. Latin America's first round of leaders could not really benefit from this opportunity, however, primarily because of a mistaken perception of priorities. This also applies to the leaders' perceptions of their own political and career priorities; the inability of the first-wave leaders to contain macroeconomic disequilibrium was the overwhelming cause of their political failure.

Yet both the Argentine and Bolivian stories of the second presidential episodes show us forcefully that extraordinary politics can also be created in a situation where there is no spectacular political breakthrough, but where the macroeconomic situation is "desperate enough" for the leadership's shock therapy approach to gain its constituency after the fact—even if the results have been achieved by policies containing a considerable degree of not-very-legal actions. It can be argued, therefore, that the *potential* for extraordinary politics exists in any desperate macroeconomic situation. The potential may be weaker in Brazil, since social and political institutions (including indexing) have had too much time to adjust to gradually developing hyperinflation—i.e., the situation is not perceived as very desperate.[12]

At the time of democratization, most of the region's elites were reluctant to face the fundamental economic challenge confronting Latin America: Excessive state involvement in the economic process had failed. This difference between Eastern European and Latin American perceptions was probably largely due to the fact that, in Eastern Europe, the failure of the statist economy was linked to the socialist ideology. In Latin America, in the early 1980s, many analysts of social life still either interpreted the misfortune of the region in the categories of dependency theory, or at least tried to preserve as much as possible from that heritage, which blamed domestic economic failures on the capitalist world economy. This perspective did not allow its intellectual supporters to recognize how different the Latin American economic systems are from the developed capitalist economies (most significantly, precisely in the ways market rules and contractual obligations determine economic action). Since then, it appears that a more fundamental change has occurred in the perceptions of the Latin American elites—of course not independently from the ideological impact of the collapse of the Soviet empire.

   URGENT BUDGETARY PRESSURE AND PRIVATIZATION. A second very strong linkage between politics and property rights reform results from the fragility of public finance in both regions. In post-stabilization situations, governments are often caught between continued budgetary constraints and public pressures to increase welfare spending. Governments must also take into account the need and expectation to contain inflation within "civilized" limits. In this situation, they frequently decide to sell high-value public assets. If this is in keeping with prevalent ideological perceptions, there is a double reason to privatize; but even governments that are initially very populist—for example, President Carlos Menem's government in Argentina—can pursue a very radical privatization policy to save the country (and their own political fortunes) from the resurgence of runaway budget deficits. From this perspective, the best targets of privatization are of course large public utilities, such as national telecommunication companies, gas and electricity utilities, and national airlines. The sale of these industries brings in very high prices that help offset even large budget deficits. This approach also fits in well with the current international environment of deregulation as well as the trend toward globalization in the airline industry. In Latin America, Argentina is the leader in the privatization of utilities, but many other countries followed suit. In Eastern Europe, Hungary was the first to sell shares in its airlines and, more important, in its telecommunication company. The latter transaction basically saved the country's balance of payments in 1993 and largely offset the impact of real overvaluation of the national currency.

   However, periods of extraordinary politics are brief, and fiscal pressures encourage privatization but have less impact on other elements of property rights reform. In general, the political chances of property rights reform are fragile in spite of some encouraging experience. Politicians tend to neglect them; initial ideological consensus on their importance may vanish as early stabilization triggers renewed group struggles for resources in the political environment of "normalized politics"; dedicated politicians—such as Poland's Leszek Balcerowicz, Russia's Yegor Gaidar, and Bolivia's Gonzalo Sánchez de Lozada—get out of the game; and the needs of long-term reform are more often than not in conflict with politicians' shorter-term career interests. Institutional reforms that in the long run lead to modernization are therefore very unlikely to prevail without major external support.

Even with external support, the politics of property rights reform needs more complex consensus-building than does macroeconomic stabilization. Consensus on property rights reform needs to be directed not toward the outcome but toward the rules. This is a task similar to consensus-building on the consolidation of political democracy: although no one can predict the specific outcome, players need to agree on the rules in the belief that none will have a particularly bad outcome. This is more difficult in economic than in democratic reform because it involves actions by sections of society that fear they will be undue victims of the changed rules; these fears must somehow be overcome. Finally, positive coalitions built on *rules* rather than outcomes also require that the public accept considerable uncertainty.[13]

Influence of Property Rights Reform on the Political Landscape

This section turns from how newly democratic politics affect property rights reform to the reverse connections: how property rights reform influences the shape of the political landscape. The linkage in this direction is indirect and complex. The sale of a bank, let alone a new bankruptcy law, will not directly and visibly change the country's political party structure. Moreover, there is a lack of empirical evidence about how reforms other than privatization bear on the core property rights issues—let alone how they impact on politics.

Privatization can have a positive impact on shaping electoral dynamics, especially in Eastern Europe. Czechoslovakia's popular voucher scheme (more recently operative in the Czech Republic alone) is said to have contributed to the repeat electoral victory of Klaus's party in 1992 as it "gave" a piece of the inherited state property to every citizen. The voucher scheme in that country has contributed to the fact that the Czech Republic is the only country that has avoided a return to power of the post-communist parties. (Another reason for this, however, is that the Communist Party in Czechoslovakia, as the most reliable ally of the Soviet Union, was deeply mistrusted.) It can also be argued that, had the Hungarian government's (or that of the United Democratic Front (UDF) in Bulgaria) economic reform drive been bolder in the afterglow of early electoral victory, their political performance might also have been more successful. Privatization success has strengthened some Latin American leaders as well. President Menem's victory in mid-term legislative elections, his successes in achieving changes in the electoral rules, and finally his probable re-election are certainly to a large extent attributable to his bold reform—most notably privatization—drive.

One should, however, vigorously refute the simplistic linkage offered in most of the Western (especially the U.S.) press, tying the strong comeback of the post-communist parties to the harshness of economic reform. Again, the Czech Republic demonstrates that if reforms are convincingly presented, and if a self-confident policy team is seen to be actually carrying out the promised reforms, even if these are very radical, the public is likely to go along. The reasons for the strong performance of the post-communist parties are more complex. Besides economic hardship, factors that have contributed to these parties' return to power include their political experience, their organizational advantage, and their presence in all elites of the post-communist societies.

As an economist, the author of this paper tends to bias in his thinking on the ways politics creates obstacles to property rights reform. However, it is important to note that the democratic setting also offers a chance to openly debate highly complex reforms. Even if large parts of the population will not directly engage in parliamentary debates about banking reform, those democratic debates, or even the democratic institutions themselves, can legitimize policy decisions that may in the short run cause hardship to the population. Thus, the democratic setting also offers a chance for those highly complex reforms to succeed. It is impossible to imagine that the Balcerowicz reforms could have been introduced in Poland in 1982—during martial law—to use a very obvious example. Moreover, deepening economic reforms after the initial measures certainly presupposes some degree of public debate, which has been facilitated by the democratic setting of post–1990 politics.

As noted earlier, privatization and other property rights reforms also have longer-run effects on politics, because they change the incentives for interest group pressures and alter social structure. In the course of discussing specific types of property rights reform, the remainder of this chapter will note several examples of these effects.

PRIVATIZATION AND THE DEMOCRATIC PROCESS

The most obvious target of economic reform aiming to get the state out of its discretionary interference with business is the privatization of state companies, and the most obvious part of the world to privatize is clearly Eastern Europe, where the economic system based on state ownership has failed on a historical scale. The major impetus for privatization is not to be found in the particular political setting of different countries—privatization in the 1980s and 1990s is a worldwide phenomenon—but rather in deep international economic and ideological currents (plus the budgetary pressures mentioned earlier). As the Appendix traces (see pp. 37–46), the roots of statist expansion go back to the Great Depression, and even farther. Moreover, the deficiencies of statist expansion have also accumulated in many geographical areas of the world economy if not totally simultaneously, then very close to each other in time.

The increasing ineffectiveness of the state in the performance of economic functions since the 1970s meant at least two major shifts in both Eastern Europe and Latin America. In its function of owner of different industries, the state became increasingly unable to fulfill its assumed role as the supplier of certain goods and services. Moreover, because of governments' extensive and increasingly inefficient engagement in these activities, it became more and more difficult to balance budgets and to provide one of the highest public goods: i.e., a stable macroeconomic environment, including a stable currency.

Clearly there are also fundamental differences in the Latin American and Eastern European settings—the most obvious being the extent of involvement of the state sector in the economy. In Latin America, state ownership in the "competitive" sectors (i.e., manufacturing, agriculture, construction, and retail and wholesale trade) had been much less widespread before the liberalization started than in Eastern Europe. A subtler and much less well-recognized difference is that, because Latin America had a semi-market environment even before the transition, state ownership in the region was less ambiguous than in Eastern Europe, where ownership of state companies in practice was very vaguely defined; in many Eastern European cases, especially where there was "socialist market reform," managers or workers had more entitlements (quasi-property rights) than agents of the state. Sorting out the legal uncertainties resulting from those socialist reforms sometimes required reformers to make difficult political decisions. One of the clearest examples of this was Poland, where workers felt they had strong rights, and where the political battle over sorting out the workers' claims in 1990 delayed vitally important legislation. In Hungary, the decentralization of some rights during privatization was also partly a consequence of earlier "managerial" reforms.

Privatization has been the most debated public policy issue in Eastern Europe since the beginning of the transition, but actual progress in this area is still modest. The development of small indigenous private businesses (which can be included in the broad definition of privatization) has been very rapid in the western-tier countries—the Czech Republic, Poland, and Hungary. The sale (or distribution) of state assets has been relatively dynamic in those western-tier countries—but the pace of sale in Poland has been disappointing so far.

In part to maximize revenue from sales some Latin American governments have focused their privatization efforts on public utilities. There is asymmetry between the two regions in this respect: in Eastern Europe, privatization is the main agenda item for establishing competition in the manufacturing sectors; in Latin America, it is more vital to establish other elements of property rights reform—such as entry and exit rules, banking reform, and other segments of market regulation conducive to competition. In both regions, privatization started somewhat spontaneously—i.e., on practical rather than ideological grounds. In the most reformist Eastern European countries, the small private sector (sorely lacking in the inherited environment of almost exclusively giant state organizations) expanded at the "grassroots" beginning in the late 1970s.[14] In Latin America, some rather isolated privatization episodes—such as the successful privatization of the Buenos Aires urban transport system—took place as early as the 1960s, but broad-based privatization gained momentum only in the late 1980s.

Evolving Goals of Privatization

In 1988, the last communist governments in Hungary and Poland implemented legislation that opened wide the doors to "spontaneous" privatization, particularly in manufacturing. These enterprises were in bad financial shape, as earlier decentralizations had established a relationship between their financial positions and the overall economic situation. They were also badly underinvested. Certainly in Hungary, and perhaps elsewhere, one of the important motives of enterprise managers in pressuring for appropriate legislation was to be able to invite outside partners (mostly foreigners) to set up joint ventures to catch up with competitors technologically and to improve their poor financial position. Subsequently, in the environment of opening the economy, this enterprise survival strategy seemed even more compelling. Since in the period just before democratization the enterprise managers' needs were driving the privatization policy in both countries, the consequence was that legislation (in Hungary, the Company Act, and in Poland, a government decree) gave excessive rights to the managers (in Poland, colored also by employee self-management rules) to shift state assets into various incorporated units.

More generally, in Eastern Europe, the following sequence of privatization took place. First, the state crisis led to isolated cases of privatization intended to achieve narrowly defined goals of the companies. This was followed by gradual recognition of privatization as an overall policy goal. In Eastern Europe in 1989–1990, this sequence coincided with democratization. In Poland, the first democratic government stopped the flow of unregulated privatization, in response to public outrage at the lawless "stealing" of state assets by managers. In Hungary, the Hungarian Democratic Forum (HDF) expressed its reservations about decentralized and barely controlled privatization in its election campaign in 1990; after gaining power, however, the HDF did not stop but merely modified the procedures elaborated by its predecessors. Over time, the methods of privatization became more sophisticated in Hungary. But the guiding philosophy under the first democratically elected government was much more a continuum than a radical change of direction. In the rest of the region, privatization was only possible after the cataclysmic changes of 1989–1990; its form to a considerable degree reflected the development of political institutions. The spectrum ranged from the mass privatization scheme of Czechoslovakia to completely unregulated grabbing of state property in Ukraine and many other new post-Soviet states.[15]

In the rapidly reforming countries of Eastern Europe after 1989, when privatization became an overall policy objective, it was in many instances defined too rigidly by policymakers. One might call this the naive phase of privatization. A "statistical" perception of privatization became dominant; both policymakers and some foreign advisers perceived privatization in a very formal, narrow sense, looking only to the nominal fulfillment of privatization and not to the actual post-privatization company governance structure. This approach has particularly characterized policymaking in countries with no socialist reform experience prior to 1989.

Macro Policies and Privatization

The history of the Polish transition provides the most striking illustration of the important linkage between stabilization policies and private-sector expansion. The privatization of state enterprises is known to be one of the weakest aspects of the Polish transition. Yet the private sector expanded very rapidly between 1989 and 1993. Although this expansion also testifies to the entrepreneurial spirit of Polish society, it could only have happened in the context of credible macroeconomic stabilization.[16]

Macroeconomic policy may have the biggest impact on short-term private-sector expansion immediately after the start of a credible stabilization program. At that point, large state organizations (as well as large parasitic private organizations in the Latin American context) are very likely to suddenly get into trouble. If they are not bailed out, and if there is enough flexibility in the system, the vacuum they create will be filled by others—most likely smaller private entities. The large firms will usually try to survive financially by selling off divisions of their empires. Consequently, privatization occurs both through expansion of the private sector at the expense of the state sector and a marked shift from large state entities toward smaller, more "market-focused" (i.e., less rent-seeking) activities.

This broader concept of privatization, embracing both conversion of state enterprises and the growth of new private firms, helps to explain the importance of systematic analysis on such issues as bankruptcy, deregulation of market entry, and size structure. Good bankruptcy regulation helps to smooth the exit of the parasites, and deregulated entry rules help the newcomers come in. A less concentrated size structure in turn helps reverse the trends of the state-centered system, in that state interference in business tends to result in size concentration. Deconcentration is vital in two ways to the theme of this volume: it helps to generate the middle classes important to maintaining a democratic political environment, and it eases political pressures on policymakers for favoritism or rent-seeking.

Two other (more obvious) ways in which sound macro policies enhance private-sector expansion should also be mentioned: First, subsidy cuts squeeze large socialist enterprises and almost always result in significant employment layoffs. A large part of the released workforce is likely to find new employment (especially if market entry is reasonably free) in smaller enterprises, thus facilitating their expansion. Second, a stable macroeconomic environment tends to increase confidence in the country on the part of investors—domestic and foreign alike.

The impressive expansion of the small private sector in Poland in 1990-93 as well as the "spontaneous" privatization in Hungary from the late 1980s provide empirical evidence of the linkage between macro policies and deconcentrated private-sector development. In Hungary, the huge pressure on the large state enterprise sector to dismantle itself would not have emerged had macroeconomic policy not become credibly tough between 1988 and 1992.[17] Financial pressure prompted passage of the Company Act during the communist era; this invited the state enterprise bosses to be creative in entering all kinds of joint ventures with primarily foreign private companies so that their businesses could escape the financial eclipse that other large state organizations were experiencing.

Examples of countries that made the lives of huge state companies' bosses easier through massive inflationary financing are also plentiful in the region. Russia and Ukraine are particular cases in point. Consequently, in those countries, the political weight of the large-enterprise bosses has remained almost intact. Industrial bosses are strong enough to create powerful political groupings that emerge as natural enemies of sound macro policies. The 1993 Russian election and the immediate post-election dynamics were painful proofs of this. What seems to have happened is that the electoral failure of the reformist group helped the industrial lobbies to occupy important positions in the political structure, resulting in a slowing of microeconomic reforms. Similarly, the easing of monetary policy in Hungary after mid–1992, accompanied by subsequent banking and enterprise bailouts (see next section), has slowed down changes in the size and ownership structure of the Hungarian economy.[18]

Strong or weak stabilization efforts not only establish the context for the rapid or slow emergence of the private sector, but also (as noted earlier) can directly prompt sales of public enterprises. Privatization led by short-term budgetary considerations encounters two major problems. One is that short-term budgetary concerns may overshadow what should be the most important long-term government consideration: establishing viable, efficient, and competitive services in the given markets. The existence of natural monopolies in these industries makes regulation of the business environment critical. This is especially important because the likely buyers are often organizations stronger (and almost always more professional in business transactions) than the national governments themselves, which are usually very inexperienced in the public regulation of private utilities. Hence the threat of political pressure or even corruption.

The second danger, also linked to privatization for fiscal motives, is that it is not at all certain that the best bidder will get the contract. In fact, in almost all such large transactions, serious questions have been raised about the process of selecting the buyer. In many cases, privatization means selling the national company (or large shares in it) to a foreign, state-owned partner; the Hungarian airlines were sold to the Italian national carrier, and the Czech, to the French state airline. Both transactions had to face very serious and legitimate questions as to whether it is in the public interest to "privatize" by selling national air carriers to other countries' *state* airlines. Since then, the performance of the two airlines has seemed to substantiate the fears. The Czech case turned out to be scandalously unsuccessful and the Czech state has already agreed to repurchase the carrier. Hungarian Telecom, on the other hand, was sold for a really excellent price; in this respect, it is a model sale of "family silver" regionwide; however even in this probably most successful case, the fact that the buyer is the Deutsche Telecom, itself a German state monopoly, raises some questions.

Despite these risks of privatization driven by budgetary considerations, one should also stress a positive potential: Through these actions, the governments of transforming countries are able to buy time. The sale of 30 percent of Hungarian Telecom saved Hungary's balance of payments in 1993; Argentina's privatization actions have had a similar effect in counteracting the impact of overvalued local currency. Although this kind of strategy cannot last long (there is only so much family silver), buying time still matters—since it provides a chance for both economic reform and political democracy to develop deeper roots.

Voucher Schemes and the Politics of Privatization

Czechoslovak (later Czech only) privatization experience offers interesting contrasts with several other Eastern European countries. The Czech voucher privatization scheme has attracted great interest, including its potential for generating broad public support and for helping to make privatization consistent with democracy.

In contrast to Hungary, where severe debt problems prompted more attention to budgetary considerations in the design of privatization policy, Czech policymakers embarked upon the boldest free-distribution-type of privatization to date. The Czech state seeks to transfer ownership of its large companies as quickly as possible. Their view is that even if there are not up-front state revenues from privatization, the privatized companies will over time contribute more to the state budget as private units than they could if privatization were a slow, case-by-case selling process. Because voucher privatization in principle gets rid of large blocks of state holdings at one stroke, the approach may also avoid another potential risk of slower processes: erosion over time of the government's willingness to sell state companies. This supposition has yet to be tested over a longer period. However, the international community (primarily the international financial institutions and independent international advisers) is increasingly leaning toward the voucher model, which is spreading to other countries—most interestingly also to Latin America.

A comparison of the politics of different privatization schemes is beyond the scope of this chapter, but domestic politics obviously affects the design, implementation, and results of different schemes to distribute shares in state enterprises. In Russia, for example, the scheme has turned into a powerful vehicle of "insider" ownership by enterprise bosses and employees because without this political concession mass privatization would have probably never happened. Poland was one of the pioneers of privatization, but a partially paralyzed political decision-making process has prevented implementation of the ambitious scheme. In the Czech Republic, in contrast, the voucher scheme proved popular, and contributed to the election victory of the radically pro-market political forces.

The ways in which voucher privatization schemes re-shape corporate structure and the links between ownership and management will have crucial implications both for economic effectiveness and for politics (mainly indirectly). The primary need in post-communist, large business organizations is a drastic change in their corporate culture. This is most likely to emerge through the splitting up and privatization of the large business organizations so as to bring ownership and management as close together as possible. Where that is done, one can expect the interests of the owner to drive managerial change.

It is an open question whether the Czech privatization scheme will translate into better management. Despite the rhetoric about "popular capitalism," the Czech scheme has in fact produced a very concentrated ownership structure. Vouchers have been submitted to "voucher privatization funds," many of which are managed by the large banks, which, at least in credit markets, represent unusually strong market power. Moreover, the company structure itself is very concentrated, since privatization did not typically lead to the splitting and restructuring of firms in the way that the Hungarian privatization did in its early phase. One can make two alternative predictions as to the longer-term outcomes of the Czech process with respect to concentration and management. On the one hand, if the macroeconomic policies of the country resist pressures from the powerful financial institutions, healthy restructuring could emerge after privatization. In this connection the recent interest of U.S. institutional investors in "emerging markets" may help, as their investment can provide badly needed liquidity for the Czech institutional investors. On the other hand, in the absence of "real" owners (i.e., owners directly involved in management control), the restructuring could become very painful, possibly forcing the government into repeated bailouts of the large organizations, companies, banks, and investment funds alike. This scenario would slow down the necessary process of splitting and restructuring.

In Hungary, the much different and slower approach to privatization is intended to deliver precisely the two aspects of reform—decomposition of large state firms and more direct links between ownership and management—that are in question in the Czech program. However, because the Hungarian approach is somewhat slower, it runs a risk of being derailed because of possible political complications.[19] Judgment as to the medium-term political dynamics and risks should determine which approach to choose. If one expects that a country's politics can sustain the enduring public tension that a slower and more orderly privatization causes, it may be beneficial to choose that more case-by-case approach.

Foreign Participation, Privatization, and Politics

The privatization process is also influenced by public sentiment toward foreign ownership. This is again a more important issue in Eastern Europe than in Latin America—simply because more assets in the region need to be privatized, and there is no national class of entrepreneurs. Within Eastern Europe, the issue has been much more controversial in some countries than in others. In Poland, early *nomenklatura* privatization (the Polish label for what was more neutrally termed "spontaneous" privatization in Hungary) was halted, for many reasons including some concern about potential foreign participation in joint ventures. Fear of foreign domination played a considerably larger role in blocking proposals for mass (voucher) privatization, since foreign investment banks would play a major role in managing the investment funds established by such schemes. Resistance to foreign involvement therefore blocked the two major potential approaches to privatization in Poland.

In Hungary, in contrast, there was relatively little resistance to foreign ownership during the initial phase; even very recently, Deutsche Telecom's 30 percent ownership of Hungarian Telecom did not cause any public protest. Part of the reason for this is that the "nationalist" government in Hungary was less vulnerable to "nationalist" criticism but did face criticism from the more "liberal" intellectuals and parties. (The privatization issue on which the liberal and nationalist parties differed most concerned the privatization of small retail and service units; on this issue, the government parties were right, since by excluding foreigners from "small privatization," they supported the emergence of a local entrepreneurial class at low cost.) This political tactic and outcome enabled the government to implement quite friendly and not particularly "nationalist" policies toward foreign investment almost unchallenged. Only very recently did it have to make concessions to local lobbies by launching programs enabling enterprise employee stock ownership plans (ESOPs) to buy out their state companies at low cost and against preferential credits.

In the Czech Republic, as in Hungary, foreign involvement has not been a major political issue, either when the plan was proposed or in the course of implementation. Indeed, from an economic perspective one potential pitfall of the Czech privatization scheme is that it does not appear to be especially conducive to large foreign involvement in the privatization process. Serious strategic investors tend to be very cautious about buying into companies whose ownership structure is as uncertain as that of most of the voucher-privatized companies. Foreign capital is flowing in, but mainly to entirely new enterprises, or to companies that have not been affected by the voucher scheme. Lately foreign involvement has also taken the form of portfolio investment into the "voucherized" companies.

An additional political dimension often interacts with foreign involvement in the privatization process. In many cases, a state bureaucracy that is weak (and sometimes prone to corruption) faces strong foreign owners who are able to efficiently bargain for concession. This has happened in each case of recent international investment in the automobile industries in Eastern Europe. Without exception, this process has resulted in excessive tax concessions giving foreign firms undue competitive advantage over local businesses.

In Eastern Europe, one should definitely differentiate between the initial phase of democracy and the consolidation period with respect to the politics of privatization. Once the rent-seeking lobbies of the state sector again become more organized, privatization becomes more difficult. In some cases, the international financial institutions have inadvertently helped *create* anti-privatization lobbies—as happened in Hungary, for example, where a state superholding responsible for producing at least 25 percent of GDP was established at the urging of the World Bank in late 1992.[20]

It is highly probable that the social environment of privatization will over time become more difficult in Eastern Europe.[21] The political dynamics of privatization may be very different in the early phase and the later, consolidation phase of democratic politics. Sub-regional differences are also noteworthy. Only in three of the region's countries—Poland, Hungary, and the Czech Republic—is bold privatization proceeding in a relatively stable macroeconomic and legal environment, and only a few other countries—Slovakia, Slovenia, and Estonia—are likely to follow suit.

Privatization in "Lawless" Conditions

In some other countries, lawlessness and hyperinflation have let the state sector disintegrate in a very uncertain way, which makes the process of privatization vulnerable to some major, later political challenges. The most interesting case is Russia, where, in a very difficult environment, privatization is the only economic reform going clearly ahead. The potential vulnerability of the Russian case to political backlash as well as the unusual high degree of uncertainty in the *economic* environment (due to high inflation especially, but also to rapidly changing regulations) provide ample reason for concern that the achievements of privatization may be unraveled and that strongly clientelist structures between privatized companies and the state may reemerge. In countries where sizable privatization still has not taken place (such as Bulgaria in this project's sample of countries), this is special reason for concern about the future transparency of business-state relationships. If more extensive subsidies reemerge in half-stabilized economies such as Bulgaria's, there is reason to question whether macroeconomic stability can be maintained. Indeed, this is a legitimate question even in the case of more advanced reforming countries such as Poland and Hungary, where the return of post-communist parties to power (though not a return of the old system) may push politics more toward subsidization and a partial unraveling of the achievements of earlier stabilization results—even if this goes against the personal convictions of the leading politicians of the left-wing parties in power.

As mentioned at the outset of this discussion of privatization, in Eastern Europe privatization so far has been impressive only in the western-tier countries and, with some unanswered questions and reservations, in Russia. One can conclude that the political structure and culture have strongly influenced privatization. In countries with a less "Western" cultural heritage, the limits of political change at the top in 1989–1991 as well as general attitudes have prevented stronger private-sector expansion. Romania's case is illustrative: In the first few years, the attitude of workers toward privatization—which in that country, without a domestic capitalist class, of course meant selling to foreigners—was hostile and prevented large selloffs. Fear of layoffs also slowed down privatization—again more so in the less "Western" parts of the region. The political risks of layoffs were a strong factor pressing governments toward free distribution schemes or, as in Russia, toward allowing a large role to "insiders." It remains to be seen what price these countries will have to pay for these compromises. This especially applies to Russia, where the role of insiders in the new ownership structure is very strong, threatening further politicization of the economy—i.e., strong demands from the working collectives to be granted financial advantages and possible bailouts in distress, and very slow implementation of bankruptcy regulations.

Privatization and Politics in Some Latin American Countries

The emergence of privatization programs in some Latin American countries followed a logic not unlike that in Hungary and Poland. As in Eastern Europe, the state crisis led to isolated cases of privatization intended to achieve narrowly defined goals. Gradually, privatization came to be recognized as an overall policy goal. Again as in Eastern Europe, initial privatization in some Latin American cases took a simplistic form—without attention to post-privatization governance structure.[22] In Chile for example, in the acute economic depression of the early 1980s, companies privatized earlier rapidly became financially unsustainable. The political leadership was forced to re-nationalize a rather large part of previously privatized companies and banks, followed later in the decade by a second round of privatization.[23] A particularly unfortunate phenomenon was the ownership connection between the large businesses and large banks, which greatly contributed to the banking crisis of 1981. That ownership connection, however, was beneficial to the big businesses since it forced the state to support them, especially because of the large-scale foreign borrowing involved. It may be that privatization in Argentina under President Menem and some Eastern European grand schemes are facing a similar risk of producing financially vulnerable large units that are prone to rent-seeking behavior.[24]

In most Latin American countries, of course, much less economic activity was directly in the public sector than in the post-communist countries. Direct and indirect subsidies to largely or wholly private firms, and a wide range of other government interventions, were more important obstacles to efficient and dynamic private sectors—and the role of privatization was correspondingly less central. Nonetheless, subsidies to state-owned firms contributed substantially to budget deficits, while public utilities often held back economic activity by providing unreliable, scarce, or poor-quality services. Privatization therefore has played an important role.

Among the Latin American countries that have moved furthest with privatization—Chile, Mexico, Argentina, Bolivia—only the last two have done so under democratic governments. Bolivia has recently announced a mass privatization scheme that is intended to combine the privatization of assets with the privatization of the state pension system.[25]

Sometimes privatization is only "nominal." Much of Mexico's privatization has in fact amounted to passing ownership from federal hands to local authorities—or possibly even to the trade unions. This is not likely to significantly improve the functioning of either the companies or the affected markets. Such "privatization" happens in Eastern Europe as well when governments play the role of Santa Claus by distributing (or, in the worst case, only promising to distribute) companies to local governments, the unions, and state social insurance organizations.

A more difficult question to address is how privatization in the two regions has affected the consolidation of the democratic political process. The Argentina country study by Adolfo Canitrot and Silvia Sigal in our project offers some important and very provocative hypotheses on this point.[26] The picture it paints is that privatization furthered the concentration of economic power in Argentina, and that this has a great potential to influence politics adversely in the future. This is so, the argument goes, because the business groups that benefited from privatization are the same ones that were given large subsidies in the 1970s and that were bailed out by the state in the crisis of the early 1980s. The case study argues that President Menem announced privatization to win the business community's support, and that he step-by-step made privatization his administration's trademark. But privatization was concentrated in public utilities and in companies that are generally regarded as natural monopolies, and it benefited mainly a few financial groups and the state budget. These groups were formed over the past two decades through the huge wealth-redistribution effect of the nationalization of the debt and hyperinflation. They are close to government officials and, given their past experience, are prone to rent-seeking behavior.

The Canitrot-Sigal interpretation of the Argentine privatization story is important—even should it turn out to be excessively pessimistic as to the way privatization has been conducted. It shows that, in certain circumstances, privatization may contribute to an overconcentration of economic power in the hands of the few, and this can have adverse effects on the dynamics of domestic politics. It also shows that governments should not lose perspective: If the sole or overwhelming aim of privatization is to fill the budgetary gap, this can cause distortions not only by adverse wealth redistribution but also by overconcentrating on selling the family silver while neglecting the sale of smaller manufacturing units—as has been the case in Argentina. The Canitrot-Sigal interpretation of Argentina's privatization leads us repeatedly to the recognition that privatization should strive to create a *broad-based* entrepreneurial and stockholding class. (This consideration should not, however, be exaggerated; the professional skills of the owners-to-be are certainly at least as important.)

This chapter's arguments concerning the impact of tough macro policies on private sector development as well as the emphasis on such regulatory issues as bankruptcy and market entry may sound rather hypothetical to students of Latin America. These arguments are certainly deeply rooted in the empirical evidence on the transition in Eastern Europe. However, it is this author's view that they are likely to prove important but greatly overlooked topics in Latin America as well.

Privatization and Politics: Concluding Remarks

As this section has shown, different strategies of privatization may have different degrees and kinds of long-term success. It would be premature to draw final conclusions on the highly debated issue of privatization. Certainly the impressive statistics on the growth of the private sector in Eastern Europe do not yet convince us about the long-term growth prospects of market competition in given fields. This section also has drawn attention to possible pitfalls of different privatization approaches and to their interaction with politics. However, these qualifications should not detract from the broader perspective.

In Eastern Europe, the overall impact of privatization on the political process has been positive. One comes to this conclusion not only intuitively, but also through the indirect proof of comparing the political dynamics of countries where economic reform (including privatization) has been successful with those of countries where it has not yet happened. The overwhelming difference is that extremist opposition parties get much less popular, support in the elections in the former countries. The recent surge of "post-communist" parties everywhere does not refute this point: In Poland as well as in Hungary, this surge is mostly an expression of conservative feelings (in the sense of cautiousness, status quo protection, lack of confidence in extremist political views) of the population. Radically anti-capitalist parties have no chance of gaining sizable support in countries with successful privatization.[27]

Moreover, in the past in Eastern Europe the state sector's dominance had an enormous impact on the general political culture of the society. Recent privatization has had a powerful "civilizing" impact on the social climate by creating a sizable social stratum of small owners whose attitude toward politics has become much more responsible since they have acquired a stake in the situation. The history of privatization certainly has had a lasting ideological impact in both regions; the perspective that private-sector preeminence is desirable in most of the economy now characterizes "mainstream" thinking in Latin America and certainly in the more reform-advanced western part of Eastern Europe.

To sum up, privatization has a huge potential to be a strong driving force not only for economic development but also for the stabilization of political democracy, especially in Eastern Europe. It is a necessary long-term precondition for consolidating democracy—though this linkage is by no means automatic. But as the Argentine case suggests, privatization can also carry risks for democratic consolidation, if it excessively favors already powerful business groups.

The following sections examine interactions between politics and economic regulation in three additional fields that are strongly interdependent with privatization in policy mixes striving to create more competitive and neutral market environments.

FINANCIAL SECTOR REFORM

Regulation of banking is exceptionally sensitive because of the high costs of business failure in this sector to the state and society. These high costs make it very difficult to establish credibly "neutral" regulation in this sector—that is, to refrain from state intervention to prevent bank failures. Consequently, rent-seeking is very difficult to prevent in banking—especially in relatively underdeveloped countries. In many countries, banks are publicly owned—or if they are not, regulation is overtly "soft"; banking and insurance supervisory bodies are supposed to watch the business performance in the sector so that they can intervene early in case of trouble.

In modern banking, bankruptcy regulation always differs from that of other types of businesses; special, "softer" rules exist all over the world due to the great risks involved in bank insolvency. In underdeveloped financial markets, and especially in Eastern Europe, where commercial banking has only recently been permitted, the risk of corruption is a very special issue because the macroeconomic impact of business failure in this sector can be huge.

Eastern European Reforms

To be successful in the long run, financial sector reform normally needs more complex state capacity than privatization in general— precisely because of the sector's sensitivity. The example of Chile in the late 1970s tells us most vividly that privatization that is not solidly based may in fact unravel, and the governments involved may be forced to re-nationalize the financial institutions in trouble. At the same time, financial sector reform is a tempting field for politicians to play favoritism; board seats are influential and pay well. Moreover, nontransparent financial transfers from state (and sometimes also private) banks may help politicians to get access to power in political competition.

In a disciplined, well-established market environment, there are cases in which banks are state owned, yet responsibly and prudently managed; this is more or less the case in France,[28] and in Germany, local and *Lander* governments have a considerable stake in the large banks. However, in business environments where rent-seeking is more of a norm than an exception, the "moral hazard" of state ownership is very great, unless countered by tight regulation. While in technical terms the Eastern European banking industry was, at the beginning of the transition, far behind Latin America, pre-reform Latin America was a textbook case of all kinds of discretionary, non-normative state interference in the financial sector. Because of this, the policy challenge in the banking sector shared certain similarities in the two regions.

In Eastern Europe, financial sector reform was not particularly high on the reform agenda in the initial phase of transition; policymakers were busy with a long list of other tasks. The development of a regulatory framework and technical skills advanced quickly; however, an overall banking reform strategy was certainly lacking—not least because (in contrast to privatization or other reform fields) consensus among international and Eastern European experts had evolved much less.

In the case of Hungary, where on the eve of the transition the business environment was the most sophisticated of the region, there was a considerable foreign interest in 1989 and early 1990 in buying into the large Hungarian banks. At that time, it was the cautiousness of the reformers more than anything else that prevented early privatization in the banking industry. The government was overcautious and did not privatize any of the large banks. Hungary's case is particularly interesting because, instead of privatizing the existing banks, the government liberally gave licenses to foreign banks in the period discussed. This has had two sets of effects on the Hungarian financial sector. On the one hand, the presence of a large number of well-regarded foreign banks has created a healthy competitive challenge by improving the quality of a broad range of services and has also encouraged foreign investment in other fields. On the other hand, liberal licensing of foreign banks has sharply reduced the potential sales value of Hungarian banks, since investors are likely to prefer starting entirely new ventures to buying into established banks of uncertain value. The uncertainty comes primarily from the shaky portfolios of the large state banks.

In retrospect, one can see how much better it would have been to start privatizing banks early on; however, lack of proper understanding of the situation and, more important, the desire of politicians and some technocrats to control the sector led to harmful delays in the process. As the next section describes, this failure of the politicians has proven to be very costly: The insufficiently radical improvement of the banks' functioning, among other things, has caused the deterioration of their asset portfolios, which in turn forced the government into subsequent partial bailouts. These have sizably increased the nation's debt. The future sales price of the banks must be expected to be relatively low for reasons mentioned above. This policy failure is serious, as its effect is not limited to the banking sector alone. In Hungary we are observing the comeback of enterprise subsidization through state support to the banking sectors; this has a very bad impact on business morale throughout the economy.

Hungary's mistakes are by no means an isolated case. No Eastern European country has so far implemented a sufficiently credible banking reform, and some have created very serious trouble for themselves by not regulating their financial sectors properly. The two most troubling examples in this respect are again Russia and Ukraine, where so-called "pocket" banks have emerged that belong to industrial firms or groups and that de facto (especially in Ukraine) have the capacity to create money. This obviously opens a huge channel for syphoning wealth out of the economy for the benefit of the few. These systems thus create a concentration of economic power that is not in evidence in the better regulated parts of the region. Another problematic aspect of the Russian and Ukrainian version of financial sector development is that it is a magnet for mafia activities; in Russia, about 80 bank managers were killed in 1993 alone. Clearly, this lawless situation is a problem of a different order than insufficiently rapid reform in Poland, Hungary, and the Czech Republic. The Ukrainian and Russian developments in the banking sector remind us again of the crucial political importance of one of the most precarious public goods: a stable macroeconomic environment. By providing the economy with cheap credit, the central banks (in effect, the governments) of these countries help to create powerful financial groups without having any capacity to exercise control over them.

In the Czech Republic, voucher privatization included the shares of the large formerly state-owned banks as well. Although this may turn out to be the best model in the region, its challenge is that not only the firms' but also the banks' corporate governance problems are not solved for long, as strong cross-ownership has been established among the financial intermediaries, and no professional investor has had direct access. A second problem is that the banks constitute a major public asset; if the privatized firms are valuable, then it is even more the case, since banks own large blocks of shares in those firms. By allocating these institutions free of charge to the public rather than selling them, the government chose to forgo potentially high sales revenues. In a country with a balanced budget and a very low public debt—such as the Czech Republic—this might be a defensible position. The approach has an "opportunity cost," however, since the forgone revenue could have been used for social or infrastructure purposes or to decrease very high marginal taxes. Yet, however sub-optimal the Czech approach may be, it is certainly superior to that of countries that have not privatized their banking industry at all, or to ones that have in effect allowed financial businesses to become criminalized. Moreover, the Czechs would argue, their way is more feasible politically, as it is fast and enhances the "popular capitalism" image that helped the pro-market-reform party to win the 1992 election.

After Hungary and the Czech Republic, banking reform has advanced most in Poland. The bank-company bailout problem will be touched on later in this chapter; here, the discussion will briefly focus on the politics of bank privatization. Up to spring 1994, the team of policy planners appointed by Balcerowicz in the field of financial sector reform were retained despite frequent government changes. This facilitated managing the so-called banking conciliation program (see next section) and also preparing the public auction of some of the best-performing banks. However, price mismanagement of the sale of Bank Slaski, one of the two banks sold, gave the new government elected in autumn 1993 an opportunity to remove Stefan Kawalec, Deputy Finance Minister and the architect of financial sector reform. This suggests that financial sector reform may slow down under the recently formed post-communist coalition.

Yet the story of the Polish banking reform shows that the positive legacy that the Balcerowicz reforms established in Polish economic policy was sufficient to protect their main designer in a government position as high as that of Deputy Finance Minister for two years after the overall economic reform's architect had resigned. In the meantime, the banks were largely protected from political influence, and two of them were privatized; moreover, the Polish banks have undergone rather impressive development in learning proper banking functions. These legacies can have still other future benefits, especially if international influence continues to be as positive as it has been. However, it is also possible that, now that political life has somewhat consolidated, the Polish banks will become more frequent targets of clientelist efforts than they were in the past few years—when none of the governing elites had either the time or the appropriate personnel to fill the banks' governing positions with their people.

Latin American Reforms

Pre-reform Latin America is a textbook case of mis-regulation and rent-seeking in the banking sector. As in Eastern Europe, reformers paid relatively less attention to the financial sector in the early reform years. There are, however, encouraging examples, such as the second-wave Chilean reforms and the recent massive privatization of banks in Mexico.[29]

Latin America provides considerable evidence that excessive market power is a greater risk in the financial sector than in most of the rest of the economy. In its "statist developmental" period, the region was characterized by under-regulation, by a high and unhealthy concentration of market power due to government preferences and high inflation, and by very close government-business relationships. In Latin America, the emphasis in financial sector reform needs to be on improving the regulatory framework. This is so because the sector's ownership structure is somewhat less distorted than in Eastern Europe, and technical skills are highly developed; indeed, in certain notoriously high-inflation countries, notably Brazil, the technical skills in financial transactions are among the best in the world. However, reform of the regulatory framework is politically difficult to achieve, since illegal links between governments and the large banks have a very long tradition. In some countries, the leading banks have enormous institutional and political power. The commonly cited example of this is Brazil, where Banco do Brazil is described as a state within the state. In such a situation, it takes unusual political courage and concentrated state effort to reform the sector. It is not coincidental that, compared to Brazil's other structural reforms (for example, in trade), the country's recent performance in banking reform is modest. In Argentina, too, large market power is concentrated in financial intermediaries that benefited from government bailouts and the country's hyperinflationary past, and this may have political repercussions in the future.

In addition, part of the problem in Latin America is misperception of the kind of reform mix needed. In Chile, Argentina, and Uruguay, deregulation got a bad name after the failure of bold financial deregulations in the 1970s. This caused the governments to react in the 1980s by imposing strong *discretionary* controls instead of choosing the more efficient alternative of increasing the capacity of the state to exercise *prudential* control and refraining from arbitrary interference in the financial markets.

BANKRUPTCY REGULATION

Microeconomic efficiency can be expected in the long run only if the threat of business failure is credible. This is an indispensable yet much neglected part of property rights. Eastern European reformers are acutely aware of the adverse effects of *excessive* organizational stability and security; consequently bankruptcy legislation has been a major concern of policymakers in the reform period. This does not seem to be the case in Latin America; despite the lack of credible bankruptcy regulation, policymakers in the region do neglect the issue.

Regulation of business failure in the particular setting of consolidating early reforms poses a particularly important and difficult question. Initial stabilization measures can be expected to cause a liquidity crunch in any country with acute macroeconomic imbalance. The liquidity crisis is likely to be more acute in the Eastern European setting 1) because financial management skills in the post-communist companies are much more modest than in a Brazilian or Argentine company and, 2) because of the double imbalance of shortages and inflation. The new macroeconomic policies caused an avalanche of financial crises in the enterprise sectors of each of the fast-track Eastern European countries—i.e., Poland, Hungary, the Czech Republic, and Slovakia. Even in the Latin American environment, a radical change in relative prices in times of macroeconomic adjustment throws a large proportion of firms into major financial difficulty.

The most instructive cases in the politics of the post-stabilization liquidity crunch and company bailouts are the Hungarian and Polish experiences. Hungary adopted the toughest bankruptcy rules in the entire region, together with banking and accounting legislation, at the beginning of 1992.[30] (These actions actually go against the common perception of Hungary's transition as "soft" or "too gradualist," compared with "shock therapy" in Poland and the "boldness" of the Czech approach.) Two aspects of the Hungarian bankruptcy legislation made it exceptionally radical and therefore worth studying. On the one hand, it instituted the "automatic trigger"—i.e., enterprises that could not meet their payments to any creditor were required to file for financial restructuring or for liquidation.[31] The other radical aspect of Hungary's bankruptcy legislation was the law that made it very difficult to reach an agreement between debtor and creditors by requiring unanimous consent of the creditors on restructuring the debt. Both measures interfered quite strongly and directly with the property rights of the businesses: It is one thing to secure the legal possibility to file against a debtor with overdue obligations, and quite another to make filing by the debtor obligatory in case of any amount overdue.

From such tough bankruptcy legislation, the policymakers expected a radical increase in financial discipline in the economy. This probably was achieved, at least in the short run. Payment arrears dramatically decreased in real terms in 1992. The bankruptcy law came into force in February 1992 and a huge wave of bankruptcy filings began in April of that year when the real application of the law was started. However, the system (i.e., courts, judges, trustees, banks, etc.) was unable to meet the time requirements of the law; even now, only about one-fourth of the liquidation cases have been finalized, and even a smaller share of filings has led to actual liquidation. Thus it is quite questionable whether the "credibility bonus"—the perception that so severe a law had to be taken seriously—can hold fast over time. Also, other dysfunctions of the legal system related to bankruptcy, such as the slow and difficult execution of claims, have raised questions about the overall effectiveness of the legal enforcement of this segment of property rights reform in the economy. A lack of policy coordination was very visible on this issue as well; despite the courts' repeated appeals to the government to invest in their technology and staffing, the government refused to do so. The size of that investment would have been incomparably lower than the losses caused by delays and dysfunctions in the courts' processing of bankruptcy cases. Lack of experience and knowledge, rather than any deeper political variable, played a crucial role in this policy deficiency. One has to remember that Hungary was the first country in transforming Eastern Europe to sanction business failure in an ordinary fashion.

From their very beginning, the Hungarian bankruptcy rules were met with broad criticism as too harsh (on account of the automatic trigger) and strict on the reorganization side, and as creating too many bankruptcy cases, given the limited processing capacity of the legal infrastructure. Changes came very late (in the summer of 1993)—providing yet another illustration of the lack of coordination and prioritization in Hungarian economic policy—and dealt only with removing the requirement for unanimous consent. However, application for reorganization became unnecessarily complicated,[32] and no additional incentives have been introduced to accelerate liquidations, which lag badly, causing many delays as well as actual abuses.

As already mentioned, the shock effect of the set of new rules, and especially of the bankruptcy law, at the beginning of 1992 revealed the extremely poor quality of the assets portfolio of the Hungarian banks. This is the fact that makes the Hungarian story additionally interesting for the theme of our project. The *systemic challenge* that this situation caused has generated a chain of actions that has unraveled some of the achievements of the 1988–1992 period. At the end of 1992, the three largest state-owned banks were able to effectively blackmail the Ministry of Finance to bail them out—by replacing a large part of the bad assets with government bonds. This in itself had a detrimental effect on bank-government relations, as the action did not appropriately reward better institutions (it actually rewarded bad management—since the worse the portfolio was, the more state subsidies the bank received), and it did not condition the help on any future performance or reform, such as privatization.[33]

Moreover, these actions were just the start of a chain of bad policy steps. In 1993, the bailout was virtually repeated, but on a larger scale (with higher budgetary costs), more banks involved, and through bank recapitalization rather than loan consolidation, as in the first case. The credibility of "hard budget constraint" toward the financial sector was damaged even further as this action looked very much like an "institutionalized repetition" of government help to the financial sector.

The third action in this chain of events was the launching of debtor consolidation simultaneously with the conclusion of bank recapitalization at the end of 1993. This was planned with a view to the general election scheduled for spring 1994. The debtor consolidation promised large enterprise bailout (in several tranches) at great organizational and financial cost to the state. Again, without going into the technical details of the action,[34] this series of bailouts in Hungary has caused serious damage because it deeply shook the credibility of the hard budget constraint. Businesses now *expected* subsidization. The message conveyed was that prudent banking and company financial management are not so important after all (especially for large companies and banks), because the state is always there to help out. Although in some situations the state indeed has no alternative but to help, in Hungary the scale of government action and lack of proper conditionality was extremely damaging. The fiasco was a combined result of a lack of government expertise in the field, and the increasing assertion of sheerly political (electoral) considerations that have gradually overshadowed earlier reform enthusiasm.

What makes the Hungarian case particularly instructive is that, while this has happened first in one of the best reformer countries, the challenge may arise elsewhere in Eastern Europe after macroeconomic stabilization. The consecutive bailouts in Hungary have invited a reemergence of the very bargaining attitudes in the business community that had been so successfully eliminated in the period of tough regulation and elite shakeup between 1988 and 1992. The government-business relationship has been somewhat re-politicized through the series of badly prepared rescue operations.

An alternative approach, called the "banking conciliation" program has been applied by Poland. In contrast to Hungary's approach, Polish policies treat the issues of insolvency and bad bank portfolios as part of a more comprehensive program. The Polish approach does not apply the "automatic trigger," and it is also very permissive toward state-owned firms that are deeply in debt. Furthermore, this approach tries to solve the problem of inefficient court capacity by allowing the lead bank of the debtor firm to organize the financial restructuring.[35] It appears that this is a more subtle, temporary regulation and intervenes in the life of the businesses less harshly than the Hungarian bankruptcy law of 1992, even as somewhat "softened" in 1993. But even the Polish banking conciliation program did not come in time; the great liquidity crisis started in 1989 and reached its peak in 1991. It is legitimate to ask whether this kind of action, had it come earlier, might not have mitigated the production decline—or, in 1992, might not have contributed to stronger industrial recovery. However, it obviously took time to elaborate the project; and it then took even more time to persuade the parliament to accept the proposed new legislative act.

Again, without going into the technical details of the Polish program, one should notice that even this elegantly planned and managed approach carries a political risk: In the meantime, the government has been replaced by a new, post-communist one made up of politicians who have stronger ties to state enterprise bosses. In its recent form, the banking conciliation program is a good balance between the reform goals (enterprise and bank privatization), the need to maintain some degree of institutional status quo (bailout of some large organizations), budgetary considerations (the action should not cost too much), and credibility (bailouts will not be repeated). However, the balance is precarious, which the new government needs to understand this if it does not want to make the operation much more costly.

In Latin America, public opinion appears to be overwhelmingly against applying bankruptcy laws—especially during the democratization process—because of their immediate negative impact on employment. This seems to be part of the region's heritage. Employees are expected to pressure the government for assistance to protect the troubled industry; this is viewed as an acceptable concern. The region also has a history replete with resort to the nationalization of troubled companies. Without changing this culture, property rights reform will be somewhat undermined. To this Eastern European analyst, it seems that a critical review of this culturally driven approach is yet to come in Latin America if reforms are not to be undermined in the future.

An additional problem is the past record (not yet overcome in Brazil) of hyperinflation. In Argentina and Brazil (as, interestingly, in Russia) interest payments are frozen in bankruptcy. The obvious consequence of this is that in a hyperinflationary situation, debt gets wiped out within a few weeks—i.e., the threat of "business failure" is seriously undermined.

The politics of post-stabilization liquidity crises and the consequent potential of bank and debtor bailouts appear to need as serious attention in Latin America as does insolvency regulation in general. Even in the boldest reform countries of Eastern Europe, this challenge has proven to be a powerful source of major compromises of the original reform blueprint and philosophy. These compromises undoubtedly foster the strong consolidation of business pressure groups. This new trend can be expected to get an additional boost from the return of post-communist parties in Poland and Hungary because of their more "natural" political ties with not only state enterprises but also businesses—through their contact with former *nomenklatura* who have become businessmen.

RULES OF ENTRY

In building a competitive market environment, the regulation of market entry by new businesses and, more broadly, a liberal approach to market access is an important and usually somewhat neglected field. In Eastern Europe, this has proven to be a very powerful vehicle of encouraging private-sector development, of competition, and of restructuring of the economy. In Poland, Hungary, and Czechoslovakia alike, deregulation in this field was enormous in the early period—again due to the fact that the collapse of communist power created a vacuum in interest representation. In the future, much more lobbying can be expected for the purpose of closing market entry. Some of this can already be seen in import regulation, where the Eastern European countries are becoming more sophisticated in applying nontariff barriers; here the driving force is pressure from domestic producers.

Entry rules are much less deregulated in the rest of the region, including Bulgaria in our sample. On this issue, historical differences within the region are very important; the attitude toward law is tremendously different between countries whose historical experience is—or is not—within the Western legal heritage. This inherited difference leaves a very strong impact on recent expectations, social norms, and therefore on policies with respect to market-entry regulation.

Most of Latin America of course does not have the luxury of the above-mentioned vacuum in interest representation in the early stage of "transition"; again, only Chile seems to have drastically deregulated entry rules. As a result, the country has experienced tremendous development in new entrepreneurship and a considerable deconcentration of business structures over the last two decades. As a recent empirical study shows, bureaucratic procedures, money costs, and time requirements for entry are much higher in Brazil than in Chile. In Brazil, there is a documented tendency for low-level bureaucrats to profit from their power to administer legal barriers to entry.[36]

Radical deregulation of entry rules is also important from a broader social (and political) perspective: The freedom to form a company leads to the very rapid development of a middle class as well as middle-class mentality, especially since the size structure of businesses has favored larger firms in this region, too—although to a lesser extent than in Eastern Europe. The formation of the *Mittelstand*, or the process of "embourgeoisement," should be seen as very desirable from the point of view of stabilizing democracy and overcoming the populist heritage of the societies' value systems.

Entry rules are a powerful tool in shaping the size structure of the economy over the long run. Generally, and in a very stylized fashion, one can say that the more centralized the economic policy is, the more arbitrary the intervention that can take place, and the more likely it is that the size structure of a country's economy will resemble an upside-down pyramid. Likewise, the more decentralized decision-making is, and the less room there is for arbitrariness in state intervention, the more likely it is that the size structure will be pyramidal (i.e., with a large number of small companies, a sizable layer of medium-size ones, and a relatively small number of large units). A more pyramidal size structure is likely to have an advantageous impact on the country's politics for two reasons: the *Mittelstand* has, on most issues, a positive impact on the political agenda and values; on the other hand, the upside-down pyramidal structure is likely to lead to the strong influence of large-company bosses on politics. The communist Eastern European countries' structures were more of an upside-down pyramid, whereas the pre-communist era had been characterized by a large number of small companies, as well as by (in international comparison) an "overdeveloped" sector of large companies—due to the coexistence of a traditional sector and a modern sector (generated by state industrialization) integrated in the world economy. In that structure, the middle strata were very weakly developed. As an indirect consequence of improved policies in the fields analyzed in this paper, one would expect the size structure of the economy to become healthier in both regions—with positive consequences for political dynamics. Clearly, however, these are changes that one can expect to evolve only over a longer period of time.[37] Even so, Table 1 illustrates the revolutionary changes taking place in Hungary in respect to decentralization and the size structure in the Central European economies.

CONCLUSIONS

Experience in the six countries studied in the project, as well as others, indicates that the success of economic reform in a democratizing environment to a large extent depends on the initial momentum gathered by the boldness and resolution of the policies. Among our sample

TABLE 1: NUMBER OF ENTERPRISES IN HUNGARY WITH LEGAL STATUS BY NUMBER OF STAFF[a]

Period	Less Than 11 Persons	11 to 20 Persons	21 to 50 Persons	51 to 300 Persons	301 or More Persons	Total
1989	—	5,105[b]	2,387	3,459	2,617	13,568
1990	—	16,465[b]	4,129	4,469	2,599	27,662
1991	—	36,809[b]	6,169	5,372	2,396	50,746
1992	—	52,825[b]	6,970	5,773	1,937	67,505
1993	39,772	28,447	7,637	6,055	1,624	83,535

Note: — indicates not available.
[a]Excluding housing and garage cooperatives, organizations being liquidated, and those with unknown number of staff.
[b]Number includes organizations employing less than 11 persons.

Source: *Statisztikai Havi Kozlemenyek,* March 1994.

countries, the best illustrations are the Polish and the Argentine cases. In Argentina, this combination of characteristics actually translated into legislative election success, backing President Menem in 1994; in Poland, the comeback of the post-communist parties has not reversed the outright victory of the Balcerowicz reforms and their legacy. There have been frequent changes of government in Poland, yet the basic tenet of the reforms—clearly in the cast of macroeconomic policy, if less so in that of radical institutional reform—remains unchanged.

Rapid initial action is even more important because it will almost automatically facilitate some of the further reforms. For instance, while this chapter has been somewhat critical of privatization efforts that focus overwhelmingly on budgetary needs (as in Argentina), it is true that governments that are committed to maintaining macroeconomic equilibrium are likely to undertake some of the right policies just out of macroeconomic considerations. And as has been said, "buying time" is helpful in itself, since some of the distortions need time to get corrected. The economic as well as the political history of the past two decades in both regions indicates that maintaining a solid, responsible, and transparent macroeconomic regime is an overwhelming public good—and by no means solely an economic concern. A sound macroeconomic regime encourages (without guaranteeing) economic structures that, although they may be very far from optimal, nevertheless are conducive to the long-term sustainability of a democratic regime.

In Eastern Europe, democratization has proceeded in tandem with economic reform; moreover, the more democratic a country is, the more reformist it is. However, this does not indicate that more democracy automatically translates into better economic systems elsewhere, although in the long run this linkage will likely prevail in broad terms.[38] First, Eastern Europe's experience under Soviet domination makes the linkage of the two processes stronger in this region than elsewhere. Second, it is also true that Eastern Europe's geographic closeness to Western Europe as well as its cultural traditions correlate strongly with both economic reform and democratic political processes.

In addressing the way property rights reforms have influenced democratization, this chapter has identified three main linkages: first, the impact of those reforms on electoral politics in the short run; second, the way property rights reforms shape incentives for pressure group activity; and third, the way these reforms affect changes in the social structure.

As to the first point, this chapter has repeatedly argued for the importance of macroeconomic policy for democratic consolidation. Macro policies are not property rights reform but, as discussed in the chapter, if maintained in a longer period of time they generate positive changes in the property rights regime. Vigorous macroeconomic reforms (i.e., comprehensive stabilization programs) more often than not help the parties that sponsor them to be reelected. Václav Klaus's Czech Republic and Carlos Menem's Argentina are the obvious cases in point in our regions, but the recent powerful comeback of Gonzalo Sánchez de Lozada in Bolivia should also be noted here. The situation with privatization is similar: The linkage is even more intimate as we have seen that the drive for privatization often stems not only from ideological/professional conviction but from the commitment to maintain macroeconomic sanity once it has been achieved. Since other property rights reforms discussed in this chapter have a longer maturation period and their impact on the macroeconomic situation is also more indirect and complex, their influence on electoral politics is less direct and less strong.

A second way property rights reform affects politics is through its influence on pressure group activity. One would expect not only more democracy but, very importantly, less narrowly self-interested politics as the result of successful and bold property rights reform. In reality, however, this result is not at all clear cut. The area where it is more visible is privatization, which decreases (although by no means eliminates) lobbying for state resources. Here again we must include in the picture the significance of sustained solid microeconomic policies, which contribute to deconcentration of business structures which, in turn, helps to ease lobby pressure on governments. Deregulation of entry rules is also a powerful means of relaxing that pressure. It is not often realized how important financial sector reform is in the context of the democratization process. This is the area of business activities whereby subsidization can most easily return through the back door; banking can be very easily overpoliticized. Cutting the cord between the budget and the banking sector is a very important field of democratic reform. Strong property rights reforms also lead to a rearrangement of political strength of different organized groups; most likely (especially in reforming Eastern Europe) representatives of emerging new private businesses will gain in strength relative to old groups representing troubled large state industries.

Deregulation of entry rules and emergence of new firms are likely to contribute to stabilization of democracy though a third route: strengthening the middle classes, especially the entrepreneurial strata. This class is usually "conservative" in the sense of disliking political extremism and generally favoring the status quo; at the same time it strongly values democratic openness. The extent to which governments follow through on the privatization process in Eastern Europe also strongly determines the pace and shape of this social process.

In sum, the links between democratization and property rights reform are complex. Although property rights reforms contribute to consolidation of democracy, the long-term character of the required policies, as well as the lack of intellectual consensus concerning them, make these reforms very vulnerable to organized political and other group interests. As the crucial role of deep structural reforms leading to more stable property rights is increasingly clearly recognized, the desirability of much more scholarly research on the interaction between democratizing politics and those property rights is also emerging.

Notes

The author would like to express his thanks to the other participants in the project— Marcelo Cavarozzi, Jacek Kochanowicz, Oscar Muñoz, and Miguel Urrutia—as well as to Catherine Gwin at the Overseas Development Council for their valuable comments on the draft of this paper. He would also like to express his gratitude to Jean de Fougerolles for research support and detailed comments on the paper. The author is particularly indebted to Joan Nelson for her devoted help throughout the process of writing this paper, which has more than exceeded the usual support of project directors in similar situations.

[1] The term "Eastern Europe" is used in this chapter in the sense of post-communist Eastern Europe with the exception of the former Soviet Union. On occasion, however, examples from Russia are also used to illustrate specific points. The six country case studies included in the first stage of this project were Bulgaria, Hungary, and Poland in Eastern Europe, and Argentina, Bolivia, and Brazil in Latin America. It is important to emphasize that in Latin America the "simultaneous reform" criterion "disqualified" countries such as Chile and Mexico from inclusion in this study because their economic reforms preceded their political democratization. However, the economic reforms of these countries will also be referred to for illustrative purposes.

[2] As the next section discusses in greater detail, property rights reform is reform that

tries to reduce state ownership and discretionary state regulation and intervention in the economy.

[3] Albert Fishlow, an outstanding expert on Latin American political economy, used the notion "structural reform" in the sense of wealth distribution: "[in the 1960s] assistance was provided to finance structural reforms. These were still much oriented to the domestic economy and in the spirit of public intervention. . . . the Alliance [for Progress] emphasized land reform and greater income equality." See Albert Fishlow, "The Latin American State," *Journal of Economic Perspectives*, Vol. 4, No. 3 (Summer 1990).

[4] This does not mean that it was immediately recognized, especially in the Latin American countries of our sample; in fact, the typical reaction of the first democratic governments was to neglect economic stabilization and concentrate on restoring democratic, civilian order. See Marcelo Cavarozzi, with Joan Nelson and Miguel Urrutia, "Economic and Political Transitions in Latin America: The Interplay Between Democratization and Market Reforms," *A Precarious Balance: Democracy and Economic Reforms in Eastern Europe and Latin America*, Vol. II (San Francisco: ICS Press for International Center for Economic Development, 1994), Chapter 1.

[5] Indeed, the factor that defined both foreign and economic policy throughout Eastern Europe in 1989 was the wish for integration with the European Community and with the North Atlantic Treaty Organization (NATO). Much of Eastern Europe's current political instability stems from the fact that integration with the West and economic reform have not yielded the hoped-for spectacular results. Much of the earlier political consensus is being replaced by more paternalistic, populist voices, which (especially in the easternmost parts of the region) threaten to slow down or arrest democratic and market reforms.

[6] The notion is here used in the broader sense, referring mainly to the new institutional economics. See, in particular, S. Pejovich, *The Economics of Property Rights: Towards a Theory of Comparative Systems* (Boston: Kluwer Academic Publishers, 1990); and E.G. Furubotn and S. Pejovich, "Property Rights and Economic Theory: A Survey of Recent Literature," *The Journal of Economic Literature*, Vol. X, No. 4.

[7] William Glade also makes the point that it makes sense to use the term "privatization" more broadly than "merely the removal of assets from the public sector and their placement under private control." What is really interesting, he further notes, is "the effects of different regimes of asset control on the quality of asset management." For him, the key criterion in judging the different privatization schemes is whether they decrease the degree of rent-seeking behavior or not. William Glade, "Privatization in Rent-Seeking Societies," *World Development* (U.K.), Vol. 17 (May 1989), pp 673-682.

[8] These are also the most important areas in which deep structural/institutional reforms as well as long-term changes in state-business relationship (i.e., trends toward narrowing arbitrary state intervention and supports to businesses) can most easily be detected. Precisely because of the complexity and long-term nature of these changes, however, it is much more difficult to get good analyses in the literature about the linkages between some of these policy issues (with outright privatization a possible exception) and politics. However, these issues are certainly crucial when tracking the evolution of the relationship between government and business.

This chapter omits many reforms that also greatly influence the long-term process of reducing discretionary state involvement in business decisions. For example, the issue of financial subsidies and preferences (tax breaks, export incentives, etc.) will be disregarded; so will the issues of capital market regulation or the way the state lets or prevents owners of large public organizations exercise control over management decisions (the agency problem).

[9] The methodological difficulties of this kind of comparative undertaking, especially the historical ones and those relating to pre-reform structures, are convincingly analyzed in B. Slay, "Latin America in the 1980s and Eastern Europe in the 1990s: Useful Parallels or Mixed Metaphors?" unpublished manuscript.

[10] A similar view has been expressed in the very instructive study by Geoffrey Shepherd and Paul Holden, "The State and the Private Sector in Brazil" (Washington, DC: World Bank, November 1993).

[11] This is not to suggest that pressure groups are less significant in non-democratic

politics; on the contrary, the chance of favoring certain groups is even greater in authoritarian politics simply because politicians are not constrained by the pressures of public opinion.

[12] In *A Precarious Balance,* Marcelo Cavarozzi has emphasized the political implications of different hyperinflationary paths in Argentina and Brazil. See Cavarozzi, op. cit.

[13] I am grateful to Marcelo Cavarozzi and Joan Nelson for the ideas in this paragraph.

[14] Kálmán Mizsei, "Experiences with Privatization in Hungary," unpublished manuscript, 1990.

[15] Thus far, the only implemented mass privatization schemes in the region are those of Czechoslovakia (recently the Czech Republic has launched a second wave of voucher privatization) and of Russia.

[16] The critical first months of 1990, when the psychological pressure on the Polish government was enormous, are especially memorable. This was the first stabilization program of its kind. The economic profession was extremely skeptical about the fate of the Balcerowicz program. The state firms were drastically squeezed financially. While the official retail chains were dying, a huge number of private entrepreneurs (mostly street traders) appeared and replaced the state sector. There was a huge outcry—in which even some leading Polish economists took part—about street peddlers ruining the Warsaw landscape. Now everyone takes it for granted that the Polish retail network has gone through an absolutely fundamental transformation compared to four years ago. But it took the conviction, political courage, and nerves of the Balcerowicz team to resist demands to ease the pressure on the state retail chains and to clear the streets of peddlers.

[17] See comprehensive analysis in Mizsei, "Experiences with Privatization in Hungary," op. cit.

[18] A series of pioneering Hungarian empirical studies have contributed to the understanding of the impact of politics on the size structure of industries in socialist economies. These have implications for post-socialist situations and, more generally, for environments in which bureaucratic coordination of the economy is extensive.

[19] In Hungary this has not happened in a critical way so far. However, other governments might have to face a less tolerant public; in that case, the "big bang" in privatization might have additional political advantages.

[20] Such a large business organization clearly has more political clout to press for tax concessions or subsidies. Over time, the existence of positions on such a superholding and its large enterprises offers politicians opportunities to reward their clients by putting them in these positions—thereby creating a strong interest *against* privatization.

[21] On the other hand, a generally favorable *international* environment toward privatization is helpful to convince politicians, who are not motivated only by the political scientist's ideal world of group interests, but also by many other things, including international demonstration effects.

[22] See J.A. Gonzalez Fraga, "Argentine Privatization in Retrospect," in William Glade (ed.), *Privatization of Public Enterprise in Latin America* (San Francisco: ICS Press, 1991).

[23] Glade, op. cit.

[24] See Adolfo Canitrot and Silvia Sigal, "Economic Reform, Democracy, and the Crisis of the State of Argentina," in *A Precarious Balance,* op. cit, Vol. II, Chapter 3.

[25] See "Bolivia Plans Far-Reaching Privatization," *Financial Times* (1 February 1994).

[26] Canitrot and Sigal, op. cit.

[27] A possible exception is Russia, where privatization is moving ahead, but in a somewhat isolated way, without the support of other components of radical reform. In Russia, the lack of democratic political traditions, as well as the trauma of losing the empire, also contribute to the surge of extremist political forces.

[28] Although the recent scandals of Credit Lyonnais show quite high prices to the taxpayer for the luxury of state-owned banks—even for a developed country.

[29] Guillermo Barnes, "Lessons from Bank Privatization in Mexico," Policy Research Working Papers, Financial Policy and Systems Division, Country Economics Department (Washington, DC: World Bank, November 1992).

[30] Kálmán Mizsei, "Bankruptcy and Banking Reform in the Transition Economies of Central and Eastern Europe," in J.P. Bonin and I. Szekely (eds.), *The Development and*

Reform of Financial Systems in Central and Eastern Europe (Brookfield, VT: Edgar Elgar Publishers, forthcoming 1994).

[31] This is a crucial fact, since the Polish example clearly shows that in absence of such measures, introducing bankruptcy as a real option is very slow. This is not a normative but an analytical statement; we do not evaluate here which policy is better.

[32] Even for just accepting the application, the agreement of two-thirds of the creditors is required.

[33] Various other technical mistakes created huge additional problems. See Mizsei, "Bankruptcy and Banking Reform," op. cit.; and E. Varhegyi, "The Second Reform of the Hungarian Banking System," Bonin and Szekely, op. cit.

[34] For more details, see Kálmán Mizsei, "Lessons from Bad Loan Management in East Central European Economic Transition for the Second Wave Reform Countries," Institute for East-West Studies, New York, February 1994, manuscript.

[35] Banking conciliation is a temporary procedure, regulated by a single legal act. This act rules that the participating banks (predominantly large state banks) must first be recapitalized; then, for two different classes of debtors, financial restructuring can be organized by the lead bank. The restructuring is very permissive: the consent of 50 percent of creditors is sufficient for the restructuring deal. The project also provides the opportunity to arrange debt-equity swaps; in this way, it attempts to foster enterprise privatization.

[36] A recent study takes the example of the Brazilian regulation of market entry; it concludes that although the legal framework would be a deterrent to entry, "life" has produced institutions circumventing the legal obstacles: a specialized professional (an accountant or a "despachante" handles all the bureaucratic hurdles in a relatively easy, time-effective way (although obviously institutionalizing the bribing of bureaucrats). See Andrew Stone, Brian Levy, and Ricardo Paredes, "Public Institutions and Private Transactions: The Legal and Regulatory Environment for Business Transactions in Brazil and Chile," Policy Research Working Papers, Country Economics Department (Washington, DC: World Bank, 1992).

[37] It is also obvious that, besides size structure, other parameters are also important—for example, the degree of monopolization of a given market, the size of the country, technical characteristics of a given branch, and the ownership structure and level of unionization in the given sector. At the aggregate level, however, one still can expect strong correlation between the developmental *strategy* and size *pattern* of a given economy—i.e., the more "statist" development has been, the more likely it is that the size structure is "upward biased."

[38] As a recent article in *The Economist* argues. See "Democracy and Growth: Why Voting is Good for You," *The Economist,* 27 August 1994.

Chapter Three

Labor and Business Roles in Dual Transitions: Building Blocks or Stumbling Blocks?

Joan M. Nelson

Political openings and economic restructuring transform the roles of major interest groups and their relations with each other and the state. Old groups must rethink their goals, tactics, and alliances—or disappear. New groups emerging in or after the political transitions must adjust to rapidly changing political and economic challenges. How they adjust will strongly affect the sustainability of economic reforms and the consolidation of democratic government. At times their fierce opposition can derail reforms, or (more rarely) set in train events that destroy democracy. More often, their behavior affects the quality rather than the survival of economic and political reforms and shapes the nature of emerging political and economic systems.

New democratic governments undertaking radical economic reforms must decide how they are going to relate to interest groups. Old channels of communication, influence, and control are obsolete or shattered and new ones must emerge. Government attitudes and actions interact with those of interest groups; each side affects the other's tactics.

Although interest groups are clearly important for the prospects of economic and political reform, their appropriate roles are hotly debated by both academicians and practitioners. Economic interest groups, and labor unions in particular, are often viewed as stumbling blocks for economic reform, but building blocks for democracy. The first section of this chapter surveys different perspectives on how interest groups affect economic reform and democratic consolidation. The second section examines how unions have been affected by, and have reacted to, dual transitions. The third section turns briefly to the roles of business associations and business interests more broadly. The final section considers approaches to remodeling relations between the state and major interest groups, so as to facilitate consolidation of both economic and political reforms.

INTEREST GROUPS, MARKETS, AND DEMOCRACY: THEORETICAL PERSPECTIVES

Conflicting Economic and Political Perspectives

At first glance, economic reformers and democratic theorists hold diametrically opposed views of economic interest groups. The most fundamental strength of well-functioning decentralized market economies is their efficiency in allocating resources (land, labor, and capital) to their most productive uses. But economic interest groups try to protect their members from the effects of unbridled competition. Industries seek protection from less expensive imports. Professions and occupational groups seek to limit competition by requiring extensive credentials. Unions band workers together to bargain for better wages and working conditions; if they are powerful enough, they may seek to control labor access through closed-shop provisions. Agricultural groups seek protection from imports and state intervention to stabilize notoriously volatile agricultural prices. These efforts usually make resource allocation less efficient in economic terms.

In most Latin American and all post-communist nations, elaborate systems of state controls, subsidies and inward-oriented growth strategies had by the late 1970s slowed or halted growth (see Appendix, pp. 37–46). In both regions, the historical evolution of protection, subsidies, and controls was more the product of elite growth strategies than pressures from interest groups. But once these systems were in place, they generated vested interests that resisted or prevented their adjustment to changing conditions. Consequently, economic reformers have had to sideline, weaken, or dismantle economic interest groups linked to the old arrangements.

Democratic theorists and activists, on the other hand, focus on different objectives: governments that are responsible and responsive, participatory and legitimate, able to manage societal conflicts and to formulate and implement coherent decisions. From this perspective, economic interest groups are important building blocks. Representative democracy is not simply a matter of competitive elections and party systems. In complex societies, interest groups and voluntary associations act as intermediaries among individuals (or firms), representative institutions (parties and legislatures), and the state itself. Major parties cannot be built on the basis of single interests; instead, interest groups inject their members' concerns into broader party platforms and legislative debates. This more effective "voice" strengthens these groups' stake in the democratic system.

These differences in perspective are not, however, as stark as first appears. While market-oriented economists rue losses in allocative efficiency, most admit that efficiency must sometimes yield to other values, including social equity and security as well as democratic legitimacy. Moreover, as Jacek Kochanowicz argues in Chapter 4, well-functioning markets require a wide array of supportive state services and regulations. Interest groups may serve constructive roles in their design and implementation. In complex industrial societies, legislation only provides broad guidelines for executive branch programs and regulations. Interest associations often work directly with executive agencies to develop the details of implementation and to adjust these over time. The process risks special-interest "capture" of executive agencies or programs, but it is also essential to realistic design and periodic fine-tuning of detailed programs and regulations. Collaboration between government agencies and interest groups may be even more important in dual transition countries struggling to implement complex institutional reforms required for the transformation from statist to market-oriented economies.

If interest groups are not entirely negative from the perspective of economic reforms, they are also not unalloyedly desirable from the standpoint of democratic consolidation. One major problem is biased representation. Particularly where parties are weak, powerful interests gain disproportionate influence and can even control the state, undermining the integrity, capacity, and legitimacy of government. Interest groups may also fail to represent their own constituencies fairly. Often they are "captured" by particular sub-groups or become dominated by the narrow interests of their own leaders.

Demand overload is another risk to democracy associated with interest groups. In the last quarter-century, the spread of sophisticated organizing techniques and new communications technologies generated an explosion of powerful single-interest groups. In the United States and Western Europe, conflicting pressures from these groups have profoundly altered how democracy works there. Many analysts are convinced that they have made governments less representative and capable. In new democracies with weak administrative capacities, strong demands from conflicting interest groups pose even higher risks of paralyzing legislative processes or swamping the state.

In short, interest groups are Janus-faced. They serve important representative functions, but they can also be profoundly unrepresentative. They provide groups with a means of bringing their needs to the government's attention, but their demands may swamp state capacities. They can educate their members and moderate their behavior, but they can also radicalize and promote conflict. They provide channels for intermediation between specialized state agencies and specific economic or social interests, but those channels may degenerate into "private governments" shielded from examination or influence by broader public concerns.

Interest Groups in Times of Transition

Authoritarian governments generally constrain all secondary associations except those they sponsor in order to mobilize support. More extreme forms of authoritarianism seek to destroy autonomous civil society. However, the first signs of the weakening of authoritarian systems prompt the beginnings of a resurrection of civil society.[1] Thus in Eastern Europe, post-World War II communism initially dissolved most pre-existing horizontal and communal bonds. But by the 1970s, and more clearly in the 1980s, late communist governments tolerated considerably more autonomous activity, mainly by small informal groups (with the notable exception of the Solidarity movement in Poland).[2] New (or resurrected) autonomous groups often play a major role in hastening the collapse of the old regime. An explosion of additional new groups follows, together with the reorientation (and often the splintering) of organizations closely associated with the old system.

Organizations representing major economic interests are only part of civil society, but they are crucial for the central concern of this volume: the interaction between economic and political reforms. This chapter focuses on labor unions, particularly those representing industrial workers and major public services (such as teachers), and on the array of formal and informal organizations among business groups. Other groups—such as agricultural interests and pensioners—that are also active players in both economic and political reforms are not covered in this paper.

A common central theme underlies the changing role of unions, business associations, and other economic interest groups in Latin America and Eastern Europe. Where the state exercised pervasive controls and where specific decisions (on prices, wages, licenses for foreign trade or foreign exchange, subsidies, investment) were made at the discretion of state agencies and commissions, enterprises and economic interest groups focused their attention on persuading and perhaps pressuring key officials in those agencies. Political parties and legislatures were not important channels for protecting or pursuing interests in either region, nor did public opinion play a role. Conflicts between groups were mediated by state agencies.

When economic liberalization reduces state controls and intervention, these patterns change. Unions, firms, and entrepreneurial associations must shift their attention to new channels for determining resource allocation and key policy decisions: market mechanisms, labor-management relations, legislatures, political parties, and public opinion (which affects the behavior of legislatures and parties). These new channels require changes in organization and tactics. Some groups and interests are able to make these shifts much faster and more successfully than others. The pace and nature of different groups' responses to economic and political liberalization profoundly affect prospects for emerging market economies and democratic politics.

THE CHANGING ROLE OF UNIONS

The Impact on Unions of Dual Transitions: An Overview

How have democratic openings and economic reforms affected labor unions in Latin America and Eastern Europe? How, in turn, have evolving union strength, organization, goals, and tactics influenced the course of economic reforms and democratic consolidation? The discussion that follows draws on experience in selected Eastern European and Latin American nations—particularly Argentina, Bolivia, Hungary, and Poland, with some reference also to Brazil, Bulgaria, the Czech Republic, and Romania.

THE IMPACT ON UNIONS AND WORKERS OF ECONOMIC REFORMS. Economic reforms have a wide range of effects on unions and workers. Three sets of distinctions must be kept in mind:

■ Which reforms? Stabilization, liberalization (the dismantling of old economic controls and subsidies), and institutional restructuring each have different effects.

■ Effects on whom? The impact of each type of reform on workers in general may differ from the impact on unionized workers (especially in Latin America, where unions cover a much smaller fraction of the workforce). The effect of reforms on unions as organizations is yet another question.

■ Effects when? Impact varies in the short, medium, and long run.

Stabilization seeks to contain inflation or hyperinflation, which hurt almost everyone. Effective stabilization therefore benefits almost everyone, certainly including workers. Moreover, stabilization is a crucial precondition (though not a guarantee) of resumed growth, which benefits workers in the medium run. However, some categories of workers are hard-hit by the immediate costs of stabilization—through unemployment and reductions in real wages. Workers in industries or sectors particularly dependent on government contracts and subsidies as well as public service workers paid directly from the government budget (for example, teachers) are particularly vulnerable to fiscal retrenchment. These same fields are often strongly unionized.

Dismantling price, trade, and other controls can also hit workers hard. In Eastern Europe in particular, releasing price controls produced a draconian surge in consumer prices and a corresponding drop in workers' real wages. In most cases, real wages did not recover their earlier levels for some years. But workers, along with other consumers, benefited from greater availability of goods—again, particularly in Eastern Europe.

Trade liberalization may also destroy firms that cannot compete with imports. Older workers (often unionized) may have great difficulties finding new jobs. In the medium to long run, however, trade liberalization spurs export-oriented production, generating new jobs—often for workers who are not unionized.

More complex institutional reforms are likely to have mixed effects on workers in general, but adverse impact on unionized labor. Privatizing or restructuring public enterprises generally means major cuts in the (unionized) workforce, but removing the burden of subsidies and inefficient production from the economy is likely to encourage growth and expand employment in the medium and long run. Labor-market liberalization—especially reduced regulation of hiring and firing—benefits some workers, particularly women and youth who would like to be able to work part-time or take temporary jobs, and who are usually excluded from unions. But more flexible hiring increases competition for regular (and often unionized) workers.

Market-oriented reforms also reduce the strength and bargaining influence of unions as institutions. Trade liberalization in particular undercuts bargaining power. In protected markets, employers can pass on the costs of wage increases to consumers. In open economies, this option is much more limited. Privatization also usually reduces bargaining power (even when unions are not dismantled as part of the process). Political pressures that can be brought to bear on the government as an employer are not available (or are less effective) in negotiation with private management.

Labor-market liberalization strikes still more directly at the power of unions. In heavily state-dominated Latin American economies as well as in Eastern Europe, old-style labor relations and wage bargaining institutions and laws provided little or no link between productivity and wages; non-wage costs of labor were very high; labor mobility was restricted; and employers faced a maze of obstacles in removing unsatisfactory or redundant workers (and in communist countries had little incentive to do so). Liberalization of these arrangements is a vital part of the economic reform agenda. But measures that make it easier for employers to hire part-time or temporary help and to fire workers, that shift the locus of wage negotiations from the industry to the firm, or that eliminate automatic deduction of union dues from wage payments undercut union strength. So, too, do certain reforms designed primarily to ease government fiscal burdens—such as reforms of social security and pension funds that reduce union control.

In sum, the impact of economic reforms on workers depends broadly on the depth of depression and the speed of the economy's rebound. Workers who are older, less educated, and live in smaller cities or towns are particularly vulnerable to transition costs. To the extent that unionized workers are concentrated in sectors and fields that depend on trade protection or the state budget (directly or through subsidies), unionized workers may be especially hard-hit. While successful stabilization and market-oriented reforms should benefit more flexible workers and sectors in the medium run, unions as organizations are likely to be weakened.

THE IMPACT ON UNIONS OF DEMOCRATIC TRANSITION. In contrast to the impact of economic stabilization and liberalization, the transformation from authoritarian to democratic politics would appear at first glance to benefit unions. Authoritarian governments always seek to control unions, although their tactics may vary from suppression to the use of unions to mobilize workers for political or economic purposes. In abstract theory, unions have a stake in democracy. Their major asset is their numbers. Moreover, workers have little access to political decision makers through informal or individual channels. Their main channel for influencing government is likely to be unions acting directly or through political parties.

Democracy may be advantageous for unions, but unions do not necessarily understand or value democratic institutions; nor do they behave in ways that consolidate democratic openings. After decades of authoritarian rule, some unions will have been created by, or allied with, the old regime. They face immense problems of redefining their identities and restoring (or creating) credibility. Other unions have been radicalized by repression, and still others simply place little value on the norms of interaction consistent with democratic government.

Even unions that support democracy—and some fought hard to install or reinstall it—find that the political transition opens a difficult period. The more permissive atmosphere generates an explosion of new rivals, including splinters from old groups. Union leaders must decide how much of their attention and resources to devote to protecting their existing turf and trying to expand it, versus seeking to influence legislatures and governments that are rapidly changing the rules that shape their future.[3]

Labor leaders and unions dedicated to democracy may find themselves in a double bind. Their members expect concrete benefits from the introduction of democracy and may become alienated if those benefits do not appear. But it is also crucial not to jeopardize business confidence, since democracy will be eroded unless investment resumes. Business and industry circles are often skeptical about the ability of new democratic regimes to adopt and sustain supportive policies (a point discussed further later in this chapter). Based on experience with democratic transitions in the 1970s and early 1980s in Southern Europe and Latin America, some analysts have argued that labor must restrain its demands while democratic governments remain fragile, in order to reassure business sectors that democracy does not automatically imply populism.[4]

In short, democratic openings do permit much more autonomous unions. But transition also brings splits and rivalries within labor, as well as difficult strategic dilemmas. These problems are intensified where democratic transitions are followed in short order by painful economic reforms.

Unions, Economic Reform, and Democratic Consolidation in Eastern Europe

PRE-TRANSITION LEGACIES AND TRANSITION ROLES. Eastern European nations share a communist-era legacy of large official trade unions with very high nominal membership, considerable material assets, and virtually no autonomy. Unions functioned primarily as "transmission belts" conveying directives and production targets to workers. Most workers' commitment was minimal, but unions did provide important social service and recreational benefits. In the 1980s, as economic conditions worsened in most of Eastern Europe, dissatisfaction with the system as a whole, including unions, grew.

Despite these broad similarities, unions in different Eastern European countries were not carbon copies of each other. Polish labor had a history of periodic protest pre-dating the emergence of Solidarity in 1980. Bulgaria's unions were particularly all-encompassing—claiming to represent 98 percent of the workforce—largely as a result of the predominance of mammoth industries and immense agricultural collectives. In Hungary, where partial economic reforms were launched much earlier and carried farther than elsewhere in the region, trade union leaders often co-operated with the managers of large state enterprises and local party apparatchiks to resist reforms. By the 1980s, deepening economic reforms may have begun to erode union salience. The informal economy, already fairly widespread, was legalized in 1982 and grew rapidly thereafter. By the late 1980s roughly 70 percent of Hungarian households derived some income from informal activities: as a result, workers may well have focused less on their official jobs and the official work environment, including their unions.

In Poland, Bulgaria, and Hungary, a second set of unofficial, anti-communist unions emerged as part of the broader rebirth of civil society and political opening. Solidarity was of course the earliest, most powerful, and best known of these, and it rapidly expanded far beyond its original workers' base. Solidarity's role in the dramatic end of the communist monopoly on power is too well known to recount here. In Hungary and Bulgaria, independent trade unions emerged in the late 1980s—initially largely representing white collar workers and intellectuals. In Bulgaria, the new autonomous federation Podkrepa rapidly became a powerful political force pressing for the dissolution of communist rule. In Hungary as well, the new democratic unions supported political opening. Since the Hungarian transition was largely negotiated among elites with little mass involvement, however, the unions' role was minimal.[5]

ACCEPTING REFORM: UNIONS IN THE INITIAL POST-TRANSITION PHASE. In the course of political opening, the traditional trade unions in Hungary, Bulgaria, and Romania declared their autonomy from the state institutions and political parties with which they had been linked. In Czechoslovakia, some 6,000 strike committees set up during the November 1989 revolution took over the official trade unions. Political opening was also accompanied by new labor legislation that decentralized collective bargaining and freed it from earlier detailed administrative regulation; established new procedures for settlement of disputes; and recognized the right to strike, subject to various restrictions.[6]

New union autonomy and rights were accompanied or shortly followed by initial economic reforms. Stabilization and liberalization packages, introduced at different times in different countries, in each case brought dramatic cuts in real consumption wages within a month, ranging from 27 percent in the Czech and Slovak Federal Republic

(CSFR) to a staggering 57 percent in Bulgaria. By the end of the first year, Bulgarian wages were still 40 percent below their pre-shock level; CSFR and Polish wages were still down by 18 percent or more.[7] Only Hungary, where price distortions and shortages were both much milder than elsewhere in the region, was spared this initial shock.

Intense resistance from newly empowered labor unions would not have been surprising. Yet in fact unions did not strongly challenge initial economic reforms—although there were scattered strikes, including some quite major ones. Internal disarray and the larger political context combined to restrain protest. The former official unions were in a weak position to challenge the radical new policies. Most suffered splits, and membership dropped precipitously. In Hungary, for instance, the ex-official National Association of Hungarian Trade Unions (MSZOSZ) claimed about 3.5 million members in summer 1990[8] but by May 1993 had perhaps 1 million.[9] Many democratized their internal organization and procedures to varying degrees. Nevertheless, new political leaders and parties, and much of the public, questioned the ex-communist unions' legitimacy and the degree to which they could be viewed as representing labor.[10]

Rivalries among old and new unions, and within both categories, complicated the scene. In Hungary, for example, labor was soon divided among six—later seven—major confederations and a number of unaffiliated unions. Many of the rival groups were associated with different political parties, intensifying their hostilities. Moreover, bitter disputes promptly emerged over the proposed reallocation of the considerable property controlled by the former communist confederations.

More insidious, though hard to document, were changing attitudes regarding the claims of workers as a category. The rhetoric of fallen communist systems celebrated workers as the builders of the socialist society. The new market ethos sharply downgraded workers' importance and instead praised private entrepreneurs as the engine of growth and prosperity. Initially much of the public was willing, even eager, to try "the magic of the marketplace" and to endure sacrifice during the transition. The atmosphere was not supportive of protests, either by special interests or in the name of the broader working class and public.

The newer, anti-communist unions were also constrained by the prevailing public mood. Moreover, where they were strongly associated with the democratic forces that took power, they were inhibited from challenging their close allies. In Poland, Solidarity unions and their delegates in the Sjem initially pledged their support for economic reforms. Even somewhat later, when protests or strikes mounted, they were staged "in ways that allowed workers to vent their frustrations without jeopardizing either political stability or the economic health of firms. The strategy of painstaking negotiation [was] preferred to one of strikes and confrontation."[11] In Bulgaria, both Podkrepa and the former Communist Confederation of Independent Trade Unions of Bulgaria (CITUB) entered agreements with the Dmitar Popov government (December 1990-October 1991), signing an "Agreement on Social Peace" that implied a 30 percent drop in real average wages as a result of price liberalization at the beginning of 1991.[12] In pre-partition Czechoslovakia, the new peak labor association (Czech and Slovak Confederation of Trade Unions, CSKOS), claiming four-fifths of the workforce as members, entered into a tripartite agreement to enforce wage restraint when radical economic reforms were launched in January 1991. CSKOS continued to honor the agreement despite the fact that real wages fell three times more than had been agreed.[13] In Hungary, the most dramatic protest—a drivers' strike in October 1991 in reaction to fuel price increases—was organized by mainly self-employed taxi and truck drivers, not by unions.

CHALLENGING REFORM: UNIONS IN LATER PHASES. In most of Eastern Europe, initial union acquiescence or even cooperation with economic reforms gradually gave way to more aggressive, sometimes confrontational, roles. Several factors contributed to the trend: the rising social costs of economic transformation, changes in the reform agenda itself, the recovery of the ex-communist unions, and the reorientation of the non-communist unions.

Most fundamentally, the rising and unanticipated costs of economic transformation weakened public support for reforms, giving unions more space to press their criticisms. Except in Hungary, consumption wages at the end of 1992 remained about 20–35 percent below pre-transition levels.[14] Moreover, by mid-1993, registered unemployment as a percentage of the labor force was in the range of 13 to 15 percent in Hungary, Poland, and Slovakia and was closer to 17 percent in Bulgaria. In the Czech Republic, however, unemployment had peaked at 4.3 percent at the end of the first year of reforms and was down to 2.8 percent by mid-1993.

Not only the levels but also the nature of unemployment began to show troubling trends. In initial stages of economic transition, many state firms reduced wages, but held on to workers; many of the first drops in public employment were early retirements. Involuntary layoffs increased later, as budget constraints tightened and more firms recognized the imperative to restructure. Mass layoffs, however, continued to be rare.[15] The proportion of unemployed who have not worked for a year or more sharply increased; in the second quarter of 1993 it reached more than half in Bulgaria, roughly a third in Hungary, and 43 percent in Poland. Thus a pool of marginalized unemployables seems to be emerging. In addition to high open unemployment, labor force participation rates dropped, particularly in Bulgaria (from 87.4 percent of the working age population in 1989 to 74.2 percent in 1991).[16]

Government measures to assist the unemployed varied considerably among Eastern European countries and evolved in different directions. Hungary provided comparatively generous benefits (relative to wage levels), but cut back on both duration and level of benefits in 1993 to reduce fiscal pressures. Polish and Romanian benefits were intermediate in level, and their duration was extended in 1993 in both countries. Bulgarian benefits were comparatively low—and had not been substantially changed by mid-1994. Czech benefits, interestingly, were still lower relative to wages, and covered only 6 months. But the Czech government also provided vigorous job placement and retraining programs. In most countries, effective coverage of the unemployed dwindled as the duration of unemployment grew. In Bulgaria, by June 1993, only 30 percent of the unemployed received some form of unemployment benefit. In Poland, coverage dropped from about three-quarters of the unemployed in mid-1992 to 40-50 percent a year later.[17]

In addition to reduced real wages, high unemployment, and the overstrained social safety net, the quality of life of most ordinary people in Eastern Europe suffered from the continued decay of health, education, and other public services and facilities. Moreover, as the Overview in this volume notes, increased inequality and anxiety over growing crime and corruption added anger to frustration over hardships. Union activism was spurred not only by growing pressures from members but also by the altered public mood.

At the same time, the flux and rivalries within and among unions diminished. Former communist unions reorganized and gradually regained credibility among their reduced members and in public opinion. In Bulgaria, the former official communist union adopted new statutes and replaced about two-thirds of its leaders at special sessions in late 1989 and early 1990. Though still allied with the Bulgarian Socialist Party, it has significantly democratized and is largely independent.[18] In Hungary, the leader of the main successor to the former official trade union, MSZOSZ, regained considerable credibility when he was asked to negotiate on behalf of the striking taxi drivers in October 1991. Despite its loss of members, MSZOSZ was still the largest federation, enrolling about 39 to 45 percent of all Hungarian union members (depending on whether one accepts low or high estimates of other federations' members). It won an overwhelming victory in the union elections held in May 1993 to determine which unions would represent employees on new joint councils of unions and employers responsible for managing health care and pension funds. Similarly, in

Poland, the old official All-Poland Alliance of Trade Unions (OPZZ) continued to be easily the largest.

In part because of rivalry from the former official unions, the newer non-communist unions also had to rethink their roles and alliances, distancing themselves from governments run by their former allies. Solidarity probably changed most markedly. During and after the political transition, many of the intellectuals and professionals associated with the Solidarity movement in the difficult underground years moved into government positions or became active in the bewildering array of new political parties, losing close contact with their old labor union associates. As the trade union elements of Solidarity became increasingly isolated, the leaders of the 1980s lost influence to younger, more radical leaders with little memory of the shared anti-communist struggle and little understanding of, or patience with, the costs of structural adjustment.

In Bulgaria, Podkrepa remained associated with the anti-communist United Democratic Front (UDF) during and after the elections of September 1991 but began to distance itself from the increasingly doctrinaire and high-handed UDF government that then took power. And in Hungary, Liga and other pro-democratic federations grew more frustrated over time with the lack of government response to union views.

In several countries, resolution of the conflict over distribution of the properties of ex-official unions removed a divisive issue from the labor union scene. This was particularly clear in Hungary. In 1992, the government passed legislation that appeared to perpetuate the dispute, thereby weakening unions in general. In reaction, six of the seven main federations resolved their differences regarding the disputed property: The former official union agreed to share about half of its properties while the new unions conceded the legitimacy of their old enemy. Even earlier, the new unions had begun to cooperate with MSZOSZ in dealings with the government.

Reflecting all these factors, by mid or late 1992, unions began to play a much more critical and influential role. In Poland, union militance erupted in 1992 in a wave of serious strikes involving all the major federations; Silesian coal miners called a general strike in December 1992; and some 600,000 teachers went on strike in May 1993. Union militance also prompted political action. The Solidarity Caucus in the legislature was increasingly strident, and in late spring called for a no-confidence motion that brought down the Hanna Suchocka government.

In Hungary the union federations jointly pressed claims on the government, threatening a general strike for the first time in November 1992. The Minister of Finance reluctantly negotiated a pact conceding a variety of social benefits and ratifying the unions' own agreement regarding allocation of properties. The concessions were expected to absorb the entire increase in revenues anticipated from the newly instated value-added tax in 1993.[19] In Bulgaria, both CITUB and Podkrepa were active in the coalition that pushed the UDF government out of power at the end of 1992, after little more than one year in office.

The Czech Republic was an exception to the broader pattern of increased union militance. At first glance, the government seems to have ignored, perhaps even betrayed the unions. The tripartite pact of January 1991 had included commitments that real wages would fall no more than 12 percent and that the minimum wage would be increased. The pact also guaranteed the right to strike (after mediation), limited the work week, instituted generous unemployment benefits, and required employers to consult with unions before laying off workers. But most of these concessions were never fulfilled. Average real wages fell drastically (by at least 23 percent) in 1991; minimum wages were not raised as promised; and in 1992, the government cut the duration of unemployment benefits by half. In July 1993, the government reintroduced wage controls after a brief hiatus—over vocal opposition from unions (as well as employers).[20]

In other ways, however, the government was sensitive to the concerns of workers and unions. More than half of the state funds for labor were spent on programs to create employment, generating over 100,000 jobs per month after April 1992 and employing over 60 percent of the monthly registered unemployed. In addition, the government imposed regulations restricting employers' discretion to fire workers, and it delayed implementing the new bankruptcy law for eighteen months after its passage in August 1991. Even then, additional measures to limit unemployment were introduced, including selective credit to large state enterprises that were major employers in their localities. These and other factors—including the separation of Slovakia from the Czech Republic[21]—helped to keep unemployment low. Moreover, by 1992, the economy had begun to recover and real wages rose 9 percent. Union and social protest were minimal; for example, the unions chose to contest the government's reimposition of a wage cap in the courts, rather than through protest or political action. In effect, the Czech government pursued policies that minimized direct trade-union influence by successfully addressing workers' most pressing concerns. Its ability to do so was due in part to initial advantages—low debt and macroeconomic stability—compared to other Eastern European countries.

DEEPENING REFORMS AND EVOLVING UNION ROLES. Unions in Eastern European countries are still very much in the process of redefining their goals and desired roles, in both industrial relations (at the firm and national levels) and the broader political arena. Their reassessments are shaped not only by their own internal evolution but also by the changing economic and political contexts in each country.

In the industrial relations arena, including reform or privatization of state enterprises, most of the major union federations broadly accept the need for far-reaching changes. The most bitter resistance understandably comes from those industries and firms with the least promising prospects for survival in open, market-driven economies. Unions obviously want a voice in policies affecting restructuring and in the process at the level of individual firms. They also want clear agreements regarding their role in restructured or privatized firms; many are pressing for some sort of voice in management. Regarding wage policies, the caps on wage increases in Poland and in the Czech Republic have been particularly unpopular. On this and other industrial relations issues, specific unions' demands have ranged from moderate to more extreme.

Many workers and unions find it very difficult to accept the concept that the virtually total job security of the old system cannot continue. They approach industrial relations from the perspective of non-negotiable rights rather than pragmatic goals. For instance, striking Polish teachers in May 1993 insisted that their pay demands be conceded as a condition prior to negotiating with the government regarding reforms in the education system. In contrast, especially in the Czech Republic and Hungary, a good deal of union attention has focused on the longer-run and more moderate goal of acceptable roles in privatized or restructured enterprises. Union tactics have emphasized negotiation.

In several countries, including Bulgaria, the Czech Republic, and Hungary, policies regarding wages, prices, employment, and social welfare are coordinated, at least in principle, by tripartite councils at the national level. The councils' roles have varied across countries and changed within countries over time. In Bulgaria, the National Tripartite Council on Coordination of Social Interests was established by the Popov government early in 1991, at the same time that major economic reforms were launched. During that period, "The government rarely introduce[d] major policy changes without securing consensus from the Commission."[22] However, after the anti-communist electoral victory in autumn 1991, the new government of Filip Dimitrov disbanded the council, apparently feeling little need to consult with labor. When the Dimitrov government fell 16 months later, new Prime Minister Lyuben Berov quickly reestablished the tripartite forum, which he had chaired in 1990 and 1991.[23] In Hungary, a formally similar tripartite forum had little significance until the end of 1992. Unions complained that it was used mainly to convey government decisions to union representatives.

In Poland, as already noted, initial close links between the transition government and the trade unions associated with the broad anticommunist Solidarity movement gradually gave way to much more tense relations. The Suchocka government faced down a series of severe strikes in the summer of 1992. Aware that the uneasy peace could not hold without more systematic channels for consultation with labor, Minister of Labor and Social Policy Jacek Kuron then sought to work out a broad agreement with the unions regarding privatization and related issues. The so-called Pact on Enterprises, consisting of some 14 draft laws and amendments to existing laws, addressed a range of substantive issues; it also proposed procedures for fuller consultation and participation of workers on issues of direct concern to them.[24] After months of discussions between the government and the unions, legislation was submitted to the Sjem in spring 1993. However, it had not been passed when the Suchocka government fell in late May.

By mid-1993, non-communist center-left political parties had emerged as serious power contenders in Poland and in Hungary. That shift in the broader political context offered new options for union participation in the political (as distinct from the industrial relations) arena. In particular, it created opportunities for the by now reconstituted successors to the old official unions. Before the Polish elections of September 1993, both Solidarity and OPZZ had had groups of deputies in the Sjem or lower house. In autumn 1993, OPZZ cooperated with the winning coalition of parties and emerged as the second-largest force within it, represented by 61 of the Democratic Left Alliance's 171 deputies. Solidarity, in contrast, miscalculated the effects of new election laws and refused to enter a coalition. Their delegates failed to top a 5 percent threshold required for seats in the Sjem. Shut out of the legislature and with no strong party allies, Solidarity has since pursued the tactics of protest. It has been losing members steadily and seems to be increasingly isolated and ineffective politically.

In Hungary, meanwhile, the Hungarian Socialist Party (HSP) had been gaining strength throughout 1993. In February 1994, the party signed an electoral agreement with MSZOSZ, the successor to the former communist union federation and by far the largest federation. The HSP designated MSZOSZ chairman Sandor Nagy to run in second position on the party's national list. When the HSP won an unexpected landslide victory in May, the MSZOSZ clearly was well-positioned to influence the new government.

Both economic reform and democratic consolidation will be affected by how union influence in governing parties or coalitions is exercised. In Poland, OPZZ delegates promptly took aim at the hated tax on excess wages (the popiwek).[25] The new government repealed the law early in 1994. Wages surged 10.7 percent in the second quarter of the year; different statistical agencies and economists disagreed on whether the wage increases were due to lifting controls or other reasons. After bitter arguments and political maneuvers, a new version of the excess wages tax went into effect on August 1.[26] In Hungary, HSP and MSZOSZ agreed on many aspects of economic policy, including continuation of privatization under closer parliamentary control. But the HSP, like the Polish Democratic Left Alliance, includes both moderate factions that give high priority to containing fiscal deficits and more populist factions urging concessions to a wide range of social groups.[27] In both countries, union influence is likely to bolster the more populist tendencies. From the perspective of democratic consolidation, union participation in government councils means that unions must negotiate directly with coalition partners whose priorities differ—a process likely to moderate union demands. Their participation may also increase the legitimacy of policy outcomes in their members' view. But unionists belonging to federations with different or no party affiliations may be less persuaded.

While the evolving party systems in Poland and Hungary offered major portions of the union movement new channels for responsible participation in legislatures and governments, the failure of workable party systems to emerge in some other countries contributed to much more aggressive and disruptive patterns of direct political action. In Romania in particular, weak and ineffective government and confused and rapidly shifting party politics have perpetuated—perhaps intensified—the use of large-scale strikes to demand specific government actions. In winter 1994, three of Romania's most powerful labor confederations, together representing the bulk of state sector workers, for the first time cooperated in a general strike. The unions demanded faster economic reforms, but at the same time protested an IMF agreement that would sharply increase unemployment. The miners' confederation was also involved—even threatening a repeat of the scenario of September 1991, when miners swarmed into Bucharest and toppled the government. The weak political system not only encouraged the unions to continue their pattern of direct action, but also perpetuated unrealistic and inconsistent demands in the absence of responsible and credible debate within and among parties regarding policy options.

Unions, Economic Reform, and Democratic Consolidation in Latin America

Unions in Eastern Europe and Latin America contrast in several basic ways. First, while Eastern European unions enroll extremely high proportions of workers, membership in most Latin American countries is much lower. In Argentina, unions represent about 35 percent of the economically active population (but half of all workers on wages and salaries—a level higher than that of Germany or France). In the mid-1980s, Venezuelan unions also claimed about a third of the labor force; Jamaican unions, a quarter; Mexican unions, roughly a fifth; and most other Latin American union movements, a still smaller proportion. Union membership is concentrated in sizable (and mainly private, in many countries) industries and in government services. Most of the poorest, including many agricultural laborers and the urban informal sector, have no union representation (though some informal-sector workers have other kinds of associations).

Second, the break between authoritarian and post-authoritarian systems was much less sharp in Latin America. All unions in Eastern Europe have had to rethink their goals and roles; most Latin American unions generally have faced a less fundamental reassessment. Indeed, the point applies not only to unions, but to civil society and political parties more generally. The shift away from military governments has greatly broadened individual political and civil liberties and opened the field for political competition, but most of the organized contenders—including parties, unions, and business associations—are held over from the pre-transition era. There are relatively few major new actors, and not many of the old actors have undergone major internal reforms.

PRE-TRANSITION LEGACIES AND TRANSITION ROLES. In the three Latin American countries emphasized in this study—Argentina, Bolivia, and Brazil—the traditional power of unions differed dramatically, as did the ways in which union movements related to pre-transition authoritarian governments.

In Bolivia, the labor confederation Centro de Obreros Bolivianos (COB), and especially its core in the powerful tin miners' union, was virtually a state within a state. Founded during the 1952 revolution and intensely Marxist-Leninist, the COB was not subordinated to the National Revolutionary Movement (MNR), but functioned as a workers' assembly backed by its own armed militia and court system. At the peak of its political power, in 1971, COB head Juan Lechin Oquendo was elected president of the presidium of the Popular Assembly, a Soviet-like assembly installed within the Chamber of Deputies of the National Congress. Led by Lechin, the COB played a major and controversial role in Bolivian politics, forming shifting alliances with parties and the military and enduring periods of harsh repression by the military. During the turbulent late 1970s and early 1980s, the COB spearheaded opposition to military rule, operating underground after its headquarters were stormed and demolished. The COB therefore could claim much of the credit for the process that put Hernán Siles Zuazo and his populist coalition in office in 1982. It expected the new civilian government to treat it as a full partner in government as well as to meet demands for worker co-management of the tin mines.[28]

In Argentina, unions also have a long history as powerful political actors. Traditionally large, well-organized, and wealthy, many were also highly undemocratic and corrupt. Until very recently, it was true that "The leader of a large union in Argentina is almost automatically a prominent national politician; the secretary general of the General Confederation of Labor (CGT) holds political power that is probably equal to that of the leader of a major Argentine political party."[29] However, the Argentine labor movement was (and is) complex and faction-ridden. In contrast to the Bolivian COB's shifting alliances, most Argentine unions were closely tied to and dominated the Peronist Party. Unions claimed (and sometimes achieved) a strong voice in government during periods of Peronist rule, but they never tried to operate as an autonomous entity co-equal with government.

Like the COB, factions among the Argentine unions at various times collaborated with the military and at other times were harshly repressed. When military rule began to unravel at the end of the 1970s, the CGT split, but by early 1983, both major factions joined in protests to hasten the political transition. For the Peronists, however, the return of elected civilian government combined liberation and defeat. For the first time in post-World War II Argentine history their candidate failed to win a fair election.[30]

In Brazil, large unions developed in public services such as ports and in giant state enterprises in the late 1950s and early 1960s, but they were closely regulated by, and maintained tacit understandings with, the Ministry of Labor. While unions were coopted and controlled, those in strategic sectors gained comparatively good wages and fringe benefits. During the 1970s, much more militant and autonomous unions emerged, with core support from the rapidly expanding automotive and metallurgical industries of greater São Paulo. The São Paulo unions were in the vanguard of labor opposition to military rule, including the unprecedented strike waves of 1978–79.

REJECTING ECONOMIC REFORM: UNIONS AND THE FIRST DEMOCRATIC GOVERNMENTS. Despite their roles in hastening political openings, and in sharp contrast to their counterparts in Eastern Europe, Latin American unions in general did not cooperate or even acquiesce in the economic stabilization and reform efforts of the initial post-transition governments. The reasons are instructive.

First, the Latin American labor movements were much less disoriented and disorganized as a result of the political transitions than were the Eastern European unions. In contrast to Eastern Europe, the transitions were far more clearly anticipated, and the bulk of the union movement was not discredited by intimate association with the outgoing regime.

Second, again in contrast with Eastern Europe, unions did not view economic reform as part of the new era they had helped to usher in. Along with much of the general public, unions blamed the economic difficulties of the late 1970s and early 1980s on military mismanagement, not on structural weaknesses of their countries' economies. They expected new democratic governments to improve the economic situation without much sacrifice. Their role was therefore much the same as it had always been: to struggle for a larger share of the economic pie, taking advantage of the new and more favorable rules of the political game.

When Siles took office in Bolivia, the country was already in an acute economic crisis. Despite his own and his coalition's populist leanings, the situation left little room for maneuver: Siles repeatedly attempted to introduce stabilization measures. The COB response was adamant opposition, made more turbulent by ideological factions within the movement, which competed with each other in declaring strikes and demonstrations. "Between 1982 and 1985 the hapless Siles government was subjected to daily strikes and marches which paralyzed Bolivia . . . in March 1985 . . . hundreds of miners marched to La Paz and virtually occupied the capital city for 20 days."[31] The strikes crippled the government, but they also exhausted and disillusioned rank-and-file unionists and alienated the broader public.

In Argentina, the Raúl Alfonsín government did not at first confront so desperate an economic situation and therefore did not adopt provocative policies; indeed, real wages were sharply increased as part of a strategy to woo workers away from Peronist loyalties. Moreover, the labor movement was deeply split by personal rivalries and disagreements over political strategies. These divisions were temporarily set aside in early 1984, when the Alfonsín government introduced a bill designed to democratize the unions' internal procedures and to break the power of the Peronist bosses. The bill was defeated by a single vote in the senate (where the government lacked a majority). Thereafter, the government "alternated stick and carrot tactics with the labor movement,"[32] while growing economic crisis prompted a series of abortive stabilization and reform attempts. Saul Ubaldini, leading the most radical elements of the labor movement, won leadership of the CGT, and the nation was subjected to thirteen general strikes. A brief and partial respite came in 1987, when the government engineered a short-lived accord with the right-wing labor faction, led by Jorge Triaca, which viewed Ubaldini's radicalism as a growing liability. This group won control of the Ministry of Labor and special wage deals for their unions in exchange for support of the government's current economic program. But in 1988 the weakened government was forced to reinstate provisions regarding collective bargaining and professional associations that had earlier been revoked. These concessions further limited executive power to intervene in union affairs, and strengthened the union bosses' power.[33]

In Brazil, autonomous central labor organization had been barred under military rule. In the early 1980s, as the end of military rule drew closer, unions advocating a sharp break from the corporatist system formed the Central Unica dos Trabalhadores (CUT), closely affiliated with the Workers' Party (PT). More politically cautious unions were represented by the Central Geral dos Trabalhadores (CGT).[34] The CUT viewed the political transition via indirect election as illegitimate, was suspicious of the José Sarney Costa government, and criticized its stabilization plan when it was introduced in 1986. Much of the CGT was associated with President Sarney's party and broadly supported his government and the Cruzado Plan. The plan featured a wage and price freeze billed as temporary; it was preceded by wage increases and succeeded in virtually halting inflation for a few months, thereby sharply increasing real purchasing power. Repressed inflation surged, however, when controls were lifted in late 1986. Half-hearted Sarney government efforts to establish a tripartite pact to maintain more flexible controls foundered—in part because of divisions within both labor and business. The CUT, and to some extent the CGT, turned to strategies of confrontation. The government responded by repressing several major strikes. Tense industrial relations added to the paralysis and confusion of the end of Sarney's administration.[35]

ACCEPTING REFORM: UNIONS AND SECOND-ROUND DEMOCRATIC GOVERNMENTS. As the first round of elected governments neared the end of their terms, inflation accelerated into hyperinflation in both Bolivia (in 1985) and Argentina (in 1988). Hyperinflation triggered a desperate desire for a government that could control the economic tailspin and restore enough stability to permit people to resume their ordinary lives. Hyperinflation also intensified growing public impatience with union intransigence. Even much of the union rank and file now recognized that excessive confrontation could paralyze the government but was not improving their welfare. In the changed context, government handling of labor changed dramatically.

In Bolivia, Víctor Paz Estenssoro was elected president in August 1985 and promptly announced a New Economic Policy (NPE), including draconian stabilization measures. The COB attempted a general strike; Paz (a long-time enemy of COB leader Juan Lechin Oquendo) countered by declaring a state of siege and arresting and exiling or banishing key COB figures, including Lechin. The federation was further weakened when 22,000 mine workers were laid off as part of the restructuring of the nationalized mining sector. Unable to launch a general strike, the COB in July 1986 sponsored a popular referendum on the NPE. The results were devastating to the COB. Urban areas in particular strongly supported the Paz government. While the COB never acquiesced in the government's policies, its internal divisions and loss of support prevented a general strike throughout the remainder of the Paz administration. Meanwhile the government's economic policies were dramatically successful in halting hyperinflation—bringing it from over 16,000 percent to 92 percent within one year, and to roughly 16–18 percent by the end of the 1980s. In the May 1989 elections, all major parties adopted platforms promising to continue the broad thrust of the NPE; 75 percent of the electorate voted for those parties. For the moment, the unions were excluded from political influence.

In Argentina in 1988, initially only the conservative Triaca labor group supported Carlos Menem as the Peronist Party's candidate for the upcoming presidential elections. Later, all factions swung over to support his candidacy, but Triaca's group played a key role in funding and organizational networks. Labor in general hoped an electoral victory would restore their paramount power, and their expectations were fanned by Menem's campaign promises to create more jobs and sharply increase wages.

Upon taking office in July 1989, however, Menem promptly took a totally unexpected course, signaled by appointing as Minister of Economy a vice-president of Bunge y Borne, the largest multinational firm in Argentina and a symbol of "sell-out capitalism" to all Peronists.[36] Repeated stabilization programs followed, with only temporary success until April 1991, when newly appointed Minister of Economy Domingo Cavallo announced a fresh attempt dramatically anchored in full dollar convertibility. Alongside its stabilization efforts, the Menem government launched radical and rapid measures to: privatize virtually all of Argentina's substantial publicly owned industries, transport, and communications; downsize the national government; decentralize major government services; remove industrial subsidies; and liberalize the labor market. In summer and autumn 1991, 70,000 jobs were cut from the public payroll, with another 130,000 scheduled to follow by mid-1992.

The Menem program promptly produced a split in the CGT. The officially recognized CGT-San Martin reluctantly acquiesced in the government's sweeping program; the CGT-Azopardo, headed by the militant Ubaldini, fiercely opposed proposals for liberalization and privatization. Considering the turbulent history of Argentine labor, however, even the militants' response was surprisingly muted. Despite considerable protest and a number of small strikes (not backed by the main CGT), no general strike was attempted until November 1992—more than three years after Menem had taken office.

Many factors contributed to this restraint. Long-term trends in economic structure had weakened Argentine industrial unions (though not the public service unions). Industrial employment had declined almost 40 percent between 1974 and 1983, and another 5 percent by 1988.[37] Union strength within the Peronist Party had also dwindled. The electoral defeat of 1983 was blamed on union hegemony, and the party began to seek a broader social base. As part of that shift, it changed its by-laws to considerably reduce the power of union representatives in the party hierarchy. Especially after Cavallo's "miracle" had taken hold in the second half of 1991, public opinion strongly supported the general direction of government economic policies. Many rank-and-file unionists no longer favored militant tactics.

A less obvious shift in the political context also discouraged union militance. The traditional "military option" of Argentine politics—the threat to create such instability that the military would be tempted to step in—was no longer available. In contrast to the Alfonsín years (when three military uprisings were attempted), and despite one isolated and promptly repressed uprising, no significant group considered military coups acceptable or likely.

Menem's reforms and tactics in dealing with the unions took full advantage of, and deepened, these weaknesses. Strikes by individual unions were stonewalled or repressed; railroad workers were dismissed after a long strike protesting privatization, and neither telephone nor steel workers gained concessions. More compliant union leaders were coopted with desirable appointments or other concessions. New laws and decrees restricted strikes in the public services, authorized temporary hiring in private industry, and shifted the locus of collective bargaining to lower levels, including the individual firm.[38]

Unions seemed able to set aside their differences only in defense of their financial resources. In 1992, the CGT factions reunited and held the only general strike of the period in response to a government threat to union control of welfare funds. On this occasion the government backed down. A second general strike was threatened for January 1994, after the government used its decree powers to reduce employers' taxes paid into union welfare funds. The strike was averted by promises to compensate unions for the loss of employer contributions and to nationalize certain debts resulting from measures by the old military government. But the government also launched tax investigations of the welfare funds, the unions, and even union leaders' personal accounts.[39]

In Brazil, in contrast to Bolivia and Argentina, inflation remained high but did not erupt into hyperinflation. Pervasive indexing and elaborate additional devices for living with high inflation diminished the public's sense of urgency about halting price rises. Fernando Collor de Mello, elected in 1989 to replace Sarney, attempted both to stabilize the economy and to launch serious structural reforms. He promptly met strong resistance from both unions and employers, continuing the pattern established under Sarney. It is a moot question whether or not he could have persisted and prevailed, since corruption charges first crippled him and then led to his impeachment. His successor had little interest in economic reform; there were no further serious stabilization efforts until mid-1994.

DEEPENING REFORMS AND EVOLVING UNION ROLES. In Latin America as in Eastern Europe, unions are still in the process of reassessing their objectives and roles in reaction to economic and political changes. Their reactions are shaped by many of the same factors that are at work in Eastern Europe: economic progress, social costs, and the impact of both on public opinion as well as on unionized workers; the evolving pattern of party politics and union links with parties; and ideological legacies and organizational characteristics within the union movements themselves.

As in Eastern Europe, economic progress in those countries that have implemented vigorous economic reforms has been accompanied by high social costs. In Bolivia by the end of the 1980s, inflation was moderate and falling and the economy was growing, albeit slowly. Real wages, after tumbling by more than 20 percent in 1985 and again in 1986, rose in each year through 1992 (in 1988 alone by almost 20 percent).[40] But growth was tentative and from an extremely low base. Gains in wages affected a small fraction of the labor force; from 1987 through 1990, growth in real income per capita hovered close to zero.[41] Social services remained minimal, as did social safety net provisions, although a temporary program of small decentralized public works and social projects, financed through an externally funded Emergency Social Program, provided some relief.

After the 1989 elections, broad public support for the new economic strategy clearly began to erode. Privatization, in particular, was viewed with a great deal of skepticism. Polls suggested that most people viewed the process of divestment as tainted with corruption and doubted that the goals of increased efficiency and investment would be realized. In this changing context the COB, like the labor movements in

Eastern Europe, grew more aggressive. Major strikes again became frequent, protesting privatization in particular. By 1991 the COB once again sought to play a leading political role, facilitating (or perhaps engineering) a coalition of opposition groups in the legislature to block approval of the 1991 budget. COB protests did not succeed in altering basic policies, but did slow privatization and joint-venture initiatives involving foreign capital.[42] Although it is much weaker than before 1985 and linked to new (in part agrarian) allies, the COB has not basically altered its confrontational approach.

In Argentina, Menem's economic policies offered workers fewer gains. Average real wages in manufacturing had fallen dramatically during Alfonsín's term; when hyperinflation peaked in 1989, wages were roughly 44 percent of their real 1983 level. Menem's economic program slowed but failed to reverse the fall: after an 8.8 percent drop in 1989, real wages in manufacturing fell 5.1 percent in both 1990 and 1991, 2.9 percent in 1992, and 1.7 percent in 1993.[43] Unemployment continued to be high, even after growth resumed. Despite 8 percent annual growth since 1991 and high investment, hundreds of thousands of jobs continued to be eliminated from public and private sectors. As of early 1994, it was estimated that as much as 18 percent of the workforce was unemployed or underemployed, although open unemployment was far lower.[44]

Many of those laid off from public-sector positions received fairly generous severance pay (in some instances financed by a World Bank loan). But the social safety net was far from adequate. Less than half the unemployed and underemployed received income support; support levels were extremely low; and special programs for the elderly, single mothers, or other vulnerable groups were minimal. As in Eastern Europe, most people remained committed to economic reforms but were increasingly concerned about the social costs.[45]

In contrast to the COB in Bolivia, and in part reflecting the stronger social consensus in support of economic reforms, Argentine unions for the most part seem to have abandoned confrontation for an array of more pragmatic strategies and tactics. Some union leaders have simply focused on retaining their political ties with and appointments in the government. However, a fair number of unions, including some of the largest and most wealthy, are devising new strategies. Among other measures, they are going into business for themselves, acquiring privatized firms in order to strengthen their financial autonomy while at the same time protecting jobs.[46]

In Brazil as well, some powerful unions have moved away from confrontation toward new strategies. In the São Paulo region, formerly militant auto workers have developed intricate cooperative arrangements with management; these arrangements are backed by the state and link increased wages in part to improved productivity.[47]

As in Eastern Europe, union strategies and strength are strongly influenced by changing party systems. The three Latin American countries emphasized in this study offer striking contrasts in this respect. In Argentina, the earlier close ties between the union movement and the Peronist Party are clearly weakening, encouraging less directly political strategies and prompting some unions to seek means to strengthen their financial autonomy. In Bolivia, parties have long been much weaker and more fluid than Argentine parties, and important political party groups have not (since 1985) sought close union ties. The COB's continued confrontational stance reflects not only its ideological legacy but also the limited strategic alternatives available. In this respect its behavior may be somewhat similar to Romanian unions. Brazil presents a sharp contrast. The PT—long closely linked with the dynamic and militant CUT labor federation and strongly based in industrial São Paulo—has continued to gain strength. PT candidate Luis Inácio Lula da Silva was a powerful contender in the presidential elections of 1989 and 1994. In October 1994 he lost to Fernando Henrique Cardoso, who as Finance Minister had introduced a dramatically effective stabilization program a few months earlier. Cardoso's decisive victory included substantial support from workers and testified to ordinary Brazilians' desire to escape the economic and political quagmires of the past decade. Despite Lula's defeat, and in contrast to the trends in Bolivia and Argentina, Brazil's workers and segments of its unions have become much more influential political actors in the first decade following the restoration of democratic government.

Unions' Longer-Run Prospects in Dual Transitions

No strong generalizations can be drawn from such diverse experiences, even among the small number of countries discussed. We can, however, usefully ask: How would the dual transitions in these countries have differed, had there been no unions or only a few weak unions?

On the economic reform side, in the absence of unions, some stabilization efforts that in fact aborted might have moved ahead. No unions, or only very weak unions, also would have permitted faster implementation of structural reforms, especially privatization, in countries where governments were committed to reform, including Bolivia, the Czech Republic, Poland, and perhaps Hungary, where other problems contributed to slow privatization. Union opposition has not been the major obstacle, however, in those countries where reforms have made least progress, including Romania, Bulgaria, Slovakia, and Brazil.

In all of these cases broader and deeper political conflicts and paralysis have slowed reform—and provoked union turbulence. In several of the countries surveyed, many unions actually supported reforms in crucial periods. And union participation has helped legitimize many specific decisions, often at the level of individual enterprises.

As for democratic consolidation, in most of the cases surveyed, had there been no unions, sizable groups probably would have felt unorganized and undefended during the transition period. This would have been particularly likely in those countries where political parties were most fragmented, ephemeral, and ineffective. However, the confrontational tactics of unions clearly strained new democratic governments. In several cases, unions played a major part in pushing particular governments out of power, including Siles in Bolivia, Alfonsín in Argentina, Suchocka in Poland, Dimitrov in Bulgaria, and Theodor Stolojan in Romania.

In longer perspective, the roles of unions in both Latin America and Eastern Europe will surely change over the next two decades. In most countries, their direct political influence and their negotiating strength in industrial relations will both decline. As the public sector shrinks and private employment increases, as heavy industry employs a smaller share of workers, and as international competition reshapes industries and firms, union membership and leverage will dwindle. Decentralized wage bargaining, a more flexible labor market, and the restructuring and partial privatization of social security programs are also likely to undermine union power.[48]

To survive and be effective, unions will have to shift their tactics and strategies. Reduced government intervention in industrial relations and the economy will diminish the importance of direct political channels and tactics at the national level and increase the importance of industrial bargaining. Union roles in sector-specific, regional and local institutions and networks—for instance, labor market councils such as those established in Hungary—may become relatively more important. But in a far more competitive world, unions will be under great pressure to increase their flexibility, to shift from confrontational to consultative and co-operative approaches to management, and to accept links between wages and other benefits and productivity. Signs of these trends are already clear in some of the recent collective agreements in both regions.

Unions vary tremendously in their ability to adjust. Some will shift readily to new roles, while others will prove much more rigid. Their heritages affect their flexibility; the Bolivian COB, for instance, is hampered by its intense Marxist-Leninist ideology and by bitter factional and ideological feuds within that tradition. Ironically, Solidarity's proud history of courageous anti-communist confrontation may equip it less well for new roles than the more pragmatic stance of the rival former communist unions.

Union responses also vary with their assessments of economic prospects. Workers who anticipate a better future are better able to tolerate current hardship. And where change appears not only inevitable, but on balance desirable, workers and their unions are more likely to bend their efforts to adjusting rather than resisting. For instance, the São Paulo auto workers' recent shift in strategy from militance to cooperation with management and government, noted earlier, makes sense for workers employed in a dynamic industry in a fundamentally strong (if grievously mismanaged) economy. In contrast, Bulgarian uranium miners or Slovak defense industry workers, employed in industries where the major question is how fast and thoroughly to close down, tend to be bitterly obstructionist.

The structure of union movements and of specific unions also affects unions' capacity to adjust and their choices of strategy and tactics. Local and narrowly specialized unions are likely to have narrower horizons and less sophistication than national federations. Fragmented labor movements and competition among unions may also put pressure on leaders to adopt militant goals and tactics, lest they lose their members to more aggressive rivals. Large unions or confederations exercise considerable market power, but they are also more likely to recognize that wage settlements may affect the larger economy; inflationary push may erode nominal gains. In general, associations that are more encompassing and combine internal accountability with centralized decision-making are better partners for negotiating economic reforms.[49] But generalizations along these lines are risky. Some centralized unions (such as Bolivia's COB) are highly ideological, and many specialized unions are pragmatic. Decentralized unions may also be better able to respond flexibly to the decentralization of collective bargaining.

The political roles of unions are intertwined with and conditioned by evolving party systems. This is clearly illustrated by the opportunities for unions opened by the new strength of center-left parties or coalitions in Poland, Hungary, and Brazil. Where a manageable number of fairly stable, disciplined parties fails to emerge, unions will be prompted to take on much more direct and aggressive political roles—as in Romania in the past several years. And where one strong and disciplined party captures such strong popular support that there are (temporarily) no plausible challengers, union leverage is sharply reduced and depends largely on the good will of the dominant party. The Czech Republic provides a current example.

In the long run, center-left parties with strong union affiliations are likely to deemphasize their union base and move to broaden their support among lower-middle class and middle class groups. That tendency is a result of the same economic and social shifts that are the fundamental reason for reduced union power. Argentina's Peronists have been feeling their way toward a broader social base ever since the shock of electoral defeat in 1983. In Hungary, the Socialist Party won an absolute majority in the spring 1994 parliamentary elections, but invited the liberal Alliance of Free Democrats to form a coalition government, in part to counterbalance the strength of the post-communist trade union representatives among Socialist members of parliament.[50]

Such trends need not weaken democratic systems by closing off channels of representation for workers. Changing economic and social structure in industrialized and semi-industrialized nations is diluting what might be called the working-class subculture. A century ago, industrial workers (mainly in Europe and North America) had rather little in common with middle-class people in white-collar and commercial jobs. At the end of the twentieth century, that social and psychological gap has greatly diminished. Recent research among Argentine unionists, for instance, emphasizes the extent to which industrial workers share the concerns of other middle-class groups as parents, consumers, or commuters.[51] Unions are likely to continue to serve important functions representing the interests of certain kinds of workers in their roles as workers. Other kinds of interest groups and intermediary associations and political parties will represent their concerns about other aspects of their lives.

BUSINESS ROLES IN DUAL TRANSITIONS

Business Reactions in Dual Transitions: An Overview

While labor unions serve as the main channel for organizing and exercising the collective power of workers, business associations are only part of a more diverse set of channels through which business interests pursue their goals. And while labor unions play broadly similar roles in Latin America and Eastern Europe, the character of business interests and their roles vis-à-vis economic and political reforms differ sharply in the two regions. This section briefly considers the changing role of business associations in the context of broader state-business relations in each of the two regions.

BUSINESS, MARKET-ORIENTED REFORMS, AND DEMOCRACY. Effective stabilization and structural reforms place partly parallel demands on workers and on business interests. State protection and assistance are sharply reduced. Many firms see profits reduced or eliminated; some will fail. Entrepreneurs in industry and agriculture must shift out of inefficient lines of activity into more promising ones; to do so, they must retool and sometimes relocate.

But the parallels are obviously limited. At least in early stages of reform, workers are mainly asked to tighten their belts; many aspects of economic restructuring require their acquiescence, but not necessarily their active cooperation. In contrast, adjustment cannot succeed without energetic and creative action from a substantial part of the business community. Without investment, there will be no recovery, no growth, and no new jobs. In many of the countries that have undertaken stabilization and market-oriented reforms since the early 1980s, investment remains low and recovery elusive. A flexible labor force facilitates restructuring and growth, but business confidence—not mere acquiescence—is absolutely crucial.

Sound economic policies alone are not enough to create and maintain confidence. Businessmen must be convinced that new policies will be implemented as intended and will not be reversed. The large degree of discretionary authority that officials exercise in most developing countries (and in former communist systems as well) leads owners and managers to be skeptical about new policies and reforms. Recent research suggests strong links between lack of political credibility and weak long-term growth.[52]

Business skepticism that new policies and reforms will be *implemented* as intended is based both on past experience with arbitrary discretionary authority in old regimes, and on the flux and erosion of state capacities discussed in the Overview and particularly in Chapter 4 (Kochanowicz) of this volume. If state officials, high or low, are not both well-disciplined and technically competent, they can readily subvert the intent of many reforms.

Business concerns about *reversal* relate less to state capacity than to political institutions and forces. Measures put into effect by decree can be reversed by decree. More generally, where reforms are driven by the commitment and power of a small central group of officials, it is obvious that the reforms may be at least diluted, and perhaps abandoned, if that key group loses power.

Competitive democratic politics and a large role for legislatures are not necessarily reassuring to business interests. Historically, perhaps especially in Latin America, many businessmen have been concerned that democratic politics means sharp swings in policy—due to unsustainable demands from labor or popular classes more broadly. Major chapters in Latin American history are at least partly the result of alliances between business and commercial interests and authoritarian governments to contain populist pressures. In Latin America in the 1990s, business attitudes have taken a new turn: Democratic governments are widely viewed as those most likely to be legitimate—and therefore most likely to provide enough stability for business to invest and grow. In Eastern Europe similarly, democracy is widely viewed as the only route to legitimate and stable government. But business concern persists regarding the kinds of policies democratic systems will adopt.

If business groups tend to distrust much of the rest of society, they see the feeling as reciprocal. In a number of Latin American countries, many businessmen believe that much of the public views business or capital as exploitative and in some sense illegitimate.[53] In Central and Eastern Europe, public attitudes toward business are more in flux and vary in different countries. In both regions distrust or antagonism is likely to grow as inequalities widen and media highlight stories of corruption and insider deals.

Obviously it takes time and hard work to overcome mutual distrust and to hammer out broader areas of consensus regarding economic rules of the game and basic policies. Chilean experience in the late 1980s offers a fascinating case of deliberate engineering of consensus between the business community and democratic forces. Over the period of several years leading up to the 1988 referendum that denied Augusto Pinochet an automatic extension of his rule, pro-democratic groups worked hard to persuade business groups that a return to competitive politics would not bring back the instability and polarization of the late 1960s and early 1970s. Business also sought assurance that the broad thrust of the economic reforms put in place under Pinochet would not be reversed. The success of the effort to create consensus was reflected not only in the referendum and later election results, but more specifically in agreements reached between labor, business, and official representatives after Pinochet left power, laying out the basic principles guiding economic policy.[54] In Chile, economic reforms were in place and widely viewed as working well (though needing more attention to equity) before democracy was restored. Dual-transition countries must promote confidence in both economic and political reforms simultaneously. It holds for business as for labor (as argued earlier) that many aspects of the later phases of reform, involving more complex institutional changes, need to be worked out in consultation with the groups that will be most affected. Consultation improves information for fine-tuning the design of complex changes. It also increases the legitimacy and eases the implementation of decisions. The challenge for reformist governments is how to build channels that enhance communication and trust without at the same time encouraging business interests to seek special privileges.

BUSINESS, THE STATE, AND THE ROLES OF BUSINESS ASSOCIATIONS. Workers have compelling reasons to form unions. Incentives to organize politically are much weaker for business and industrial firms, which normally have multiple channels of access to and influence over government policies and actions. Large firms and conglomerates are likely to have direct access to high-level executive and legislative leaders. Governments seeking good relations with the business community often appoint well-known business leaders to prominent posts. Campaign finance is of course a time-honored channel of influence. For large businesses, banding together to form business associations is therefore only one option among many—and may not look particularly effective as a means to pursue priority concerns.

The heterogeneity of business, industry, and financial interests also affects business associations. Peak associations encompassing large segments of the business community, such as chambers of industry or commerce, are often internally divided on many matters and can take a united stand only on very general issues. Radical economic reforms—actual or proposed—may intensify internal disputes, since market-oriented reforms have different impacts on export-oriented versus import-substituting interests, and on fixed asset holders versus more "footloose" liquid-asset holders. More specialized associations representing specific industries, size categories (such as small business), or regions or localities are more cohesive, but by definition have much narrower concerns.

Despite these caveats, business associations have played considerable roles in at least some Latin American countries, in the political and economic changes of the past decade and a half. In general, they supported democratic transitions; with some delay, they also supported stabilization measures, but their stance regarding structural reforms has been more mixed. Not surprisingly, in Eastern Europe, both business in general and business associations in particular are considerably less organized politically.

Business, Economic Reform, and Democratic Consolidation in Latin America

The structure and character of business interests and their relations with the state vary widely among Latin American countries. The different patterns have long roots—in part traceable to contrasts in the character of pre-industrial export activities.[55] Business links with the military also varied, but by the early 1980s, business elites in many countries were disillusioned with military rule. The trend emerged earliest in the Andean nations, starting with Ecuador. In the Southern Cone, closer business-military ties persisted until the early 1980s, when acute economic problems threatened many firms with bankruptcy. At the same time, turmoil in Central America led businessmen elsewhere to view military rule as a potential source of instability rather than a guarantor of capitalism.[56]

REJECTING REFORM: BUSINESS AND THE FIRST DEMOCRATIC GOVERNMENTS. Business support for democratic transitions did not, however, mean automatic support for economic reforms. When elected civilian governments took over, many business groups, like broader public opinion and technocratic views, blamed economic problems on external forces and military mismanagement, and did not see a need for fundamental changes. In Bolivia, Argentina, and Brazil, moreover, business elites did not have close ties to incoming civilian governments.

In Bolivia, the Confederation of Private Entrepreneurs of Bolivia (CEPB) had been dominant in business-state relations since the early 1960s. By the early 1980s, the CEPB favored economic and political liberalization, but when President Siles took office in 1982, they feared his populist leanings and saw their role as a counterweight to aggressive COB union demands. Prominent CEPB legislators would not cooperate with the Siles government. In early 1984, amidst deepening polarization and paralysis, the CEPB even called a two-day business strike to protest the government's failure to prevent workers' takeovers of businesses.

In Argentina as well, despite considerable business support for the return of democracy, the Alfonsín government's relations with Argentina's formidable array of business associations were cool, even tense. Alfonsín's Radical Party had few industrial allies, and even fewer links with transnational firms and international banks. The Argentine Industrial Union and the Argentine Rural Society, representing manufacturing and agro-export interests, adamantly rejected proposals to ease the fiscal deficit through tax increases. Associations representing both the international banks and the domestic banks lobbied successfully to block bills intended to penalize financial speculation and reorient capital toward productive endeavors. For its part, the government initially made little effort to consult with business groups—in part because of its own internal divisions. A change of finance ministers and the initial successes of the heterodox Austral Plan to stabilize the economy drew temporary support from much of business (in contrast to vocal opposition from labor). The government also agreed to establish an Economic and Social Conference giving privileged representation to organized labor and industrialists. By late 1986, however, as the Austral

Plan unraveled, even the peak industrial association became sharply critical.[57]

Late in its term (in mid-1987) the Alfonsín government adopted a more radical neo-liberal strategy of reduced state intervention and an opening to international markets. The shift facilitated collaboration with the Grupo Maria, an informal association of 20 prominent "captains of industry" representing many of Argentina's largest and most diversified national and transnational conglomerates. The Grupo Maria had been formed soon after Alfonsín took office to seek a more fluid dialogue with government than was possible through the rather cumbersome channels of the mainline business organizations.[58] By 1987, the government's new strategy encouraged an informal alliance with the Grupo Maria (at the cost of alienating some of the more formal business associations), but that alliance rapidly eroded as the economic situation deteriorated.

ACCEPTING REFORM: BUSINESS AND SECOND-ROUND DEMOCRATIC GOVERNMENTS. The shock of hyperinflation and much more vigorous economic reforms prompted much greater business support for the second round of civilian governments in Bolivia and Argentina. By the mid-1980s, the Bolivian CEPB was dominated by a circle of mainly U.S.-trained businessmen who strongly opposed traditional clientelist and dependent links between business and the state. The CEPB was deeply and directly involved in the design of the New Economic Policy launched by Paz Estenssoro in 1985, and it continued to have "unlimited and even decisive access to the policy-making process" in that and the following government.[59] It used its influence to press for more rapid market-oriented reforms, including privatization; in the early 1990s the association was given direct control over the newly established Office of Investment Promotion.[60]

In Argentina, no single business association was as central to Argentina's economic reforms under Menem as the CEPB was in Bolivia. But Argentine business interests provided important support for Menem's programs. Menem's appointment of a vice-president of Bunge y Borne as Minister of Economy was calculated to woo business support, and his determination to contain hyperinflation and press structural reforms won business approval. Early in his administration, 350 "price-forming" companies agreed to an accord requiring them to moderate future price increases; the government in turn agreed to lower interest rates and postpone exchange-rate and public-sector price changes. But cooperation to contain hyperinflation proved easier than agreement on longer-term strategies to dismantle the state-led and semi-closed industrialization model that had guided Argentine policies for decades. Not only the more traditional business associations but the

Grupo Maria as well voiced fears that cutting subsidies would sacrifice even internationally competitive firms. However, business groups strongly supported government proposals for radical privatization and liberalization of the labor market and pressed for more rapid implementation; some urged Menem to use his decree power more freely if the legislature would not cooperate.[61] The privatization program also may have been important in gaining business acceptance of sharply tightened tax collection.[62]

FACILITATING REFORM: BUSINESS GROUPS AND THE CONSOLIDATION OF ECONOMIC AND POLITICAL REFORMS IN LATIN AMERICA. In some Latin American countries, business groups and associations not only supported economic reforms but played a major role in the design, fine-tuning, and implementation of later stages. In Pinochet's Chile, shifting capitalist coalitions had been important from the outset of economic reforms in the mid-1970s. After major policy failures and the severe depression of the early 1980s, a new Minister of Finance considerably broadened the circle of business interests engaged in policy dialogue, encouraging more effective fine-tuning and contributing to Chile's dramatic economic recovery after 1985.[63] In Mexico, key business associations collaborated with state agencies and labor unions to implement the 1987 Pact of Economic Solidarity (since renewed several times), to contain inflation and (in later versions of the Pact) to address privatization and deregulation as well.[64] In Brazil in the late 1980s and early 1990s, at a time when economic reforms were floundering, new business associations formed by young industrialists from the São Paulo region sought to forge and articulate a voice for progressive business interests: one group focused on broad socio-economic policies, the other on industrial policies.[65]

Especially in Latin America, where tremendous inequalities underlie corrosive social conflict, broad-gauged and forward-looking business associations may also contribute to the consolidation of democratic politics. Recent research suggests that in Brazil, for instance, more than 70 percent of businessmen believe that poverty and inequality must be reduced to restore social stability and permit a viable market economy. Yet individual firms and narrow sectoral interests have every incentive to evade redistributive measures. Ben Ross Schneider argues that "stronger business associations and associated parties would be better able to aggregate interests, negotiate the terms of redistribution, police members, and reduce free-riding."[66] For instance, business interests in Chile agreed in 1990 to a surtax on corporate taxes, earmarked for social programs. Broad-gauged and vigorous business associations of course are no guarantee of such behavior. But without such associations, business elites are highly likely to shape their behavior in accord with parochial and short-term interests.

Emerging Business Interests, Economic Reform, and Democratic Consolidation in Eastern Europe

Despite the diversity of Latin American business interests, the general idea of a "business elite" is considerably clearer there than in Eastern Europe. In the post-communist countries, the normal heterogeneity of business is compounded by legacies from the communist era and by the rapid changes in economic structure and corporate forms since 1990.

In most Eastern European countries, business interests fall into several categories. State enterprises from the old regime still account for much of large and medium enterprise. Under communism, the managers of state enterprises and officials from the branch ministries responsible for their lines of activity were linked in powerful informal networks. In parts of the former Soviet Union (including Russia and Ukraine), those networks remain potent and are reinforced by ties between managers and workers. In Central Europe, the networks quickly lost their political power, although informal contacts continued to be important for both old and new firms seeking to adjust to rapidly changing circumstances.[67]

New private medium- and large-scale firms make up a second category of business interests. Outside Central Europe, that category is still limited (as measured by numbers of firms and share of production and employment, excluding those employed in the burgeoning small-scale private sector). In Central Europe, it is growing rapidly, but employment and output are still smaller than those of state enterprises. Throughout the region (though perhaps especially in Hungary, where "spontaneous privatization" was extensive in the late 1980s), former state enterprise managers and *nomenklatura* have played a major role in these new firms. Their pre-transition connections carry over, in a radically new setting, as webs of informal contacts. Some of these firms are beginning to establish more formal associations. In Hungary, for instance, the National Association of Hungarian Industrialists (MGYOSZ), organized in 1990, represents 100 member firms—primarily the largest private Hungarian firms but also some state-owned firms that have begun privatization.

The multitude of small private entrepreneurs who rapidly emerged throughout Eastern Europe are a third category of business interests. Their role has been tremendously important in early economic reforms, providing considerable new employment and rapidly filling niches neglected under the old system. Like small businesses in other parts of the world, they tend to concentrate on surviving and growing, and are usually less politically active than larger entrepreneurs. Their associations usually emphasize services to member firms, but may also seek to influence policy. For example, the Hungarian National Association of Entrepreneurs (VOSZ), founded in 1988 (before the political transition), represents about 6000 small and medium private firms with half a million employees. It focuses mainly on services to member firms, but is also active in national tripartite negotiations.[68] Small entrepreneurs also can provide a potential political base for aspiring politicians. The president of VOSZ had strong political ambitions; the Jan Krzysztof Bielecki government in Poland was formed mainly from representatives of a thriving small business circle from Gdansk.

Foreign firms are a rapidly growing presence in the Central European countries and to a lesser extent further east. While foreign interests cannot play direct political roles similar to those of local business groups, they not only press for favorable (often preferential) terms and conditions but also may exercise indirect influence regarding economic policies. For instance, in late 1993 General Electric, with investments in Hungary, prompted an article in the London-based *Financial Times* arguing that the Hungarian currency should be devalued.[69] Early in 1994 multinational companies in Hungary formed an association, which maintains a low profile but lobbies strongly for preferential treatment such as special tax exemptions and regulations.

The evolving array of business interests in Eastern Europe also includes an alarming growth of Mafia-style organizations and networks; this is still more obvious in parts of the former Soviet Union. While information is obviously scarce, there is wide agreement that such networks are large and sophisticated. The growing influence they exercise on economic evolution is somewhat analogous to that of the drug networks in Bolivia and some other Latin American nations. Their political connections and influence must also be spreading rapidly.

In contrast to the patterns in Latin America, in Central Europe none of these categories of business interests were strong contenders just after the political transitions, when major economic reforms were launched or (in Poland and especially Hungary) deepened. The state enterprise networks were disrupted. In Hungary, for instance, import liberalization between 1989 and 1991 was "possible because the previously powerful industrial lobbies had disintegrated during the political transition."[70] Medium and large private firms were still very few and new, while burgeoning small enterprise was not politically organized and active. Foreign investment was still very limited and cautious, while illegal networks were embryonic.

As reforms have deepened in the post-launch phases, both held-over and new business interests have become more organized and politically active. Old managerial networks have not reappeared in Hungary, Poland, or the Czech Republic, but managers of big state enterprises have joined with each other and with unions to temper—and sometimes block—the speed and nature of restructuring and privatization. Some new business interests have tried to form their own political parties. Thus in Hungary in 1992, about twenty large entrepreneurs formed the Republican Party, and in Bulgaria, the Bulgarian Business Bloc sought voter support. In Russia both new and old business interests have formed parties, and managers of large state enterprises and state cooperatives are powerful in several more broadly-based parties. Individual businessmen also often run for legislative office, since the post of deputy offers opportunities to develop contacts and further private goals as well as influence policies. Presumably campaign funding will be an increasing channel of influence. Working through or controlling the media is still another. In Bulgaria, for example, the Union for Private Economic Enterprise runs the 168 Hours Press Group, which publishes the largest daily in the nation, as well as a weekly focused on business and politics and two additional publications.

Business associations—including both new ones, and the re-oriented heirs of the old official communist Chambers of Commerce and Industry—thus far seem to have played limited roles in lobbying and direct consultation with governments. Some of the business associations are represented in tripartite commissions charged with advising governments on wage, price, and related policies, but their roles have generally been less prominent than those of the unions and governments. The number of specialized trade and sectoral associations has grown rapidly, and business combinations and networks are extensive, but for the most part this mushrooming associative activity is geared to specific economic goals rather than to influencing government policies or seeking political power.

Thus far, business influence through all channels has probably been less powerful in Eastern Europe than in Latin America. However, emerging private and quasi-private firms predictably will increase their efforts to shape later phases of reform to their benefit. Large firms will use direct private contacts with decision makers; political parties will also be channels for pressure; and it seems likely that business associations will also play growing roles. It remains to be seen whether new associations, or perhaps reoriented old ones, will be able to articulate broader and longer-run business interests, including recognition of the need to balance liberalization with social equity and security.

WORKERS, BUSINESS, AND THE STATE: CHANGING RELATIONS IN DUAL TRANSITIONS

Retooling State-Interest Group Relations

For market-oriented reform, economic interest groups are clearly both obstacles and building blocks. In both Latin America and Eastern Europe, unions and business associations (more generally, business opposition), have often slowed and sometimes even derailed economic reforms. But as the earlier discussion illustrates, both unions and business groups have acquiesced in or actively supported stabilization and structural adjustment under some circumstances. Moreover, collaboration between government and at least some interest groups is probably crucial in later phases of consolidation of reforms.

More broadly, reorienting relations between the state and major economic interests in society is a key element in creating a well-functioning market economy. In industrial societies, the state must intervene extensively to protect and promote a range of public goals, including public health and safety, the environment, and the competitiveness of markets themselves. The need for information, feedback, and cooperation with implementation is ongoing—not solely a transitional requirement.

But it is a delicate task to retool state-interest group relations in ways that facilitate communication and consultation but minimize opportunities for rent-seeking or, worse still, the emergence of privatized areas of government activity, where state agencies and specific private interests collude to the exclusion of broader public surveillance and guidance. Retooled relations between the state and group interests must strike a fine balance between access and autonomy for both interest groups and state agencies.

For democratic consolidation, too, interest groups are both building blocks and stumbling blocks. They are important channels of representation, supplementing political parties and (particularly for larger businesses) direct individual contacts. As the first section of this chapter noted, however, they pose two main risks: distorted representation (both within and between groups) and demand overload.

The internal organization and dynamics of interest groups are one source of distorted representation. Unions have an inherent tendency to become dominated by bosses, who sometimes represent their own rather than their members' interests. Similarly, business associations are often captured by their staffs or by small cliques of members. Laws and regulations can encourage internal democracy and accountability by requiring specific procedures—such as periodic open elections—as conditions for registration or legal recognition. However, such regulation cannot be guided by a simple belief in the virtues of direct democracy. Like legislators, union and business leaders have roles that go beyond the pure reflection of their constituents' current views and desires. Representative leaders have a responsibility to try to modify their supporters' demands on the basis of broader information and perspectives, and thus to encourage an evolving and dynamic redefinition of their constituents' own interests. Trade union bosses and business leaders also need substantial autonomy to negotiate with other groups. Thus increased internal democracy is often part of the solution to distorted representation, but itself raises complex questions.

A second source of distorted representation grows out of the inherent difficulty of organizing certain kinds of workers (domestic servants, for example) or businesses (particularly small businesses). Where the state picks particular organizations to consult or act as partners in particular tasks of regulation or management, it clearly privileges certain groups and marginalizes others. Yet state agencies cannot work with all groups at once.

Demand overload as a result of interest group activity is partly a question of the capacities of the state. As Jacek Kochanowicz argues in Chapter 4 in this volume, sharply diminished state capacities may make it difficult to handle even moderate levels of interest-group demands. Conversely, as core state functions are reformed and reinvigorated, overload becomes less of a program. Demand overload is also, obviously, affected by the extreme or moderate nature of the demands and interest-group tactics. The histories and ideologies of different groups powerfully shape their moderate or extreme demands. But more moderate positions can also be encouraged by how the state organizes its relations with major interests—and by the laws and institutions governing interactions between those interests.

SOCIAL CORPORATIST APPROACHES TO STATE-INTEREST GROUP RELATIONS. In a number of mainly small Western and Northern European countries, parallel arrangements evolved, mainly after World War II, for conciliating the interests of labor, business, and the state. These arrangements are often labeled "social corporatism." For a time, particularly in the 1960s and 1970s, they worked extremely well, delivering industrial peace and macroeconomic stability, rising standards of living and generous social welfare arrangements, and sustained ability to compete in international markets. Therefore social corporatism is often suggested as a model or possible approach for Latin American and Eastern European countries attempting dual transitions.

In social corporatist systems, each major interest is represented by one or a few peak or central associations. These associations include as members most of the relevant groups and individuals. In other words, much of the labor force is unionized and most unions belong to the peak confederation(s); most businesses are affiliated (through specialized sector, sub-sector, and/or regional associations) with one of a few peak associations. Moreover, the peak associations have considerable influence over their constituent organizations, and these in turn have considerable control over their members (union rank and file, business firms). Peak association officials are virtual partners in government decisions affecting their constituents' interests; major wage, price, and social policies are the result of discussion and negotiation among associations and the government.

In addition to its success in countries like Austria, Belgium, the Netherlands, Switzerland, and the Scandinavian nations, social corporatism probably has an intrinsic appeal to state officials, and perhaps especially to officials in post-communist countries. For state officials, especially those accustomed to communism's pervasive social controls, social corporatism organizes societal interests in a tidy manner and offers a kind of surrogate control over social forces. For those primarily concerned with protecting and advancing labor and business interests, social corporatism is also attractive because it offers an officially recognized and major role in policy. Yet despite these apparent attractions, the social corporatist approach probably is not very promising in most Latin American countries. It may be somewhat more feasible in parts of Eastern Europe but is by no means clearly the "right answer." Why not?

First, social corporatism in Western Europe was built to implement Keynesian policies in small open economies with good access to capital. The system rested on domestic structural conditions that are weak or absent in most other countries and on an international context that had changed dramatically by the 1990s. In most Latin American countries, neither unions nor business associations represent the bulk of their potential constituencies; peak associations are often multiple and competitive, and they exercise little control over their members. Eastern European unions cover a larger, though probably declining, portion of the workforce, but in several countries the union movement is quite divided. Eastern European business associations are still limited. Looking a little deeper than the statistics of membership and federation structure, it has been argued that Western European social corporatism evolved in broader political contexts that included strong social democratic parties and predictable voting patterns rooted in durable social cleavages.[71] Those patterns are also absent in most of the Eastern European and Latin American countries attempting dual transitions. Moreover, international economic conditions, especially in the 1960s, facilitated growth and reduced internal conflicts. The global economic climate in the early 1990s is considerably less supportive. Indeed, in recent years, external pressures and domestic changes have eroded the success of social corporatist arrangements in many of the Western European countries where they were for a time so successful.

Would social corporatism be a feasible and desirable long-term objective in some countries, even if the prerequisites are not now in place? Particularly in some of the Eastern European countries, the question is reasonable. The predisposition toward social corporatism is evident in the tripartite commissions created to deal with wage, price, and related issues, as well as in more specific arrangements such as the tripartite committees set up in Hungary to administer the revised health and social security programs, and the county-level Labor Market Committees established to allocate the Hungarian Employment and Solidarity Funds to local workers and firms in trouble and to job creation and retraining programs.

However, the long-term trends discussed at the end of this chapter's second section may be eroding the prerequisites for social corporatism. Those trends include changing economic structure, the dwindling strength of labor unions, and the growing premium on highly flexible business and industrial linkages in an increasingly competitive world. Trying to build new relations between the state and interest groups through social corporatist arrangements may be like building a sand castle on a beach where the tide is coming in.

TEMPORARY BIPARTITE OR TRIPARTITE PACTS AND DUAL TRANSITIONS. Whether or not the social corporatist approach is promising as a long-run model in some dual-transition countries, all of these countries must also cope with pressure from major interest groups in the short run. Both the Overview of this volume and this chapter argue that such pressure is almost certain to grow in later phases of economic reform and is an intrinsic part of democratic consolidation.

Numerous theorists have suggested and many governments have tried to manage or stave off those pressures through temporary pacts, usually involving labor, business, and the state. To some extent, such pacts depend on conditions similar to more extended social corporatist arrangements: well-organized interest groups representing and able to exercise some control over sizable constituencies. But since pacts are normally negotiated in crisis situations and are temporary (in fact, often quite short-term), they may be able to work even where the more durable and full-fledged corporatist model would not.

As noted earlier, in Bulgaria and in the Czech and Slovak Federal Republic (CSFR) in early 1991, pacts were negotiated in which unions accepted severe drops in real wages in exchange for assurances that those drops would not exceed agreed levels and additional concessions. Those pacts were highly successful from the governments' perspective, since the unions exercised wage restraint even though prices rose much more than anticipated. In Mexico as well, a Pact of Economic Solidarity was negotiated in December 1987; renewed several times since then, it proved quite helpful in reducing inflationary pressures through combined wage and price restraint. The Bulgarian and CSFR pacts were prompted by the acute sense of crisis. In Mexico, the long-established political system facilitated the 1987 pact and its successors: business associations are well-developed, and most unions are affiliated with the dominant party and substantially controlled by the state apparatus.[72]

Elsewhere, however, attempted pacts did not materialize. In Brazil, both the Sarney and Collor governments tried unsuccessfully to negotiate pacts in support of stabilization programs. Somewhat comparable efforts in Argentina and several other Latin American countries came to naught. In Poland, the Suchocka government worked for many months to reach agreement with the labor unions on a draft "Pact on Enterprises" designed to address an array of issues and to establish procedures for union participation in privatizing state enterprises. The approach was aborted when the government fell on a vote of confidence initiated by Solidarity deputies. In most cases, efforts failed because unions and business interests were fragmented and lacked confidence in each other's and the government's ability to deliver their sides of the proposed bargain.

PIECEMEAL ENGINEERING OF CONSENSUS. Social corporatism is an unlikely model in most simultaneous-transition countries in Eastern Europe and Latin America. Even temporary social pacts become less feasible as early crisis-plus-honeymoon conditions recede and issues such as labor market reforms, social security reform, and privatization of large state enterprises rise higher on the economic agenda. Therefore the piecemeal engineering of consensus may be the most realistic approach, in most cases, to enlarging the area of consensus on basic economic and political policies and institutions.

But piecemeal engineering is not the same as muddling through—that is, coping with specific disputes as they arise and promoting individual measures by whatever means seem most available and promising. Instead, piecemeal engineering implies *a strategic agenda guided by the broad goal of enlarging the area of societal consensus on basic institutions.* That overarching goal may mean giving more priority to some issues that seem solvable, if necessary at the expense of issues that might—if they could be resolved—add most to economic efficiency. The overarching goal also has implications regarding tactics. The goal of increased trust and better communications among major economic interest groups and between them and the state discourages some tactics, such as executive decrees with little consultation, or opportunistic agreements with one major group while others are excluded. It may encourage other tactics, such as tripartite workshops or travel tours to observe other countries' approaches to certain problems—techniques used by Chilean democratic forces in the late 1980s.

Piecemeal engineering rests on the assumption that state-society relations in complex industrial societies consist of complex, many-layered webs of institutions and contacts. Many of these arrangements deal with quite narrow issues and may occur at local rather than national levels. Therefore reformers must deal with a shifting array of groups and coalitions with regard to different issues. They cannot hope to rely mainly on a few established or newly created forums (such as tripartite commissions at the national level) to address most problems.

Some piecemeal engineering may result in what might be described as mesocorporatism: tripartite institutions dealing with specific issues, often at sub-national levels. Examples of mesocorporatism mentioned in this chapter are the agreements worked out between management, unions, and officials involved in the automotive industry in greater São Paulo in Brazil; and the Hungarian pension and health insurance committees and labor market councils. Vocational training is another area in which tripartite arrangements may work well. Other piecemeal engineering approaches may not establish ongoing institutions at all but simply produce agreement on specific problems.

A few broad principles can be useful in pursuing piecemeal consensus. Without pretending to provide a full list, such principles should include:

■ Incentives, and perhaps some legal requirements, for considerable internal democracy and accountability within interest associations, keeping in mind the caveats mentioned earlier about the need for some autonomy for leaders;

■ Consultative arrangements (whether temporary or ongoing) that bring a fairly broad array of interests together. Broad representation improves information available to all the groups concerned with an issue, including information on each other's positions, and increases the chances for solutions that take into account a broader public interest;

■ Preference for solutions that minimize state intervention and encourage direct communication and negotiations between groups whose interests are intertwined but may conflict. For example, regulation of labor markets, pension funds, and health and safety conditions and many aspects of promotion of research and development activities and sectoral or regional development can be down-loaded to regional or sectoral self-regulating councils formed by interest associations, with or without state representation;

■ Where regulatory, coordination, and promotion functions are shifted or downloaded to largely or wholly nongovernment regional or sectoral organizations, the state must provide for monitoring and external review (by state agencies not involved in the specialized councils and/or by private groups) to reduce risks of collusive arrangements or rent-seeking.

Piecemeal engineering will not eliminate the fundamental economic and political conflicts that are inherent in radical restructuring. Restructuring produces real losers. Many cannot be fully compensated and must be expected to resist. But piecemeal engineering can gradually widen areas of consensus on controversial public policy issues. Broadened consensus in turn is crucial to the confidence of all groups that democratic rules and democratic changes in government will not reverse already accomplished reforms nor damage their fundamental interests. In short, broadened consensus is crucial both to consolidating economic reforms through resumed economic growth and to consolidating democratic openings.

Notes

This chapter has benefited greatly from discussions over several years with Marcelo Cavarozzi, Jacek Kochanowicz, Kálmán Mizsei, Oscar Muñoz, and Miguel Urrutia. I am also indebted to László Bruszt, William Douglas, Jonathan Hartlyn, Kevin Middlebrook, M. Victoria Murillo, Peter Ranis, Ben Ross Schneider, and Susan Woodward for most helpful comments and suggestions on earlier drafts.

[1] Guillermo O'Donnell and Phillippe C. Schmitter, *Transitions from Authoritarian Rule* (Baltimore, MD: Johns Hopkins University Press, 1986), p. 48.

[2] See Jacek Kochanowicz, Kálmán Mizsei, and Joan Nelson, "The Transition in Bulgaria, Hungary, and Poland: An Overview," in Joan M. Nelson (ed.), *A Precarious Balance: Democracy and Reforms in Eastern Europe and Latin America*, Vol. I (San Francisco: Institute of Contemporary Studies Press for the International Center for Economic Growth, 1994), pp. 12–13.

[3] For a fuller discussion, see J. Samuel Valenzuela, "Labor Movements in Transitions to Democracy: A Framework for Analysis," *Comparative Politics*, Vol. 21, No. 4 (New York: City University of New York, 1989).

[4] Laurence Whitehead, "Democratization and Disinflation: A Comparative Approach," in Joan M. Nelson and contributors, *Fragile Coalitions: The Politics of Economic Adjustment* (New Brunswick, NJ: Transaction Publishers in cooperation with the Overseas Development Council, 1989), pp. 80–81; Giuseppe Di Palma, *To Craft Democracies* (Berkeley, CA.: University of California Press, 1990), pp. 93–100.

[5] András Körösényi, "Demobilization and Gradualism: The Political Economy of the Hungarian Transition, 1987–1992," in Joan M. Nelson (ed.), *A Precarious Balance: Democracy and Reforms in Eastern Europe and Latin America,* Vol. I (San Francisco: ICS Press for the International Center for Economic Growth, 1994).

[6] Lajos Héthy, "Towards Social Peace or Explosion?" *Labour and Society,* Vol. 16, No. 4 (Geneva: International Labour Organisation, 1991), pp. 350–353.

[7] Olivier Blanchard, Simon Commander, and Fabrizio Coricelli, "Unemployment and Restructuring in East Europe and Russia," forthcoming as Chapter 7 in S. Commander and F. Coricelli, *Unemployment and Restructuring in East Europe* (Washington, DC: World Bank, 1994), manuscript page 12.

[8] Lajos Héthy, "Hungary's Changing Labour Relations System" in György Széll (ed.), *Labour Relations in Transition in Eastern Europe* (Berlin, NY: Walter de Gruyter, 1992), p. 179.

[9] Judith Pataki, "A New Era in Hungary's Social Security Administration," *Radio Free Europe/Radio Liberty Research Report,* Vol. 2, No. 27 (July 1993), p. 58.

[10] Héthy, "Towards Social Peace," op. cit., p. 350.

[11] Louisa Vinton, "Polish Government Faces New Strike Challenge," *Radio Free Europe Research Report,* Vol. 2, No. 21 (1993), p. 27.

[12] Derek C. Jones, "The Transformation of Labor Unions in Eastern Europe: The Case of Bulgaria," *Industrial and Labor Relations Review,* Vol. 45, No. 3 (April 1992), p. 462.

[13] Milena K. Novy, "Dual Transition in the Czech Republic," paper written at Woodrow Wilson School of Public and International Affairs, 15 May 1994.

[14] Blanchard et al., op. cit.

[15] Ibid., p. 10.

[16] Tito Boeri, "Unemployment Dynamics and Labour Market Policies," paper prepared for the World Bank Conference on "Unemployment, Restructuring and the Labor Market in East Europe and Russia," Washington, DC, 7–8 October 1993, Tables 3 and 4.

[17] Michael Burda, "Labor Market and the Economic Transformation of Central and Eastern Europe," paper prepared for the World Bank Conference on "Unemployment, Restructuring and the Labor Market in East Europe and Russia," Washington, DC, 7–8 October 1993, pp. 17–19.

[18] Jones, op. cit.; Ekaterina Nikova, "The Bulgarian Transition: A Difficult Beginning," in J. Nelson (ed.), *A Precarious Balance,* op. cit.

[19] Judith Pataki, "Hungarian Government Signs Social Contract with Unions," *Radio Free Europe/Radio Liberty Research Report,* Vol. 2, No. 5 (29 January 1993), p. 42.

[20] The discussion in this and the next paragraph are based on Novy, op. cit., especially pp. 8–10, 15–16. Much of Novy's data are drawn from John Ham, Jan Svejnar, and Katherine Terrell, "The Czech and Slovak Labor Markets During the Transition," paper for World Bank Conference on "Unemployment, Restructuring, and the Labour Market in East Europe and Russia, 7–8 October 1993.

[21] Many of the least viable large state enterprises, including weapons factories, were concentrated in Slovakia.

[22] Jones, op. cit, p. 462.

[23] Kjell Engelbrekt, "Technocrats Dominate New Bulgarian Government," *Radio Free Europe/ Radio Liberty Research Reports,* Vol. 2, No. 4 (22 January 1993).

[24] Louisa Vinton, "Polish Government Proposes Pact on State Firms," *Radio Free Europe/Radio Liberty Research Reports,* Vol. 1, No. 42 (23 October 1992).

[25] Louisa Vinton, "Poland's New Government: Continuity or Reversal?" *Radio Free Europe/Radio Liberty Research Report,* Vol. 2, No. 46 (19 November 1993), p. 4.

[26] *Radio Free Europe Daily,* 10 June 1994, p. 5, and 1 August 1994, p. 4.

[27] Edith Oltay, "Hungarian Socialists Prepare for Comeback," *Radio Free Europe/Radio Liberty,* Vol. 3, No. 9 (4 March 1994), pp. 23–24.

[28] This and later discussion of Bolivian experience draws on Eduardo Gamarra, "Market-Oriented Reforms and Democratization in Bolivia," in Joan M. Nelson (ed.), *A Precarious Balance: Democracy and Economic Reforms in Eastern Europe and Latin America,* Vol. II (San Francisco: ICS Press for the International Center for Economic Growth, 1994).

[29] Peter G. Snow and Luigi Manzetti, *Political Forces in Argentina* (Westport, CT: Praeger, 1993), p. 121.

[30] Ibid., Ch. 4.

[31] Gamarra, op. cit., p. 54.

[32] Snow and Manzetti, op. cit., p. 133.

[33] Snow and Manzetti, op. cit.; William C. Smith, "Democracy, Distributional Conflicts and Macroeconomic Policymaking in Argentina (1983–1989)" in James Malloy and Eduardo Gamarra, (eds.), *Latin American and Caribbean Contemporary Record,* Vol. 8, 1988–1989 (New York: Holmes and Meier, forthcoming).

[34] The Brazilian CGT was not formally organized until early 1986, but a predecessor organization, CONCLAT, had been in existence since 1981.

[35] Ian Roxborough, "Inflation and Social Pacts in Brazil and Mexico," *Journal of Latin American Studies,* Vol. 24 (1992), pp. 654–655.

[36] William C. Smith, "State, Market, and Neoliberalism in Post-Transition Argentina: The Menem Experiment," *Journal of Inter-American Affairs,* Vol. 33, No. 4 (Winter 1991), p. 52.

[37] Ibid.

[38] M. Victoria Murillo, "Union Response to Economic Reform in Argentina," paper presented at the Conference on Inequality and New Forms of Popular Representation, Columbia University, 3–5 March 1994, pp. 12–13.

[39] Ibid., pp. 7–9, 12.

[40] *Inter-American Development Bank Annual Report,* Washington, DC, 1993, Table B–2.

[41] Economic Commission for Latin America and the Caribbean (ECLAC), *Estudio Economico De America Latina Y El Caribe 1991* (Santiago: ECLAC, 1992), p. 9.

[42] Gamarra, op. cit.pp. 59.ff.

[43] The Economist Intelligence Unit, 1994.

[44] "Argentina: The Other Side of the Halo," *The Economist,* Vol. 330, No. 7850 (12 February 1994), p. 39. For open unemployment data, see ECLAC, op. cit., Table 3, p. 21.

[45] "Argentina: The Other Side of the Halo," op. cit.

[46] Murillo, op. cit., pp. 16–17.

[47] See Scott B. Martin, "Forward or Backward? Corporatism and Industrial Restructuring in Brazilian Autos," paper presented at a conference on "The Politics of Inequality," sponsored by the Institute of Latin American and Iberian Studies and the Italian Academy for Advanced Studies in America, Columbia University, New York, 3–5 March 1994.

[48] For a similar assessment regarding unions in Eastern Europe, see Richard Freeman, "What Direction for Labor Market Institutions in Eastern and Central Europe?" *National Bureau of Economic Research Working Paper No. 4209* (Cambridge, MA: National Bureau of Economic Research, November 1992).

[49] For a fuller discussion of some of these points plus further references see Joan M. Nelson, "Organized Labor, Politics, and Labor Market Flexibility in Developing Countries," *The World Bank Research Observer,* Vol. 6, No. 1 (January 1991). Murillo, op. cit., is developing further ideas on these issues.

[50] I am indebted for this point to László Bruszt.

[51] Peter Ranis, *Argentine Workers* (Pittsburgh, PA: University of Pittsburgh Press, 1992).

[52] Aymo Brunetti and Beatrice Weder, "Political Credibility and Economic Growth in Less Developed Countries," *Constitutional Political Economy* Vol. 5, No. 1 (1994), pp. 23–43; Brunetti and Weder, "Credibility and Growth," WWZ-Discussion Papers, No. 9316 (Basel, Switzerland: Wirtschaftswissenschaftliches Zentrum der Universitat Basel, December 1993).

[53] Juan Lopez, "Business Elites and Democracy in Latin America: Reflections on the May 1991 Kellogg Institute Conference," (Notre Dame, IN: The Helen Kellogg Institute for International Studies, University of Notre Dame, Working Paper No. l85, December 1992), p. 5.

[54] Oscar Muñoz Goma and Carmen Celedon, "Chile en Transicion: Estrategia Económica y Politica," (manuscript paper, CIEPLAN, Santiago, Chile, early 1993), pp. 16 ff.

[55] Rosemary Thorp, "Business Groups and the Efficacy of Economic Policy in Peru, Colombia and Venezuela," paper prepared for a workshop on "The Role of Collaboration Between Business and the State in Rapid Growth on the Periphery," Princeton University, 8–9 October 1993.

[56] Karen Remmer, "Democratization in Latin America," in Robert O. Slater, Barry M. Schultz, and Steven R. Dorr (eds.), *Global Transformation and the Third World* (Boulder, CO: Lynne Rienner, 1993), pp. 101–2.

[57] William C. Smith, "Democracy, Distributional Conflicts, and Macroeconomic Poli-

cymaking in Argentina (1983–1989), in James Malloy and Eduardo Gamarra (eds.), *Latin American and Caribbean Contemporary Record* (1988–89), Vol. VIII (New York: Holmes and Meier, forthcoming), manuscript pp. 10, 21.

[58] Ibid., pp. 12, 25.

[59] Eduardo Gamarra, op. cit., p.73.

[60] Ibid., pp. 71 ff.

[61] Smith, "State, Market, and Neoliberalism..," op. cit., pp. 55, 60.

[62] Adolfo Canitrot and Silvia Sigal, "Economic Reform, Democracy, and the Crisis of the State in Argentina," in *Precarious Balance*, op. cit., p. 128.

[63] See Eduardo Silva, "Capitalist Coalitions, The State, and Neoliberal Economic Restructuring: Chile 1973–1988," *World Politics* Vol. 45, No. 4 (July 1993), pp. 526–559.

[64] For discussions of the Mexican Pact, see Roxborough, op. cit.; also Robert R. Kaufman, Carlos Bazdresch, and Blanca Heredia, "Mexico: Radical Reform in a Dominant Party System," in Stephan Haggard and Steven Webb, *Voting for Reform: Democracy, Political Liberalization, and Economic Adjustment* (New York: Oxford University Press for the World Bank, 1994), pp. 360–410.

[65] Ben Ross Schneider, "Brazil's Disarticulated Bourgeoisie: Captains of Industry Adrift in a Changing Democracy," manuscript, April 1993, pp. 16–19.

[66] Ibid., pp. 28–29.

[67] For a most interesting discussion of the evolution of informal networks and their relation to state agencies in later stages of communism, and in the post-Communist era in Central Europe, see László Bruszt and David Stark, "Restructuring Networks in the Transformation of Postsocialist Economies," unpublished paper prepared for the conference on "Economic Liberalization and Democratic Consolidation," sponsored by the Social Science Research Council, Rio de Janeiro, June 1994.

[68] Körösényi, op. cit., p. 49; interview with Peter Seirmai, Deputy Director of VOSZ, in Budapest, April 1992; letter from László Bruszt, September 6, 1994.

[69] Kálmán Mizsei, Vice President for Economic Programs, Institute of East-West Studies.

[70] Körösényi, op. cit., p. 14.

[71] Phillippe C. Schmitter, "The Consolation of Democracy and Representation of Social Groups," *American Behavioral Scientist*, Vol. 35, No. 4/5 (Newbury Park, CA: Sage Publications, March/June 1992), pp. 422–449.

[72] For a fuller discussion of reasons for the success of the Mexican pacts, see Roxborough, op. cit., and Kaufman, op. cit., p. 65.

Chapter Four

Reforming Weak States and Deficient Bureaucracies

Jacek Kochanowicz

In both Latin America and Eastern Europe, the role of the state is at the center of political debate. The state's overextension—through too much regulation, too much direct involvement in production, too much redistribution—is a cause of the present crises in both regions.[1] Reducing the state's role and expanding that of the market seems a logical policy prescription for such a diagnosis. Indeed, the advice given these countries by the international financial institutions generally has urged privatization and a reduction of state involvement. It is assumed that state intervention brings about unintended, negative consequences, and that leaving the coordination of human activity to market forces will work much better.

Yet both the short experience of post-communist countries since the fall of the old order and the longer experience of Latin American countries that democratized and started reducing the state's involvement in the economy are teaching us an additional lesson. No doubt the market's role should be expanded and reinforced, but merely shrinking the state's role is insufficient. As the state is reduced—by default, by design, and through budget slashes connected with stabilization packages—it becomes more and more obvious that what is needed is not just its downsizing but also its redesign and reconstruction. For if the state ceases to function well, both market transition and democratization are endangered.

Among political scientists and political economists in both regions, as well as in the research departments of international organizations, it is coming to be recognized that the "state should be brought back in." It is argued that, for the market to function well, it is necessary to build an underlying constitutional and legal infrastructure—both natural tasks of the state. A further argument is that efficient performance by the state is an important way to advance its legitimization. This line of reasoning can easily be extended to the problem of sustaining a democratic transition; it is hardly imaginable that democracy can thrive in a state that is not perceived as legitimate and credible. However, while the body of theoretical literature on this theme is growing, few studies have focused on the more practical level of policy design and implementation.[2]

Throughout this volume, the state is analyzed from various points of view. Here, the focus is on the role of "state machinery"—that is, on the administrative apparatus, or bureaucracy. The underlying assumption is that while the bureaucracy is not particularly important for the initiation of democratic and market reform, it is crucial for their implementation and consolidation. It is the most important "filter," or mediating mechanism, through which political ideas, programs, and projects are translated into everyday practice. If bureaucracy is deficient—inefficient, embedded in informal patronage systems, or outright corrupt—it can easily impede if not totally derail market and democratic reforms. Because the bureaucracy comes into everyday contact with the public, its performance is critical for how the state is perceived.

The main theoretical point of this chapter is that the bureaucracy is not simply a technical device for running the state, but a complicated social phenomenon—usually the product of a long-term historical process with its own dynamics and inertia. While the bureaucracy's reconstruction, redesign, and streamlining may well be crucial for democratic and market reform, making this happen is by no means an easy task. Different layers of bureaucracy may have distinct interests, and politicians—especially in a nascent democracy—generally prefer to keep things as they are if they perceive that the status quo provides them with more power.

The first part of this chapter discusses why a strong state and an efficient bureaucracy are necessary for both market and democratic transitions. The second section, a comparison of two sets of cases in Latin America and in Eastern Europe, focuses on the mechanisms that make bureaucracies in the two regions "deficient." Because this chapter is part of and draws on a wider project comprising case studies of six countries (Bulgaria, Hungary, and Poland in Eastern Europe, and Argentina, Bolivia, and Brazil in Latin America), most specific references are to these cases. The analysis concentrates on the central administration—leaving aside the problem of decentralization and local governments (which would deserve a separate study), focusing mostly on the administration (civil service) and only briefly touching on the public sector as a whole. The feasibility and potential substance of future reforms of the bureaucracies themselves is considered in a final section.

WHAT ROLES FOR THE STATE? A THEORETICAL PERSPECTIVE

State, Market, and National Community

The state, together with markets and voluntary associations, is one of the three major mechanisms of societal coordination. In any society, these three types of institutions always coexist, though their proportions and interrelations differ. Laissez-faire and command economies are both abstract models. In reality, the three types of institutions sometimes mutually support each other and sometimes compete and produce tensions. These tensions are inevitable. In particular, in any historical moment, some forces seek to preserve and others to limit or capture the workings of the market. The powerful try to turn markets to their advantage by establishing monopolies, while those who are endangered by market forces try to protect themselves against their operation. Even groups that favor reliance on market forces in principle often try to modify the specific aspects of market arrangements that affect their particular interests to reduce competition or gain some special advantage.

In the market economy, a strong state is indispensable. In advanced economies, the state has its role in providing security and public safety, enforcing contracts, regulating markets, designing antimonopoly laws, regulating drugs and hazardous materials, and regulating prices of strategic commodities—not to mention the obvious areas of monetary and fiscal policies. It also has a role to play in investment in infrastructure and human capital. In fact, the state's role both in regulation and in redistribution is enormous: as much as 30–50 percent of the GDP of the most advanced countries is processed through state budgets. Moreover, as the wartime economic conversion and the reconstruction effort after World War II demonstrated, the governments of highly developed countries are able to intervene deeply and effectively in their own economies.

The state has yet another important role to play: that of reinforcing the cultural bonds of a national community. The world does not consist solely of firms and households; other frameworks of human activity include small communities, nations, empires, cultures, and civilizations. One's perception of the world, one's identity, one's place in the universe, community boundaries, bonds of solidarity, possibilities of communication with other people, feelings of responsibility, claims to assistance—all of these are shaped largely by cultural factors rather than by the workings of the economy. In the twentieth century the nation-state seems by far the most important of these human groupings. In various ways the state contributes to the construction of cultural spaces within which people conduct their affairs. Language, codes of behavior, systems of measurement, legal frameworks, industrial standards, and the like differ more between nation-states than within them. This national-cultural context is important for the economy since communication between people is crucial for any business activity, and business is conducted within the national-cultural space. Its framework, almost invisible, is usually taken for granted, but operating beyond it can pose considerable problems (or raise transaction costs). Likewise, the operating rules of politics are usually designed to fit a particular national community. A feeling of belonging and solidarity with a nation may even be, as some would argue, a precondition for a workable democracy.

In the sweep of history, the nation-state may be a passing phenomenon. Smaller communities building their separate identities and supranational institutions may eventually assume state functions in the face of transnational challenges to humanity. But such a new world order is still very distant.

Through its institutions, the state has been a primary nation-builder. In many less advanced countries, the state has also played—sometimes successfully, often unsuccessfully—a specific developmental role, prompting industrialization and social modernization. The state's assumption of a growing role in the economy was prompted by realities such as the lack of "spontaneous" tendencies to industrialization (weak middle classes and bourgeoisie, inadequate capital), the "peripheral" position of such countries in the global economy, and the ambitions of the modernizing intellectual and bureaucratic elites, which, for various reasons, wanted their nations to advance within the international setting. Japan, South Korea, and Taiwan are the most prominent success cases of the past two decades.

In both Latin America and Eastern Europe, the state played such a specific, modernizing role in the past. It can be argued that now, during the transition, it also has a very specific role to play in the foreseeable future.

The State and the Transition

A number of important economic-institutional tasks of the transition simply cannot be performed by either markets or (at least for the time being) by nongovernmental organizations (NGOs). The most important of these tasks are the following:

- Constructing the institutional and cultural infrastructure of the market—the "business-friendly environment" (institutions as well as attitudes) that in advanced countries emerged gradually over centuries (this is of course particularly important in Eastern Europe);

- Temporarily substituting for nonexistent or underdeveloped institutions of civil society, including NGOs and voluntary associations of all kinds;

- Playing an active role in the reconstruction of welfare arrangements (this reconstruction should, among other changes, mean a withdrawal of the state from certain areas of welfare activity as alternative institutions are simultaneously created);

- Rolling back environmental devastation—which often has been an implicit cost of past growth;

- Maintaining (increasing) levels of investment in human capital in conditions of rapid education privatization and increasing inequality;

- Implementing an active policy of industrial reconstruction, of which privatization is a part;

- Investing in and reconstructing infrastructure; even if this is done in partnership with private firms, the state is still needed as coordinator and regulator;

- Administering foreign aid;

- Putting in place policies of "debt management"—ranging from negotiations with creditors to extracting resources from their own societies to repay; and

- Negotiating with outside actors—with international institutions such as the International Monetary Fund (IMF) and the World Bank in particular, and, in the Eastern European case, with the European Union.

Among these functions, by far the most controversial concerns industrial policy—whether industries need a push from a development-promoting state in order to compete internationally. Moisés Naím rightly warns of the possibility of a political tide to return to more "activist" policies. "Without a state capable of interacting with the private sector with much higher degrees of autonomy and effectiveness, targeted state support for selected industries will only bring back the corruption and the lack of incentives to become competitive that prevailed in Latin America for decades."[3]

More broadly, as Albert Fishlow observes, "[t]here are two competing models of redesign [of the state]. One starts by stripping away public functions and confidently assigning them to the private sector and the market. The other begins by confronting the central challenge of the public deficit and defining a new development strategy."[4]

All of the above-listed tasks call for active state participation in the transition process—although it is by no means obvious that the state is capable of performing these functions. The new political economy offers a very pessimistic view on this point: the state *by its very nature* produces opportunities for rent-seeking. If accepted unconditionally, this view would rule out any prospect of reform. It is true, as Fishlow points out, that both the new political economy and the theory of collective choice concentrate on *negative* consequences of state action while disregarding the *positive*. Nevertheless, many insights of an anti-state approach are useful, in that they counteract undue optimism about and reliance on the state. The question of the state's ability to play the role of agent of change remains crucial.

Strong and Weak States

In both Eastern Europe and Latin America, states are "weak," not "strong" in the sense described by political scientist Joel Migdal.[5] A strong state is able to set rules of the game, to monitor and enforce those rules, and to extract surplus. Theoretically, this could be achieved either through cooperation with citizens who share the same aims and values with state elites, or by force, as in totalitarian systems. Real cases fall between those two extremes, and coercion and acceptance are always intermixed. The state is weak when social control is atomized, fragmented, and dispersed. Informal, nonstate institutions (or individuals) resist the state or even capture and manipulate parts of it. Possible manifestations of weakness include nepotism, "clientelism," mafias, or corruption. The distinction between a strong and a weak state should not be confused with the difference between authoritarian and democratic regimes. As Tony Killick and Christopher Stevens have observed, "Some dictatorships are weak, some democratic governments are strong."[6]

As Gunnar Myrdal observed more than 20 years ago, the "soft" state has been common to many developing countries. Theories of modernization tended to treat the weakness of the state as transitional—as associated with "traditional" segments of society. During the process of modernization, strong, rational institutions were supposed to replace weak, traditional arrangements. Today we are less optimistic: In an underdeveloped country that has links with the world economy, a weak state often seems to be a permanent phenomenon—especially when its abilities are limited by alliances of local strongmen and foreign interests. Some African countries are extreme cases of "predatory states," in which corrupt officials are interested mainly in outright exploitation of their subjects.[7]

Historically, the "West" (Western Europe, North America, Australia, and New Zealand) developed a unique pattern of a strong state—one that does not consist of a strong executive and a weak society, but of a high legitimacy and functional cooperation between the state and the civil society. Informal habits and customs and historical traditions are as important for the functioning of this social order as legal arrangements. The emergence of a strong and respected state in these countries was a gradual process built upon civic traditions of medieval towns and representative Ständestaat—a process in which a strong Asian burgher class was crucial. While absolutism in the early modern era restricted representation, it contributed to the building of nation-states and a strong, efficient executive. Constitutionalism in the nineteenth century, and then mass democracy in the twentieth, gradually broadened access to political power and allowed links with the civil society to crystallize.

The development-promoting states of East Asia provide yet another example of strong states. The concept of a "developmental" state is used loosely, but what is usually cited as one of its features is the relative independence of ruling elites from societal pressures in designing and implementing policies. Except for Japan after World War II, strong Asian states were built under authoritarian regimes. Even in the case of Japan, it is difficult to talk about full-fledged democracy. While economic policymaking is insulated from society, the ruling elites endeavor to spread the effects of growth as widely as possible and thus to fend off possible resistance. The social conditions on which this model was built are very specific to this particular set of countries; no doubt centuries or even millennia of cultural identity, social cohesion, and discipline helped.

The Bureaucracy

The state is not a monolith. It is composed of a political structure (formal system of representation and political organizations), a judiciary, and an executive branch. The executive consists of constitutionally responsible executive organs (a president, a head of a cabinet, ministerial agencies, and the administrative apparatus). But a state is more than that—since it also operates a vast public sector ranging from the provision of security (army, police), to social services (education, health), to manufacturing enterprises. This state bureaucracy is the primary, though not sole, concern of this paper. Why is the bureaucracy perceived to be so important?

First, the bureaucracy is a main mediating mechanism between the formulation of policies and their implementation. Policies are based on information and analysis provided by bureaucrats, who also put them into effect. Bureaucrats design the laws the government submits to parliament. In fact, the bureaucracy plays a much more serious role in drafting legislation than the constitutional division of power assigns it. Each of the permanent and transitional tasks of the state listed earlier requires highly competent people who can grasp essentials, write clear assessments, draft laws and regulations, and finally implement political decisions. The best policies are worth next to nothing if they go through a poor administrative apparatus. As Rueschemeyer and Evans put it, "[a]n effective bureaucratic machinery is the key to the state's capacity to intervene."[8]

Second, the bureaucracy manages the public sector health clinics and schools, communications and transportation systems, and, too often, even manufacturing enterprises. It is also supposed to introduce and implement reforms of the public sector. This means that, in terms of GDP, the bureaucracy directly controls as much as half the economy.

Third, the bureaucracy plays not only a technical but also a symbolic role. Like the flag, the national anthem, an army uniform, or a presidential mansion, it is a symbol through which the state—and the nation—is perceived. Citizens who have to deal with inefficient or corrupt officials will not respect the state, and the links tying the national community together will loosen. Increasingly, with the waning of mythical legitimizations of the state (a dynasty, an idea of a nation), the efficiency of the state machinery becomes a means to legitimize it in the eyes of citizens. As Stavrakis observes, "the state capacity to deliver promised goods and respond to specific demands of the population are essential for sustaining this credibility or the ruling elite's claim to power."[9]

A fourth reason why bureaucracies are important is directly connected with the process of reform. The political situation in all transforming countries will most probably remain unstable (beset by frequent elections, changing coalitions, and political scandals). The quality of newly emerging political elites may be low, especially in Eastern Europe, but not much can be done to improve politics from this angle. Though extremely difficult, reforms of the bureaucracy—reforms making it more competent, more independent of undue business influences and political meddling, more autonomous—could be a way to strengthen the legitimacy of the state.

The classical concept of bureaucracy—legal rules of operation, nonpersonal character of decisions, requirement of specified professional qualifications, entrance by examination, lifelong tenure, a fixed salary schedule, identifiable promotion paths—was developed by Max Weber.[10] Weber's ideal type is worth keeping in mind when looking at actual bureaucracies. Bureaucrats are by no means idealists or altruists. The advantages of a civil service modeled on Weberian lines over other types of administration rest on its members' identification of their private interests with the long-term stability of the state rather than with particular groups of politicians or business groups. A long-term view of a civil service career can outbalance temptations of fast enrichment. Also important is a corporate identity or *ésprit de corps*.

Deficient bureaucracies clearly differ from the Weberian model. The Nazi and Stalinist periods provide obvious examples of such bureaucracies. In both cases, the state was pervasive, and personnel were recruited for political loyalty, not professional merit. Bureaucratic structures were not separated from political structures. Neither did they operate according to formal rules—on the contrary, they had wide discretionary powers, expressly for realizing political aims. Another clear, extreme case of deficient bureaucracies is provided by the kleptocratic administrations of "predatory states," of which Zaïre serves as an example.[11]

In Western Europe, civil services are relatively well insulated from business and politics and able to operate efficiently. This insulation stems partly from the important concept of the separation of powers. Bureaucracy is supposed to be apolitical and impartial. Historically, such systems were rooted in absolutist monarchies—although at that time the conduct of office was still treated as a legitimate source of income from subjects, and today's idea of corruption would have been hard to understand. In Prussia in the time of Frederick the Great, and in France under Napoleon, the modern concept of civil service was molded as a corps of servants loyal to the state as such, not to a particular ruler. The British civil service—which was developed gradually through reforms between 1780 and 1870, and in which entry is based on a system of highly competitive exams—is one example of this modern concept. The elaborate system developed by France is another interesting civil service example, and "[the] prestige and self-esteem of the top French administrators . . . has remained second to none."[12]

Outside Europe, Asian developmental states offer other modern civil service examples. Japan started its modern civil service after the Meiji restoration, blending its own cultural tradition with European 'imports' and introducing examination systems in 1887. Senior civil servants and politicians were distinguished by law in 1899. Referring to the ancient Chinese exam system, Ezra Vogel has noted that the "development of a meritocratically selected bureaucracy was one of the great contributions of East Asia to world civilization."[13] The most famous example is the Japanese Ministry of Industry and Trade (MITI), which recruits its staff mainly from highly prestigious Tokyo University and has a rejection rate of over 90 percent.[14] The Japanese state is not big—MITI, for example, has only about 300 officials—which facilitates control and insulation.[15] Promotion depends on merit, and early retirement guarantees a lucrative job in the private sector. Other Asian countries have modeled their bureaucracies on the MITI example. Korea, Singapore, and Taiwan have been particularly successful; while Thailand, Malaysia, and Indonesia are in the process of improving their civil services.[16] All of these countries introduced highly competitive systems in which recruitment and promotion are based on merit; compensation is competitive with the private sector; and the top people are well rewarded. The Korean case is of particular interest, since that country, infamous for corruption during the 1950s, managed to build an efficient and honest service in less than 20 years.

In addition to the competitive selection procedure, three other aspects of East Asian experience should be stressed. First of all, the reward system is not too far from private sector standards, with security of employment and prestige making up for any gap in salaries between the sectors. Koreans systematically survey pay rates in private business to keep pay and allowances in the bureaucracy at par. The second aspect is prestige. The Asian countries make a conscious effort to endow public bureaucracy with as much prestige as possible, including various symbolic measures. The third aspect is a strong emphasis on building bureaucratic institutions so as to prevent the possibility of individual or group corruption.

In comparing various types of administration, Schneider stresses that career paths shape the preferences of officials—particularly their identification with the state: "In simplest terms, bureaucratic autonomy will be greater if top bureaucrats train at a small number of prestigious universities, follow predominantly public careers (state elite), circulate rapidly through many different agencies, advance through impersonal merit promotion, and do not retire to positions in the private firms they used to regulate."[17]

Placing so much emphasis on the role of bureaucracy, one cannot neglect the problem of its relation to democratic government. Elitist, technocratic bureaucracy tends to be undemocratic even when it is competent, loyal to the state, and law-abiding. To a degree, such a tendency is unavoidable, even if a tradeoff occurs between technocratic efficiency and democratic accessibility to power. Yet the idea of an elitist, apolitical bureaucracy can also be defended in the name of democracy, along the lines of the separation of powers argument. Democratic parliaments create the rules (laws), while day-to-day government administers, executes, and safeguards the stability and continuity of the operation of the state.

WHAT WENT WRONG? A COMPARATIVE PERSPECTIVE

Latin America and Eastern Europe face a similar challenge: the need to reduce and reconstruct the state at the same time. States in both regions fall far short of the Weberian ideal; they usually can be classified as weak. The particular shape of states and societies is a product of the "historical route" each region traveled. A comparative look at these routes is necessary to explain the present and to analyze the possibilities for the future.

State Overextension and Exhaustion

In the last two centuries, in both regions, ruling elites, leaders, and governments made repeated efforts to mold their societies and to push them onto the path of modernization. No doubt considerable successes were achieved, but links between rulers and ruled were different from those in Western Europe and North America, and civil society was relatively underdeveloped. Modernizing efforts often ran into trouble, political systems developed crises, and state machinery malfunctioned, while parts of these systems were captured by private interests.

Clearly the record varies both between and within the two regions, and there are obvious differences between the communist command economies of Eastern Europe's past and state capitalism in Latin America. Still, a pattern evident in most countries in both regions has been the state's trying to achieve everything—industrialization, social modernization, welfare protection. In Eastern Europe, the reasons for this overextension were clearly ideological and political: communism in practice meant a rational organization of society from above, not a spontaneous building from below. In Latin America, the rationale was instead a perception of the region's structural differences from the politically and industrially developed countries of the West, and, in consequence, of a need for the state to fill the gaps. Efforts made during the 1950s included developmentalism with strong populist undertones, and later, resorting to bureaucratic authoritarianism. Proponents of the latter

> assume[d] that the exclusion of the popular sector and
> its demands would make possible a reconversion of the
> socioeconomic structure that would stimulate economic

growth by a general increase in efficiency and by allowing political hegemony and capital accumulation in the more "dynamic" sectors.[18]

Despite differences, optimistic assumptions were made in both Latin America and Eastern Europe about the limitless capacities of the state. These assumptions were proven wrong, in a costly way, by prolonged crises that started in both regions in the 1970s. The last two decades in both regions were marked by states extending themselves beyond their capabilities, which ultimately led to their exhaustion and their enormous problems with fulfilling even basic functions.

Specific patterns of state involvement in the two regions differed considerably. In Eastern Europe's thousand-year history, many of its nations had powerful states. In the modern era, however, Eastern Europe was ruled by foreign empires, and during the crucial nineteenth and twentieth centuries, countries in the region were unable to develop either civil societies or credible government structures comparable to those in the West. World War I ended the Austrian and Ottoman empires, and during the interwar period, the nations of the region tried to build the institutions of modern states from scratch. The results were mixed because in most of the countries there was a significant shift toward authoritarian rule in the 1930s. Under communism, the fragile pre-communist state traditions were destroyed, and an attempt was made to impose a totalitarian system upon the region's societies.

As the Appendix in this volume notes, the economic role of the state in Eastern Europe was already considerable before World War II. Like their Latin American counterparts, countries of this region responded to the Great Depression by protectionism, statism, and economic nationalism. With the introduction of the communist system after the war, prior social elites and government structures were totally shattered, and the bourgeoisie and middle classes—never very strong in this region—disappeared completely. Postwar reconstruction and then massive industrialization were organized by the state, through a command economy. Except for Polish agriculture and small remnants of commerce and crafts, the private sector in Eastern European countries practically vanished. Achievements in terms of increased industrial production were quite considerable, although—as later history showed—at enormous costs.

A declared social aim was a "classless future." In practice, Communist parties tried to achieve complete control over their societies, either through cooptation or through repression. Communism, though egalitarian socially, was profoundly antidemocratic politically. Only in its late stages did it develop some structures of limited social consultation. Cooptation was achieved by building an extensive, though primitive and bureaucratized, welfare state, of which public enterprise was a cornerstone. This welfare state became overextended, costly, and inefficient. It produced high expectations, but its ability to deliver was low.

The almost complete subordination of economic and social life to the state resulted in the growth of a bureaucracy tailored to manage a centrally planned, command economy through an extensive set of administrative agencies. Functional ministries (such as finance, foreign trade, domestic trade, and labor) and sectoral ministries (such as heavy industry, chemical industry, and agriculture) drafted plan projects (usually in the form of material balances of inputs and outputs) that were then coordinated by a superministry—the planning committee. At the level of the enterprise (the word itself is misleading), "management" became administration.

The administrative organization of the economy paralleled the political organization of the Communist Party. Regional and central committees of the Party were divided internally in a way similar to the branches of the economy, and Party *apparatchiks* had a decisive voice in all important matters. The often used concept of *nomenklatura* refers to the manner of recruitment and promotion within both Party and state bureaucracy. Technically, *nomenklatura* was a (secret) list of posts and jobs for which candidates needed approval. A person (whether a Party member or not) could not be made a boss of a provincial department store without the approval of a local Party committee; a chief executive officer of a big shipyard had to have the approval of the personnel department of the Party's Central Committee. Political loyalty came before professional skills and experience.

Anything reminiscent of civil society was also bureaucratized and politicized. All associations—from trade unions, professional societies, and cooperatives to art or regional associations—became subject to the state through the dual control of the appropriate administrative agencies and Party committees; the material needs of all of these associations were met mostly through state subsidies.

Although the system was overregulated, in no sense can it be said that the bureaucracy operated within the rule of law, or even formalized rules. On the contrary, bureaucrats had considerable discretion with issuing regulations. The legal status of the regulations was often unclear, and rules were constantly changed. Navigating through the resulting maze demanded special skills; in fact, bureaucracies had considerable rule-*creating* capacities, and ministers acquired legislative functions.[19]

Early in the history of this system, most new managers and bureaucrats were of lower class origin, due to the destruction or elimination of prewar elites and to the expansion in education under the new system. Under "late communism," the system differed considerably from its Stalinist origins. The level of professionalism was rising because of better education, and ideology lost its importance. A survey of 6,000 Hungarian communist bureaucrats notes that the system of entry was based on personal favoritism and loyalty—though also on increasing professionalization.[20] With contacts with the world as well as internal reforms, more modern segments of bureaucracy emerged, especially within ministries of foreign trade and finance.

In less than two generations, however, communism collapsed. The states evolving since this breakdown are still weak, not only because they are being constructed on the shaky foundation of a disintegrating system, but also because under communism people developed myriad ways of circumventing the state. Thus, during the crucial period of the nineteenth and twentieth centuries, Eastern Europe experienced the emergence of numerous powerful state structures, but these were not firmly anchored in the societies and therefore tended to disintegrate.

In Latin America, in contrast, there was no such sharp discontinuity in political histories. New elites—products of modernization in the late nineteenth and first half of the twentieth century—gradually replaced traditional, oligarchic elites. Most Latin American nations did not succeed in including all segments of their populations either in the social modernization process or in the political structures of power; instead, elites coopted segments of the population. Although formally most of the countries adhered to democratic principles, for many reasons democracies could not function, and there was frequent resort to authoritarian rule. Civil society was less developed than in Western Europe, and therefore a strong state could not develop in a gradual, organic way. Leaders and governments tried to impose civil society from above.

Latin American markets were also deficient compared to those of Western Europe or the United States. The bourgeoisie and the middle classes were weak, which hindered possibilities for the spontaneous accumulation of capital. After the Great Depression—as was the case with Eastern Europe—states started to dominate economies. The 1950s witnessed a surge of developmentalist ideologies and policies that further reinforced the role of the state. The state was given an "organic-statist" role.[21] In this view, while private enterprise was to fill an important function, the state had a "moral obligation" to intervene in resource allocation if the free play of market forces aroused strong social dissatisfaction. The state was also expected to step in place of private enterprise to speed development when necessary.

In Argentina during the 1960s, for example, the central bank (created in 1935) closely controlled credit and money supply; public sector banks accounted for two-thirds of all loans and for more than a half of deposits.[22] The public sector had major ownership and control of railroads, electricity, air and ocean transportation, primary gas and oil, the telephone system, pipelines, petroleum refining, and steel manufacturing. The state set rates for utilities. Protectionism, strong from the 1940s to the 1960s, was backed by public credit—often allocated according to favoritism at negative real rates. Under the presidency of Arturo Frondizi, further programs were undertaken to accelerate industrialization.

In Brazil, intervention and statism started with the first presidency of Getulio Vargas (1934–1945) and his Estado Novo program, and accelerated in the 1950s and 1960s, particularly during the presidency of Juscelino Kubitschek (1956–1961). The growth of state enterprises was also spurred by concern with national security; defense-related industries were promoted vigorously.

Attempts to introduce planning were made during the second Vargas presidency (1951–54). American missions helped to draw up lists of investment priorities. In 1956, Kubitschek formulated an ambitious program of development goals to be achieved during his five-year term. After 1964, the military supported ideas of planning to legitimize their rule through economic success. The number of state enterprises rose to around 700; most of these were in capital-intensive industries—electricity, communications, steel, iron ore, petrochemicals, and utilities. Like Italy's IRI or ENI, they were often run as big state holdings. In 1979, although public enterprises accounted for only 7 percent of all firms, they employed 18 percent of the labor force, and their share in capital investment was around 50 percent.[23]

In Bolivia, import-substitution industrialization was initiated by the revolution of 1952 through nationalization of tin mining and state control over natural resources. Regional development corporations and state enterprises were set up. After 1956, almost every government followed the state capitalist development strategy. During the presidency of Hugo Banzer Suárez (1971–78) a conscious effort was made to emulate the Brazilian authoritarian-bureaucratic model—with considerable success, in that the country achieved a relatively high rate of growth (over 5 percent) during the Banzer presidency.[24] If Bolivia differed from other Latin American countries, it was because of its relative underdevelopment. There, the state became the main source of employment, and contracts to private business were distributed to political clients in a neo-patrimonial style.

In Latin America, state-led industrialization had considerable success. This was especially the case in Brazil, where very high growth rates were achieved over a long period, and where state firms put in place the essential, modern infrastructure. Statist regimes in Latin America also had definite political aims: to mobilize support while at the same time diffusing possible protests stemming from contradictions and problems created by capitalist development. This was achieved by creating employment possibilities in the urban sector—as in Juan Perón's Argentina. In Bolivia, expanding public employment became the most important means of coopting the urban middle class.[25] Another mechanism was establishing social security systems, usually in the form of autonomous agencies, providing a wide range of services (such as health care and pensions).[26] In Argentina, Perón extended the pension system for state workers, introduced in 1904, to everyone who wanted to join. In Brazil, in recognition of the emergence of new social forces in the 1950s and 1960s, attempts were made to anticipate possible problems by tying unions to government before autonomous labor movements had a chance to pick up momentum. Cooptation of union members was achieved through the extension of welfare benefits.

The growing role of the state resulted in an increase in the size and complexity of the state machinery. This growth was a worldwide phenomenon during the 1950s, 1960s, and later. In Latin America, however, it was greatly enhanced by the logic of the statist model and by the pressure on state employment, since it was harder than in more developed countries to find jobs outside the state sector. As Moisés Naím writes, "discharging the formal functions that justify an agency's existence weighs much less in determining its daily operations than does the need to serve as a welfare agency for its employees and their families. Often this is [the agency's] tacit, but dominant mission."[27]

In Brazil, bureaucracy started to expand under the first Vargas presidency and accelerated later. Public agencies employed 2.9 million people (8.1 percent of the labor force) in 1973, and 3.3 million (7.7 percent of the labor force) in 1980.[28] Bureaucracy expanded beyond the government sector into the decentralized administration—including quasi-autonomous institutes, funds, foundations, and, of course, state enterprises. In 1985, the (ironically named) Ministry of Debureaucratization counted some 20,000 agencies, which it estimated to be only one-third of the total national state agencies.[29] Rising strata of generally able and competent managers of state enterprises developed vested interests in protecting their firms.

Thus in both regions there developed—at different intensities—a pattern of imbalance between state and society. The state tended to dominate and to expand. Perhaps that was difficult to avoid—given the social structures (weak middle classes) and the secondary position of both regions within the world economy. The results of that state involvement were by no means only dismal; the state did contribute to development and modernization. In both regions, however, this tendency led to an overextension of the state, and ultimately to its breakdown.

As part of the historical trajectory described in the Appendix, in Eastern Europe state exhaustion was visible by the late 1950s, but—due to the relaxation of international tensions after 1956—a shift of resources from armament industries as well as management improvements through decentralization eased the burden. In the 1970s, many countries tried a strategy of vast infusion of Western technologies, mostly bought on credit. This brought about an abrupt crisis, mainly caused by the inability of those countries to compete in world markets and, in particular, to adapt to conditions brought about by the shock of increased energy prices. The crisis was visible as well in declining capital/output ratios, mounting balance-of-payments problems, shortages, and repressed inflation. The extension of social benefits—a way to coopt a disgruntled population—only worsened matters in the long run.

The same years brought beginnings of the end to Latin American "bureaucratic developmentalism." Excessive government spending lay at the roots of fiscal crises and inflations, while foreign debt aggravated the situation. Political pressures made it difficult to keep the public sector within the limits of reasonable finance. In Brazil, for example, the official doctrine of solvency of state enterprises "was stretched thin in terms of financial resources and managerial talent."[30] The state, overextended beyond its possibilities, started to shrink. In Brazil, disposable state income as a share of GDP fell from 17 percent in 1970–73 to 10 percent in 1980.[31] In Bolivia, where the state was large in size, it was weak relative to the volume of resources it consumed. During the growth period of the Banzer era, the state was unable to create a workable regime, and all major political institutions tended to disintegrate. "Even the military had degenerated into a congeries of factions dominated by ambitious officers . . . and Bolivia reverted to a system of unstable patrimonialism."[32] Inflation became the most visible manifestation of the collapse of the state.

In Latin America (in the 1980s) and in Eastern Europe (after 1989), "shock therapy" (that is, a combination of stabilization and liberalization programs) was the main response to the crisis of the state. In both regions, most of the elements of state crisis that had been building for a decade became even more acute with the introduction of shock therapy. Interestingly, while these measures have to a large extent aggravated rather than solved state malaise, only in a limited sense have structural reforms of the state been addressed. The state started to disappear. This deterioration became visible first of all in such basic services (provided or co-organized by the state) as internal security, education, health care, and pensions. In Poland and elsewhere in Eastern Europe, the press was flooded with stories of unheated schools, underfed prisoners, police departments unable to buy gas for their obsolete cars, and understaffed state employment agencies. In Latin America, real spending on infrastructure collapsed, and access to safe water, health care, and education deteriorated. Ironically, at the same time stabilization caused massive layoffs, increasing demand and need for welfare programs.

Shrinking employment opportunities are one reason for increasing criminality—another symptom of state deterioration. With respect to rising criminality, including organized crime, the Latin American region—especially the great cities in Brazil—is well ahead of Eastern Europe, but this phenomenon is now also common to all of the post-communist countries. A story about a border crossing from Poland to Ukraine—in which Ukrainian "custom officials . . . [operate] as completely free agents, extracting arbitrary tolls without appeals and for themselves alone"[33]—provides an apt metaphor for the disappearing state.

Another example of state deterioration is evident in the condition of infrastructure, especially roads. Eastern Europe provides a striking contrast between a fast-developing small private sector and a still disintegrating physical infrastructure. New, shining gas and service stations are built along highways full of holes and detours.

In Eastern Europe, education and research are also deteriorating—mainly because of very low pay. Academics are either emigrating or taking much better paid jobs in private business. In Latin American countries (perhaps with the exception of Mexico), the situation in this respect is similar—perhaps aggravated (as in Argentina) by a legacy of repression of intellectuals during the military regime.

Finally, the situation is also similar in both regions with respect to lower- and mid-level employees of state agencies—the very people who are the "technicians of reform." In Brazil, salaries for public employees declined by 37 percent in real terms between 1970 and 1980.[34] Part of the problem in Latin America has stemmed from the tendency to sustain employment levels within the public sector (only Argentina and Chile seem to be exceptions), which has led to salary squeeze. Between 1980 and 1989, Latin America's real public sector wages fell 30 percent, or more than three times as much as wages in the private sector.[35] Faced with deteriorating real incomes, employees have fled the public sector, resorted to moonlighting (often during their official working hours), or become corrupt and taken bribes.

Past Efforts at Bureaucratic Reform

Awareness of low efficiency emerged in both regions well before their political transitions to democratic political systems. While there are deep reasons for a lack of resolve in tackling the state crisis (including vested interests and the hostility of public employees' unions), the present low interest in restructuring the state for new conditions may partly stem from awareness of the limited success of many previous reforms.

In Eastern Europe under communism, the structure of administration was in continual flux. Three overall tendencies can be distinguished in these changes. The first was a relative de-politicization as the political system moved from totalitarianism to authoritarianism. The second was a spontaneous expansion—and segmentation—of the bureaucracy. And the third tendency was piecemeal reform—largely consisting of partial re-organizations: similar ministries were merged only to be split later once again; various extraordinary party-government committees, as well as inter-ministerial committees were established on an ad hoc basis to deal with specific emerging problems; power was delegated to lower levels—often only to be removed again; and waves of decentralization were followed by recentralization.

In Latin America, attempts to improve the efficiency of the state apparatus also have a long history. Successive Brazilian governments have attempted to create "pockets of efficiency."[36] This process started in the 1930s under the presidency of Vargas, with reform of the civil service; entrance examinations were introduced, and the new Administrative Department of the Public Service (DASP) became a sort of superministry under the Estado Novo program.[37] After World War II, many attempts were also made to create an elite civil service, but the political needs of the day usually interrupted these efforts, and patronage prevailed.[38] In 1964, the new military government inherited a financial crisis—the result of conflict between Goulart's political objectives and the country's possibilities. The military tried to rationalize the state sector. Politics was to be legitimized in terms of technocratic neutrality.[39] Many bureaucrats were dismissed, and a major governmental reorganization put the technocrats in the foremost positions. Decree-law 2000 of 1967 aimed to improve the performance of the federal bureaucracy by allowing greater decision-making autonomy and improving material rewards. Some agencies were converted to more autonomous public enterprises; salary restrictions within the civil service were loosened; and, consequently, highly qualified staff were attracted.[40] While the government of President Castelo Branco praised meritocracy in administration and succeeded in creating new policy instruments and revamping financial agencies, it achieved little in personnel policy.[41] Some institutions performed better, but—in a context of clientelism and dependence on a particular president's protection—improvements were ephemeral, and the overall structure lacked coherence and strategic selectivity. However, since a merit system had been introduced in some segments of the administration while other segments remained under political patronage, what is called a "dual democracy" emerged.[42]

The difficulties of the 1960s also prompted military authorities to strengthen state enterprises. Later, during the 1970s, macroeconomic imbalances led Brazilian leaders to enlarge the central government's power to control spending by these enterprises; government was also empowered to make important decisions on pricing, investment, and personnel. In 1979 a special agency (SEST) was established to control public companies.

In Argentina, attempts to reform the state started much later than in Brazil. No central agency was in charge of the civil service, and no universal rules were in place in the 1930s. That situation continued under Perón, when posts were filled with political supporters. The vast expansion of the state was not paralleled by an increase in efficiency, or by the introduction of general rules or a merit orientation.

Reform Efforts Since Democratic Transition

The transition to market economies and democracy changed the context of bureaucratic reforms in two respects—perhaps making it even more difficult than before. First, due to democratic opening, reforms of state machinery became a part of a political game much more than under authoritarian or communist regimes. Second, fiscal squeeze—while producing a pressure to increase efficiency—at the same time financially constrained the possibilities of improving the state machinery.

The beginnings of transition were misleadingly easy. There was a striking similarity among the ways in which the first economic reforms were introduced in some countries in both regions. Stabilization plans were often designed and implemented by small teams of technocrats, strongly backed by political leadership and isolated not only from political pressures but also from the rest of the bureaucracy. In Poland, Leszek Balcerowicz handpicked a group of associates, mostly from outside the existing bureaucracy, and charged them with designing and implementing the new rules of the economic game. Well insulated from the influences of still powerful industrial lobbies, the group enjoyed strong political backing and held considerable power. Bolivia is a similar Latin American example: President Víctor Paz Estenssoro "created two separate governments, one technocratic and one party political."[43] Thus, extremely important economic changes were quickly introduced without any overall redesign of the state apparatus. Later it became apparent that the latter task might be more difficult than shock therapies.

True, fiscal deficits have given rise to pressure to reduce the size of the public sector, limit expenditures, and improve efficiency. In Latin America, this has prompted efforts to reduce the number of employees in the state apparatus and in parastatal agencies. Nonetheless, Lawrence Graham has observed that "concrete results to date in the implementation of these policy priorities have been just as meager as attempts to design effective new strategies capable of recapturing economic growth and funding for needed social services in health, education, and social security."[44]

Although attempts at wider reforms of bureaucracy were rather half-hearted in both regions, they went farther in Eastern Europe for two reasons. First, because of the legacy of the command economy, institutional change had to be deeper than in Latin America. Second, political change from Soviet-dependent communism to sovereign democracies was also deeper than Latin America's change from authoritarianism.

Since changes in Eastern Europe were more significant, they deserve more space here. One important dimension was the restructuring of state economic agencies. Some of those agencies—ones connected with the command economy—were liquidated. In Poland, for example, a number of industrial sectoral ministries were folded into a single ministry of industry, and there are plans to reduce the number of ministries even more, by creating instead a single Ministry of the Economy. Economic administration was made more compatible with "the Washington consensus"—particularly by the creation of ministries of privatization. With Western help and expertise, these new agencies were quickly set up, and skilled personnel was attracted. However, organizing fiscal agencies, necessary to administer new taxes—personal income tax and the value-added tax (VAT)—turned out to be quite difficult and took time.

In the area less connected with the economy, both political change and the rising crime rate necessitated reforms of the police—although these steps were constrained by budgetary problems. Such reforms were introduced in Hungary and in Poland, where the police were de-politicized, and part of the staff changed.[45]

In most of the post-communist countries, however, administrative reforms did not extend to the systematic introduction of a merit-oriented bureaucratic system well insulated from undue political influence or pressure from interest groups and safeguarded from corruption. While in many countries the government bureaucracy's constitutional position remains unclear, so too does its relation to politics. It is not decided which posts and what levels of government are political, and which are administrative. There is no legal separation between professional posts and political activity, so that some members of parliament are also bureaucrats. Yet there is at least awareness of the problem and some ideas for change are being put forward.

In the case of Russia—which is outside the scope of our analysis, but instructive because of its tendency to manifest the problems of post-communist countries in the large—at least three proposals have been advanced for new civil service laws, some even looking back to the table of ranks of Peter the Great for their inspiration. Some of these proposals have made the distinction between professionals and political appointees. Yet the state leaders, compelled to seek the support of followers, have continued to neglect institution building and separation between politics and administration.[46]

Poland, with the advice of several World Bank missions, has also toyed with the idea of introducing a formalized, apolitical civil service, with requirements such as entrance examinations.[47] But a draft bill prepared by the former government of Hanna Suchocka has not been submitted to the parliament, and the present government is working on yet another proposal. As a result of the lack of reforms, with each cabinet change, there has been a tendency to reshuffle many of the higher staff positions in government agencies. While claiming a desire to construct an apolitical bureaucracy, the leftist coalition government that took power in Poland in September 1993 replaced many top nonpolitical officials with people connected with the pre-1989 regime. The same happened in Bulgaria, where the Socialists (former Communists) rehired former Communist officials once they had won the elections in 1993.[48] Clearly, a "spoils system" is developing instead of a meritocratic, apolitical administration.

Parallel to talk of the need to de-politicize bureaucracy, there are also debates about the dangers of corruption, and some countries have started to introduce safeguards. Poland's laws against corruption include a ban on officials serving as partners in companies, as well as a requirement that they declare assets and property before taking office and when leaving service. These regulations are proving hard to enforce. Such laws have been proposed in Russia—including a code of ethics for civil servants; a ban on accepting outside money, presents, free travel, or soft loans; and rigid restrictions on civil servants' personal activities, such as reporting requirements for property, assets, and income.

Changes in Eastern Europe were complicated by the issue of "de-communization." Excepting former East Germany, which is a separate instance, the most extreme case seems to have been Czechoslovakia. In October 1991, a "lustration" was voted, with the aim of removing or excluding from government jobs people who had held certain positions or belonged to certain Communist-run organizations—and to remove or exclude anyone who had worked for the secret police.[49] Similar tendencies emerged in other countries, shedding light on the major and frequent dilemma of having to weigh the professional experience of members of the existing bureaucracy against their political trustworthiness. Although the professionalism of old-regime bureaucrats was not outstanding, replacing expertise on any large scale was not feasible; there simply were not enough qualified candidates. At the same time, staff loyalty to the new regime had to be considered, especially as long as the stability of the new arrangements could not to be taken for granted. The problem has not been solved; the tendency has been to restaff the higher levels of the bureaucracy on a case-by-case basis, with new and old people working together—often with the new officials relying on the practical knowledge and expertise of their held-over colleagues. Initially, the new entrants have come mostly from academia or pre-transition opposition movements, with both of these backgrounds offering little practical experience in administration. In Russia, significant changes were made in the administration already during the Gorbachev period. In 1992, Boris Yeltsin's government founded a special organization (Roskadry)—drawing on German, British, and French examples—for the rapid training of higher-level civil servants. In Poland, the government founded a National School of Public Administration modeled on the French ENA—but this institution has been established in the absence of a wider system of merit-oriented bureaucracy.

Recession and the fiscal squeeze, combined with the rapid growth of the private sector, have seriously influenced the functioning of the bureaucracy. Senior officials have come under constant public attack for their agencies not functioning well—even as they have been pressured by their subordinates for more staff and financial resources.

At the same time, low pay, low prestige, and other opportunities have made working for the state unattractive. In Eastern Europe, the state can not compete as an employer with the emerging private sector's demand for highly qualified people. Legal experts, particularly important in the transition period, can easily find much better jobs with the booming private sector. In Poland, pay raises for top personnel (giving a high ministerial official a salary of around $10,000 per year) helped a bit, but these adjustments have not been combined with any overall reform of the civil service structure. Attempts to hold on to qualified people have also resulted in a tendency to expand out of proportion the number of relatively well-paid, high-level posts, while the number of mid-level (but well-qualified) staffers tends to be inadequate. The still very low pay of high-ranking officials leads to various types of links with private business in the state sector that are dangerously close to corruption.

In the last respect, Eastern Europe is similar to Latin America, where the pay of high-level civil servants is also low. Ministerial salaries in most Latin American countries are in the $20,000–$30,000 range (whereas in Taiwan, for example, they are around $70,000). Naím aptly points out that "getting the prices right" has not been applied to the wages of public servants.[50] That is one (but not the only) reason for Latin America's extremely high rate of turnover of ranking officials; since 1988, ministers have kept their jobs for an average of less than 15 months.

Why is Bureaucratic Reform So Difficult?

Neither Eastern Europe nor Latin America has achieved much in reconstructing the state and public bureaucracies. The one exception may be the institutions charged with fiscal policy. Writing about Argentina, Adolfo Canitrot and Silvia Sigal conclude: "The final picture is one of an increasingly segmented state where the services necessary for fiscal equilibrium are made more efficient and those necessary to meet basic service obligations (public safety, education, health) are deteriorating."[51] This observation applies to many countries in both regions— with the qualification that even the fiscal institutions are more efficient in tightening the money supply and slashing expenditures than in collecting revenues due to the state.

Institutions in both regions still remain weak, and bureaucracies are poorly insulated from both interest groups and political pressures. There are at least three kinds of reasons for the lack of appropriate reforms.

First are the current negative perceptions of state capabilities and the record of failed rationalizations in the past. As a result, political commitment to change is weak in both regions. Instead, privatization is perceived to be a remedy for state ailments—beginning with manufacturing enterprises in Eastern Europe, and with utilities and some public services as well as manufactures in Latin America. Most intellectual and political resources are therefore concentrated on matters of privatization, to the neglect of bureaucratic reforms.

The second set of reasons relates to the fiscal squeeze, with which both regions are struggling hard. However, while it is true that new bureaucracies should be "leaner and meaner," mere downsizing is not enough, and certain investments are necessary. Pay scales should be comparable to the private sector (especially if they are to attract managerial talents); but it is difficult to argue on either financial or political grounds for higher salaries for officials when blue-collar workers are being laid off and when pensioners are starving. In Eastern Europe, this issue is particularly touchy because of the legacy of egalitarian attitudes.

Reasons in the third category are deeper and relate to social and historical legacies. They are different for each of the regions. In Latin America it is the perseverance of neo-patrimonial arrangements, manifested in the forms of patronage and clientelism, mostly consisting of public-sector job distribution to political supporters. As Evans observes, "the Brazilian state is known as a massive *cabide de emprego* (source of jobs), populated on the basis of connection rather than competence."[52] In Bolivia and Peru, the distribution of power to coalition partners and patronage networks within the parties themselves allows Haggard and Kaufman to speak about an "informal colonization by business elites, local notables and even drug lords and terrorists."[53] The problem is particularly acute in Bolivia, since—because of the low level of development—state employment has been the most important way to coopt the middle class, and the political parties are mainly mechanisms to distribute patronage. Even the Paz Estenssoro government, despite its achievements with macroeconomic stabilization, did not succeed in reducing the number of the public employees. Peru is another obvious example.[54]

Such mechanisms of social advancement—mainly through the state—were not uncommon in pre-communist Eastern Europe. However, the heritage of pre-industrial times, and the importance of old elites in particular, was completely erased by war and communist revolution from abroad.

Many other difficulties stem from the 40 years of communist rule. The habits of communist bureaucracy run counter to Weberian principles such as the rule of law, meritocracy, or professionalism. There is no system of recruitment and training of state administrators. Eastern Europe also had much less training in modern managerial techniques than did the more developed countries of Latin America. The inefficiency of the state and the rudeness of its representatives compromised it in the eyes of the public. While expectations about what the state should deliver are still high, respect for it—as well as understanding of the mechanisms of modern government—are low even among the political elites. Consequently, local perceptions of what should be done still seem to be unclear.

CONCLUSIONS

Analysis of recent economic history of the industrial era shows how great a role the state has played in development. Considerable challenges also face the state in countries that have recently started a transition to a market economy and democracy. In conditions of relative backwardness, however, the state has frequently been extended beyond its capacities to deliver. This overextension has hindered the state from fulfilling even basic functions.

In both Eastern Europe and Latin America, state machinery needs restructuring. As part of this restructuring, the state should shed functions that may be better and more cheaply performed by either private business or NGOs. But reshaping the state machinery is also important for both economic recovery and democracy, since a democratic state needs efficient means to collect resources for its functioning as well as effective ways to execute its decisions.

Clearly this is easier said than done. Decades of attempts to improve bureaucracies in Latin America have produced few results because old patrimonial and clientelist informal structures have been able to recapture the state. In Eastern Europe, the task may be easier, since the political break with the past in this region was more decisive and abrupt than in Latin America. There is a lack of traditions of efficient state services to rely upon, however, and pressure groups from both the old system and the newly emerging capitalism often attempt to capture parts of the state.

Study of Latin America's experience strongly suggests a pattern of "path dependence," making it very difficult to break entrenched patterns of social behavior. Although Eastern Europe has no burden of patrimonial politics like Latin America's, the tendencies toward corruption and patronage built into the mechanisms of transition, together with the heritage of communism, could lead the region to drift toward the Latin American model.

Determinism does not, however, offer sound advice for the politics of reform. Some Asian countries provide examples of success in building efficient state institutions under even seemingly adverse conditions.[55] In both of the regions under study, there is also a chance of change for the better. There is, moreover, the demonstration effect of more capable states in well-established democracies; many of these examples can be transferred and implemented. Public opinion is also demanding more effective services and more accountability from the state. Better education and mass communication make society more transparent and facilitate the influence of public opinion upon political elites.

Restructuring the state must be part of wider constitutional change aiming at the rule of law and the separation of powers. The three branches of power—the legislative, the executive, and the judiciary—should be independent. The same principle should be extended to other segments of power structures. One of these is central banking, where independence from the executive is a safeguard of sound monetary policies. Another is the civil service, which should be made merit-oriented and apolitical. Yet another, which is not addressed in this chapter, is decentralization and the development of local governments.

There is no general recipe for reform of the bureaucracy. Moisés Naím remarks that—unlike macroeconomic reforms—there are no well-developed theoretical underpinnings for institutional reforms.[56] However, certain obvious questions must be addressed when design is considered. These concern the timespan of administrative reforms, the levels of bureaucratic structures to be reformed first (only "staff," or staff and "line" as well), the agencies of particular importance, and the costs involved. Reforms have to be given enough time—perhaps several years. It is probably better to start from the top down and reform the "staff" before restructuring the "line." The judiciary, central banking, and the fiscal systems should probably be assigned top priority.

Since reforms are needed in countries that are at the same time attempting to decrease their budget deficits, reducing the number of people employed in the administrative services should also be a goal. There are procedures to approach this task.[57] Fewer but better paid and better qualified public employees are likely to be more effective. If civil servants are recruited through difficult, competitive examinations, the chances are that—apart from remuneration—the prestige factor will attract good entrants. In addition, high pay for senior civil servants—a necessary element of the reform—will be easier to accept by the public if the right to receive it is earned through hard study and passage through a merit-oriented selection system. One can imagine a two-layer system of bureaucracy, in which the upper layer consists of a corps of well-paid and carefully selected top civil servants, while the lower level consists of contract staff. The size of the corps could then be gradually expanded downward, contingent upon the resources of the state. It is critical, however, to define very clearly the legal status of the corps and to keep its number limited and its pay high. In other words, it is crucial to keep high quality and the elitist nature of the service through competitive selection, and to keep its *ésprit de corps* and loyalty to the state through insulation from political patronage and from bribery by business. Setting statutory limits on the size of the civil service should also be considered.

The experience of countries that introduced successful reforms shows that it is advisable to establish a special agency for recruiting, managing, and supervising the civil service. Among such an agency's tasks should be the setting up of pay scales as well as rules for promotion and for the performance assessment of both agencies and personnel. Another of its responsibilities should be to run educational institutions or programs to train civil servants.

Reforming countries at the mid-level of development might also consider investing in high technology to improve the work of state administration. Computers and data banks reduce costs of data processing, make feasible the use of economies of scale through the centralization of information and data processing, and facilitate budgetary control. While decentralization of administration may be argued for on the basis of the trend toward democratization, there are limits to this because of the lack of properly trained staff. High technology may be a help.

A parallel effort should be reforming and streamlining the public service sectors (including utilities, health, education, social security). Without attempting to address this here in detail, the basic lines of such reforms should include: privatizing parts of the public sector and commercializing others (that is, adopting user fees); introducing strict budgetary measures in public enterprises considered unsuitable for either privatization or commercialization; and, finally, turning some state responsibilities over to NGOs. While the state should certainly play a considerable role in organizing and delivering public services, it should do so in a way that is both more efficient and more compatible with market reform.

Prospects for such reforms depend in large measure upon politics. Much has been said in this chapter about the political tendencies that interfere with the chances of redesigning the state. But politics is not just a mechanical process. Its course is also affected by how elites perceive the challenges facing them, and in that sense, study and debate might do a positive service. While it is true that politicians can reap short-term benefits from structures that assure patronage, the path of legitimization through efficiency and honesty of the state offers them other, longer-term benefits. Stable and efficient state machinery is also indispensable if democracy is not to be reduced to an anarchic, populist travesty.

Finally, success also depends upon sheer luck—on the presence of imaginative, far-sighted politicians who understand the importance of an efficient public bureaucracy, and on the emergence of a coalition of forces willing to agree on reforms.

Notes

The author would like to thank Luiz Carlos Bresser Pereira, Marcelo Cavarozzi, Catherine Gwin, Jonathan Hartlyn, Robert Kaufman, Marcin Kula, Kálmán Mizsei, Oscar Muñoz, Joan Nelson, Barbara Nunberg, Barbara Stallings, Ben Slay, and Laurence Whitehead for valuable comments and suggestions.

[1]Of course, state overextension is an issue not only in less developed and post-communist countries but even in highly developed countries.

[2]Peter B. Evans, Dietrich Rueschemeyer, and Theda Skocpol, eds., *Bringing the State Back In* (Cambridge: Cambridge University Press, 1985); Stephan Haggard and Robert Kaufman, *The Political Economy of Democratic Transitions* (forthcoming); World Bank, *World Development Report 1991,* (New York: Oxford University Press, 1991); World Bank, *Governance and Development* (Washington, DC: World Bank, 1992); Gordon C. Rausser and S.R. Johnson, "State-Market-Civil Institutions: The Case of Eastern Europe and the Soviet Republics," *World Development,* Vol. 21, No. 4 (1993); Peter J. Stavrakis, "State-Building in Post-Soviet Russia: The Chicago Boys and the Decline of Administrative Capacity" (Washington, DC: Kennan Institute for Advanced Russian Studies, n.d.), mimeo; Barbara Nunberg, "Managing the Civil Service: What LDCs Can Learn from Developed Country Reforms," *Policy, Research and External Affairs Working Papers: Public Sector Management and Private Sector Development* (Country Economics Department, World Bank, August 1992); Barbara Nunberg and John Nellis, "Civil Service Reform and the World Bank," *Policy, Research and External Affairs Working Papers,* op. cit., May 1990.

[3]Moisés Naím, "Latin America's Liberalization: Will the Pendulum Swing Back?" mimeo (1993).

[4]Albert Fishlow, "The Latin American State," *Journal of Economic Perspectives,* Vol. 4, No. 3 (Summer 1990), p. 71.

[5]Some authors conceptualize this problem in a slightly different way, speaking of either "hard" and "soft," or "autonomous" and "subordinate" states. Joel S. Migdal, *Strong Societies and Weak States: State-Society Relations and State Capabilities in the Third World* (Princeton: Princeton University Press, 1988); Gunnar Myrdal, *The Challenge of World Poverty: A World Anti-Poverty Program in Outline* (1970); and Dani Rodrik, "Political Economy and Development," *European Economic Review,* No. 36 (1992).

[6]Tony Killick and Christopher Stevens, "Eastern Europe: Lessons On Economic Adjustment from the Third World," *International Affairs,* Vol. 67, No. 4 (1991), p. 621.

[7]Peter Evans, "The State as Problem and Solution: Predation, Embedded Autonomy, and Structural Change," in Stephan Haggard and Robert R. Kaufman (eds.), *The Politics of Economic Adjustment: International Constraints, Distributive Conflicts, and the State* (Princeton: Princeton University Press, 1992).

[8]Dietrich Rueschemeyer and Peter B. Evans, "The State and Economic Transformation: Toward an Analysis of the Conditions Underlying Effective Intervention," in Evans, Rueschemeyer, and Skocpol, op. cit.

[9]Stavrakis, op. cit., p. 5.

[10]Hans H. Gerth and C. Wright Mills (eds.), *From Max Weber: Essays in Sociology* (New York: Oxford University Press, 1947), pp. 196–244.

[11]Evans, op. cit.

[12]G.E. Aymler, "Bureaucracies," in Peter Burke (ed.), *The New Cambridge Modern History,* Vol. IX, *Companion Volume* (Cambridge: Cambridge University Press, 1979), p. 180; Ezra N. Suleiman, *Politics, Power and Bureaucracy in France: The Administrative Elite* (Princeton: Princeton University Press, 1974).

[13]Ezra F. Vogel, *The Four Little Dragons: The Spread of Industrialization in East Asia* (Cambridge: Cambridge University Press, 1991), p. 93.

[14]Chalmers Johnson, *MITI and the Japanese Miracle: The Growth of Industrial Policy, 1925–1975* (Stanford: Stanford University Press, 1982).

[15]Ben Ross Schneider, "The Career Connection: A Comparative Analysis of Bureaucratic Preference and Insulation," *Comparative Politics* (April 1993), p. 344.

[16]Robert Wade, *Governing the Market: Economic Theory and the Role of Government in East Asian Industrialization* (Princeton: Princeton University Press, 1990), pp. 195–227; World Bank, *The East Asian Miracle: Economic Growth and Public Policy* (New York: Oxford University Press, 1993), p. 161.

[17]Schneider, "The Career Connection," op. cit., p. 344.

[18]Guillermo A. O'Donnell, *Modernization and Bureaucratic-Authoritarianism: Studies in South American Politics* (Berkeley, CA: Institute of International Studies, University of California, 1973), p. 92.

[19]Stavrakis, op. cit., p. 19.

[20]Ferenc Gazso, "Cadre Bureaucracy and the Intelligentsia," *Journal of Communist*

Studies, Vol. 8, No. 3 (September 1992).

21Alfred Stepan, *The State and Society: Peru in Comparative Perspective* (Princeton: Princeton University Press, 1978).

22Carlos F. Diaz-Alejandro, *Essays on the Economic History of the Argentine Republic* (New Haven: Yale University Press, 1970).

23Thomas J. Trebat, *Brazil's State-Owned Enterprises: A Case Study of the State as an Entrepreneur* (Cambridge: Cambridge University Press, 1983), pp. 35 and 56.

24Eduardo Gamarra, "Market-Oriented Reforms and Democratization in Bolivia," *A Precarious Balance: Democracy and Economic Development in Eastern Europe and Latin America,* Vol. II (San Francisco: ICS Press for International Center for Economic Growth, 1994).

25James M. Malloy, "Democracy, Economic Crisis, and the Problem of Governance: The Case of Bolivia," *Studies in Comparative International Development,* Vol. 26 (summer 1991), p. 46.

26Lawrence S. Graham, *The State and Policy Outcomes in Latin America* (New York: Praeger, 1990), p. 7.

27Moisés Naím, "Latin America's Journey to the Market: From Macroeconomic Shocks to Institutional Therapy," paper prepared for the Ninth Plenary Meeting of the Inter-American Dialogue, Wye, Maryland, April 1994, mimeo.

28Rugiero F. Werneck, "Public Sector Adjustment to External Shocks and Domestic Pressures in Brazil," in Felipe Larrain and Marcelo Selowsky, *The Public Sector and the Latin American Crisis* (San Francisco: Institute for Contemporary Studies Press, 1991), p. 61.

29Ben Ross Schneider, *Politics Within the State: Elite Bureaucrats and Industrial Policy in Authoritarian Brazil* (Pittsburgh: University of Pittsburgh Press, 1991), p. 6.

30Trebat, op. cit., p. 237.

31Ibid., p. 55.

32Malloy, op. cit., p. 41.

33Lawrence Weschler, "Deficit," *The New Yorker,* 11 May 1992, p. 43.

34Werneck, op. cit., p. 62.

35Naím, "Latin America's Journey to the Market," op. cit.

36Evans, op. cit., p. 168.

37Kathryn Sikkink, *Ideas and Institutions: Developmentalism in Brazil and Argentina* (Ithaca, NY: Cornell University Press, 1991), pp. 174–175.

38Lawrence S. Graham, *Civil Service Reform in Brazil: Principles Versus Practice* (Austin, TX: University of Texas Press, 1968), p. 1.

39Elisa P. Reis, "Bureaucrats and Politicians in Current Brazilian Politics," *International Social Science Journal* (February 1990), p. 24.

40Trebat, op. cit., p. 48.

41Schneider, *Politics Within the State,* op. cit., p. 25.

42Graham, op. cit., p. 170.

43Malloy, op. cit., p. 52.

44Graham, *The State and Policy Outcomes,* op. cit., p. 17.

45Edith Oltay, "Hungary Reforms Its Police Force," *RFE/RFL Research Report,* Vol. 2, No. 4 (January 1993).

46Stavrakis, op. cit., and Victor Yasman, "The Russian Civil Service: Corruption and Reform," *RFE/RL Research Report,* Vol. 2, No. 16 (16 April 1993).

47Information from Barbara Nunberg, World Bank.

48Kjell Engelbrekt, "Bulgaria's Communists: Coming or Going?" *RFE/RL Research Report,* Vol. 2, No. 21 (May 1993).

49Jeri Laber, "Witch Hunt in Prague," *The New York Review of Books,* April 1992.

50Naím, "Latin America's Journey to the Market," op. cit.

51Adolfo Canitrot and Silvia Sigal, "Economic Reform, Democracy, and the Crisis of the State in Argentina," in Joan Nelson, ed., *A Precarious Balance,* op. cit, Vol. II.

52Evans, op. cit., p. 167.

53Haggard and Kaufman, op. cit.

54Malloy, op. cit.; Alan Angell, "The Difficulties of Policy Making and Implementation in Peru," *Bulletin of Latin American Research,* Vol. 3, No, 1 (1984); Carol Graham, "Peru's APRA Party in Power: Impossible Revolution, Relinquished Reform," *The Journal of Interamerican Studies and World Affairs,* Vol. 32, No. 3 (Fall 1990); and Carol Graham, *Peru's APRA: Parties, Politics, and the Elusive Search for Democracy* (Boulder: CO, Lynne Rienner, 1992).

[55]World Bank, *The East Asian Miracle,* op. cit.

[56]Naím, "Latin America's Journey to the Market," op. cit.

[57]Nunberg and Nellis, op. cit.

About the ODC

ODC fosters an understanding of how development relates to a much changed U.S. domestic and international policy agenda and helps shape the new course of global development cooperation.

ODC's programs focus on three main issues: the challenge of political and economic transitions and the reform of development assistance programs; the development dimensions of international responses to global problems; and the implications of development for U.S. economic security.

In pursuing these themes, ODC functions as:

■ *A center for policy analysis.* Bridging the worlds of ideas and actions, ODC translates the best academic research and analysis on selected issues of policy importance into information and recommendations for policymakers in the public and private sectors.

■ *A forum for the exchange of ideas.* ODC's conferences, seminars, workshops, and briefings bring together legislators, business executives, scholars, and representatives of international financial institutions and nongovernmental groups.

■ *A resource for public education.* Through its publications, meetings, testimony, lectures, and formal and informal networking, ODC makes timely, objective, nonpartisan information available to an audience that includes but reaches far beyond the Washington policymaking community.

ODC is a private, nonprofit organization funded by foundations, corporations, governments, and private individuals.

Stephen J. Friedman is the Chairman of the Overseas Development Council, and John W. Sewell is the Council's President.

About the Authors

Project Director

JOAN M. NELSON is a Senior Associate of the Overseas Development Council. Her work at ODC during the past several years has focused on the politics of economic stabilization and adjustment, and most recently on interactions between market-oriented economic reforms and democratization in Eastern Europe and Latin America. A second area of recent emphasis has been the uses of and limits of conditioned aid as a means to promote non-economic as well as economic reforms. Dr. Nelson worked with the policy planning division of the Agency for International Development during the mid-1960s. Later she taught at Massachusetts Institute of Technology and co-directed a research program in political participation in developing nations at the Harvard Center for International Affairs. From 1974 to 1982 she established and directed the program in Comparative Politics and Modernization at the Johns Hopkins School of Advanced International Studies. Since 1982 she has been at the Overseas Development Council. She consults for the World Bank, AID, and the International Monetary Fund on problems of governance and the politics of economic adjustment, and on rural-to-urban migration. During the mid-1980s she served as a member of the National Academy of Science Population Committee; she is currently a member of the Academy's recently established Committee on Democracy and States in Transition. Among her publications are *Aid, Influence, and Foreign Policy* (MacMillan, 1968); *No Easy Choice: Political Participation in Developing Countries* (with Sam Huntington; Harvard, 1976); *Access to Power: Politics and the Urban Poor* (Princeton, 1979); *Fragile Coalitions: The Politics of Economic Adjustment* (editor and contributor, ODC, 1989); *Economic Crisis and Policy Choice* (editor and contributor, Princeton, 1990); *Encouraging Democracy: What Role for Conditioned Aid?* (ODC, 1992); *Global Goals, Contentious Means: Issues of Multiple Conditionality* (ODC, 1993) and most recently *A Precarious Balance: Democracy and Market Reforms in Eastern Europe and Latin America*, Vols. I and II (editor and contributor, ICS Press for International Center for Economic Growth, 1994).

Contributing Authors

JACEK KOCHANOWICZ is an associate professor of economic history at Warsaw University. His area of specialty includes the comparative economic and social history of Eastern Europe in the nineteenth and twentieth centuries. From 1990 to 1991 he was a member of the Institute of Advanced Studies for Princeton University's School of Social

Sciences. He has also been a visiting professor of economic history at the University of Washington, Seattle, and at the University of Chicago. He chairs the supervisory board of the Bank of Social and Economic Initiatives, founded to aid small businesses in Poland. Among his publications are *A Controversy over Peasant Economy* (in Polish, Warsaw 1992); "Transition to Market in a Comparative Perspective: A Historian's Point of View," in Kazimierz Z. Pozananski (ed.) *Stabilization and Privatization in Poland: An Economic Evaluation of the Shock Therapy Program* (Kluwer Academic Publishers, 1993); and *The Market Meets Its Match: Reindustrialization of Eastern Europe* (coauthored with Alice Amsden and Lance Taylor, Harvard University Press, forthcoming).

KÁLMÁN MIZSEI is the Pew economist-in-residence and Vice President for Economics Programs at the Institute for East-West Studies in New York. He has been a participant in the international project of the World Institute for Development Economics Research on East and Central Europe transformations. From 1990 to 1992 he was deputy director of the Institute for World Economics of the Hungarian Academy of Sciences, where he served as an advisor to the president of the National Bank of Hungary. He was also an expert on the International Blue Ribbon Commission for advising Hungary on economic reform in 1990. His publications include "Hungary: Gradualism Needs a Strategy," in *Economic Transition in Central Europe* (Centre for Economic Policy Research, 1993); *Bankruptcy and the Post-Communist Economies of East Central Europe* (Institute for East-West Studies, 1994); and *Developing Public Finance in Emerging Market Economies* (Institute for East-West Studies, 1994).

OSCAR MUÑOZ is a board member of the private, nonprofit research institute Corporación de Investigaciones Económicas para Latinamérica (CIEPLAN), where he contributed to the foundation of the corporation in 1976, was executive director from 1978 to 1980, and president of the board from 1989 to 1993. His main areas of research and publications are industrialization processes and policies, and roles of the state and the private sector. He was professor and coordinator of the graduate studies program of the Institute of Economics at the University of Chile from 1968-1970. From 1971 to 1976 he was an educator for the Center for the Study on Economic Planning at the Catholic University in Santiago, Chile. He is also a private consultant for both national and international agencies and a member of the council for the National Science and Technology Development Fund in Chile. Recent publications include *Economic Reforms in Chile,* (editor, Inter-American Bank, 1992); and *Después de las Privatizaciones: Hacia el Estado Regulador,* (editor, CIEPLAN, 1993).